Creating Boundaries

Creating Boundaries

The Politics of Race and Nation

Kathryn A. Manzo

LYNNE
RIENNER
PUBLISHERS

BOULDER
LONDON

Published in the United States of America in 1996 by
Lynne Rienner Publishers, Inc.
1800 30th Street, Boulder, Colorado 80301

and in the United Kingdom by
Lynne Rienner Publishers, Inc.
3 Henrietta Street, Covent Garden, London WC2E 8LU

Library of Congress Cataloging-in-Publication Data
Manzo, Kathryn A.
    Creating boundaries : the politics of race and nation / by Kathryn
A. Manzo.
        p. cm.
    Includes bibliographical references and index.
    ISBN 1-55587-372-3 (hc : alk. paper)
    1. Nationalism.   2. Race awareness.   I. Title.
    JC311.M345 1996
    320.5'4—dc20   95-41218
                                                                      CIP

British Cataloguing in Publication Data
A Cataloguing in Publication record for this book
is available from the British Library.

Printed and bound in the United States of America

        The paper used in this publication meets the requirements
 ∞   of the American National Standard for Permanence of
        Paper for Printed Library Materials Z39.48-1984.

    5   4   3   2   1

Contents

Preface

This book is a personal odyssey as well as an academic project. I am a U.S. citizen by birth; a "permanent resident" of Australia (although I no longer live there); and an actual resident of Britain. Because of the place of my birth and the fact that my first father was an American, I am not officially of British descent. Yet I was raised in England by my British mother and second father, with the speeches of Enoch Powell, Irish jokes, and the music of Tamla Motown. In history classes at my Catholic high school, I learned of nothing but warfare with Europe until I optioned in medieval history, at age sixteen. For the next two years I took notes on suzerainty relations between England and France from the perspectives of King John and Richard the Lionheart. My social identity comprised three life-facts: religious affiliation (Catholic); class position (middle); and soccer team loyalty (Manchester United). I was not aware of being a member of a white race or living in a once imperial country until I left home to study at the University of Manchester.

I learned a great deal in Manchester. From Nigerian and Ghanaian friends I learned that Britain had once had an empire. From Welsh friends I learned that their first language was not English and that something called Welsh nationalism existed. And in so-called black and Asian areas I learned to enjoy reggae and the taste of curry. I don't remember much about my European Studies degree except that I spent the third year in France. I never quite understood why so many of my fellow Britons seemed to hate the French simply because they "refused" to speak English. Nor did I ever hear a sophisticated explanation for why Manchester woke up one morning in 1981 to find shops burned in Rusholme (an area of mainly Indian settlement) and a police station under seige in Moss Side (where many students lived alongside people of Afro-Caribbean descent). Since there had been no racial tensions before (at least none that we students were aware of), the rumors soon circulating about agents provocateurs sent from London solidified quickly into accepted fact.

National identity means a great deal to some people and precious little to others. My purpose in writing this book was not to decide whether nationalism is inevitably good or bad (it is always both), but to understand how and why it operates. Given twenty-four years of life in Britain, twelve years in the United States, and my previous work on South Africa, I felt I could not do otherwise than set nationalist practices within a larger global and historical context than that of the individual, modern nation-state. Whatever the reader may think of this book, the writing of it has provided me with new insight into how the Britain of my experience was created; how it differed from the world of my parents; and thus how my own, composite identity has been socially constituted. I finally understand what the political fights within the family were all about.

The people I wish to acknowledge are dispersed in time and space. My biggest expression of gratitude must go to Lynne Rienner. Without her faith in my abilities the manuscript would never have been started, and without her patience it would not have been completed.

Apart from the many scholars whose thinking has shaped my own, I owe an intellectual debt to several people: first to David Campbell, for suggesting that I read about nationalism instead of ideology; second to Roxanne Doty, for her thoughtful comments on the manuscript; and third to the postgraduates at Johns Hopkins University—those who invited me to present my research and also participated in my seminars. Because their written work was as valuable to me as their classroom comments, I would like to mention Marjorie Opuni-Akuamoa, Jason Phillips, Mark Franke, Kara Shaw, and Adam Lerner.

I could not have completed the necessary research for this study without a legion of research assistants. At Williams College I was fortunate to be able to hire Tom Kimbis, Neville Alexander, Bethany Moreton, and Megan McCracken to work for me. In Australia, I exploited shamelessly the library expertise and cheerful willingness to help of my mother-in-law, Shirley Campbell. What she can do with a cryptic keyword is a wonder to behold for the CD-ROM illiterate.

Last but not least I thank the postgraduate students at the Australian National University. I was fortunate there to have the opportunity to contribute to their Identity and Governmentality lecture series, and benefited greatly from the supportive scholarly environment they fostered. My thanks to all.

—K. A. M.

1
Nationalism and Global Politics

The Scripture says not a word of their Rulers or Forms of Government, but only gives an account, how Mankind came to be divided into distinct Languages and Nations.
—John Locke, 1698[1]

This book is an attempt to make sense of the power of nationalism in a world seemingly incapable of realizing homogeneous nation-states. Within the twinned disciplines of international relations and comparative politics, scholarly attention to questions of state sovereignty and national identity has been concentrated for several decades in four main subfields. One is international political economy, where a "sovereignty at bay" literature has theorized the demise of state power in the wake of the postwar expansion of transnational capital.[2] Another is development studies, devoted since its appearance in the late 1950s to comparative analyses of state-building and national development in Western Europe and the so-called Third World.[3] The third is a more general but related literature on nations and nationalism, one that E. J. Hobsbawm thinks "entered so fruitful a phase about twenty years ago."[4] And finally there is critical international relations theory, a genre that "unties the sovereign state" while inviting inquiry into the construction of all political boundaries and identities.[5]

These literatures have emerged in a context of decolonization, when processes of "globalization and fragmentation are transforming the nature of political community across the world."[6] Although there is no simple cause and effect relationship, changing global power relations have brought challenges to the boundaries of seemingly autonomous disciplines as well as to the sovereignty of nominally independent nation-states. With one notable exception, each of the subfields mentioned has been home to critical questions about dominant intellectual traditions and practices. Should any discipline rely on conventional readings of a few key texts? Is it possible to understand and explain the world without poaching in the provinces traditionally reserved for other disciplines, especially sociology, economics, history, political theory, and comparative literature? Are all academic disciplines informed by modern assumptions and dichotomous modes of thought? How useful are ideal type categories such as tradition and modernity, political society and state of nature, if their employers "slide from treating [them] as heuristic devices to thinking of them as fixed empirical states of affairs of a rather uniform kind"?[7] And if the object of analysis is a phenomenon considered abnormal or pathological (Nazism, for example), where should its roots be sought?

The notable exception is the literature on nations and nationalism. Certainly there are critical voices throughout the social sciences, individual scholars who have questioned the boundary production and maintenance at work in eminent texts. The most influential theories discussed in this chapter are not themselves without merit or insight. But their capacity to account for contemporary nationalist practices is limited by too ready acceptance of modern ideas that presuppose a secular/spiritual dichotomy. Within that intellectual frame, the main preoccupation has been with the origins and spread of the modern nation-state, not with the historical nation in global context analyzed by early modern thinkers. The dominant academic tradition remains the modernization theory used in older accounts of state-building and national development, along with a sprinkling of the Hobbesian realism no longer hegemonic in international relations. And the prevailing approach to nationalism is still binary classification: the production of a fixed boundary between a modern (ungendered and nonracial) Western model of the nation and a deviant type now identified as "ethnic."

Etienne Balibar has argued that "there is always a 'good' and a 'bad' nationalism."[8] But that split is internal to the concept of nationalism itself, not original to one particular branch or modernizing society. Medieval attempts to understand the origins and nature of human diversity were sparked by European travel into distant lands and given sustenance by colonial relationships. Christian thought, political philosophy, and racial science have long been home to debates about identity and difference; through cross-fertilization and interbreeding they have spawned ideas that continue to echo within nationalist thought and practice.

Nationalism has been spread through (and been dependent on) imperial networks of power and knowledge. The conditions that foster its appeal are in global politics. They are in power relations associated with the operation and management of the world economy; with the institutions and imperatives of postcolonial development; and with international relations of war and diplomacy. Neither its historical genesis nor contemporary forms can be understood unless nationalism is situated within a larger historical and political context than that of the sovereign nation-state.

Colonial powers, according to Balibar, prided themselves "on their particular humaneness, by projecting the image of racism on to the colonial practices of their rivals. . . . The other White is also the Bad White."[9] That colonial practice has been revived, in attempts to cast either Germany or some part of Eastern Europe as the source of "ethnic" mythology. Unless it is acknowledged that (in Paul Gilroy's words) "the power of [these] imperial dreams remains considerable, partly because they have been so forcefully repressed and so actively forgotten,"[10] it is not possible to understand why "racism is constantly emerging out of nationalism, not only towards the exterior but towards the interior."[11]

Remembrance of how colonialism has shaped the national identities of colonizer *and* colonized (not just of the latter) can also contribute to the political project advocated by V. Y. Mudimbe for critical intellectuals—that of decolonizing the human and social sciences.[12]

The premise of this book is that nationalist practices, for all of their diverse forms and locations, are political religions that create boundaries separating sacred kin and alien kind. Nationalism's dominant conceptual partners are not simply nation and state. They are also race and alien, for without the racialized kind of alien there can be no national kin. Nation and alien are relational terms, interdependent and inseparable in nationalist thought and practice.

A historically variable concept, "race" has bound man to nature (either a mythical state of human nature or other living things in the natural world) through the twin categories of species and family. Unlike Charles Darwin's natural species, human races can transmute into ethnic groups through political selection. No boundary is ever immutable, and the alien races of today may become the ethnic minorities (or hyphenated nationals) of tomorrow.

But it is not the case—as Ernest Gellner has claimed—that "ethnicity has replaced kinship as the principal method of identity-conferment."[13] Nations are imagined as kinship groups under the authority of a godlike and frequently masculinized state; those outside the boundaries created and maintained by nationalism are treated as a different (sometimes feminized but also hypermasculine) species of either human or animal; and the sanctioned movement of people across nationalist boundaries is referred to as naturalization (of aliens) and transplantation (of nationals).

The following chapter shows that common spiritual and racial elements cut across the boundaries of ideal types of nations. Thereafter are three historical country studies—of South Africa, Britain, and Australia. These are designed to demonstrate in greater detail, and to seek to explain, how racialized understandings of identity and difference operate within nationalist practice. Race remains alive in collective memory and common sense, even though inscriptions of permanent difference and hierarchy are increasingly coded as either "culture" or "ethnicity."

The remainder of this chapter situates the "fruitful" phase of writings about nations and nationalism in historical and global context. This literature serves as testimony to how national boundaries are constituted in the present and reinvented in moments of global change. But as explanations for the power of nationalism—for a phenomenon that promises the domestic security of home and family as a way to cope with globalization—these stories are less than convincing. For it is not the specifically modern in isolation that accounts for nationalism's authority, but the continued dependence of modern political principles, like nationality, on racial and religious traditions.

MYTHICAL ORIGINS OF MODERN NATION-STATES

> Recently, everyone has been harking back to his or her origins—you have noticed it, I suppose?   —Julia Kristeva, 1993[14]

Nation and State

If the proliferation of books and journals is any indication, transformations attendant upon the cessation of the Cold War between the United States and the Soviet Union have done nothing to diminish growing attention to nations and nationalism. Looking forward in time, some have asked what is to become of nationality as a political principle. Historians such as William McNeill have argued that polyethnicity is destined to become the norm of the future, as it was before the French Revolution of 1789 signaled the "triumph of nationalism."[15] Then again, the incorporation of nations into larger transnational communities, as seems to have happened in Western Europe, cannot be discounted as a possibility.[16] While it was once fashionable to anticipate the demise of national identities ("the more industrialism, the less nationalism," according to Gellner[17]), those who predicted the rebirth of nationalism may take cold comfort from events around the globe.[18]

More enticing than prophecy has been the urge to look back, to an original moment when the idea (and ideal) of the nation was supposedly born and spread. Hobsbawm has argued that the nation "belongs exclusively to a particular, and historically recent, period." As far as he is concerned, "It is a social entity only insofar as it relates to a certain kind of modern territorial state, the 'nation-state,' and it is pointless to discuss nation and nationality except insofar as both relate to it."[19]

Many such discussions are not theoretical at all—hence the influence of a fairly small number of eminent scholars. Numerous works in the field offer little more than classification of national types, rather than theoretical accounts of the politics of nationalism across time and space.[20] According to Hobsbawm, the most common question is the same one that Ernest Renan asked in 1882, namely, "What is a nation?"[21]

Although there is no definitional consensus, "most serious writers" have apparently agreed with Karl Deutsch's 1953 claim that "nationality is not biological and has little if anything to do with race."[22] The most frequently recurring element of nationhood cited is a common culture; as Gellner has expressed it, "Two men are of the same nation if and only if they share the same culture."[23] After that comes shared time (usually historical or ancestral ties and myths but also "homogeneous, empty time"[24]), followed by common territory or shared homeland.

Within nation-states thought of as "empirical states of affairs," nationalism is more often located in subnational organizations and parties than in the social and political institutions of the dominant culture. One form of theoretical analysis that does exist (in studies of comparative government and electoral systems) takes the form of reflections on how democratic states can best manage the nationalist objectives of "ethnic groups" in "plural societies."[25] Broader theoretical questions are also posed about the concept of nationalism—about why it proves so difficult to define,[26] about whether it creates nations or vice versa, and about how models of the nation invented in parts of the Western world (usually in England, France, or what is now the United States) were transformed in the process of dissemination from one society to another.[27]

Language and Capital

> It is language, more than land and history, that provides the essential form of belonging, which is to be understood.
> —*Michael Ignatieff, 1993*[28]

Efforts to explain the origins of the national idea in the West typically focus on what Liah Greenfeld has called its "specificity,"[29] on what it did *not* share with traditional (religious and racial) conceptions of identity. Benedict Anderson, for example, has claimed that "from the start the nation was conceived in language, not in blood, and one could be 'invited into' the imagined community."[30] The distinction between language and kinship, however, has never been that stark. It is not only that ideas about "common stock" have been disseminated in popular languages and mutual intelligibility deemed a marker of relatedness. European languages were themselves divided into kinship groups at the beginning of the seventeenth century. According to Yuri Slezkine:

> In 1610, Joseph Justus Scaliger had divided the European languages into four major families: Greek, Romance, Germanic, and Slavic. . . . All languages and hence all nations had parents, siblings, and offspring (dialects); all linguistic elements could be divided between congenital and acquired; hence a correct method of distinguishing between the two would result in flawless genealogy.[31]

National identity, for Anderson, was made possible by a conception of modern time and then circulated by nationalists using capitalist modes of communication. It was incompatible with the messianic time of the medieval era and with the Christian communities and dynastic realms the nation-state supplanted. To be successful, the nation seemingly required "a secular transformation of fatality into continuity, contingency into meaning."[32] It also needed the fall of Latin as a sacred language and its displacement by territorially based vernaculars.[33]

Industrial capitalism purportedly required a common education system and uniform language; in modern factories and commercial print a mass citizenry was invented and manufactured. Meanwhile, the state was gaining authority over education, religion, and law. For Gellner the role of the educative state in developing a common culture, rather than other activities such as taxation, warfare, or bureaucratic incorporation, enabled the engendering of nations.[34]

The relationship of capitalism to nationalism needs to be rethought—as Gellner's later work acknowledges.[35] Neither the structural needs of capitalism nor its capacity to disseminate an original idea in a shared tongue were deemed productive of nationalism in the writings of early modern thinkers such as Marx, Lenin, and Weber. Yet if there is no simple causal connection between them, the two great "isms" of the modern age do share three common features.

First, both capitalism and nationalism are modes of life and systems of meaning now existing on a global scale. They constitute a global "culture" if that term is understood in the way that Gellner has used it, to mean "a system of ideas and signs and associations and ways of behaving and communicating."[36] Production never ceases within these global cultures; it occurs daily in multiple sites that are linked together to some extent in what Immanuel Wallerstein has called a world-system. Organizational structures both within political boundaries (state machineries) and across them (transnational alliances of classes and countries) work to institutionalize relations of power by managing conflicts and repressing opposition.[37]

But as Max Weber recognized, the most effective way to maintain culture that is "in reality so little a matter of course" is not to seek "a conscious acceptance" of its maxims, let alone to silence dissent. Cultures that present themselves to the individual as "an unalterable order of things in which he must live" appear most natural and outside of conscious thought. Unconscious common sense is the product of "a long and arduous process of education,"[38] one that operates continuously in social institutions (schools, universities, media, and churches, for example) that need not be under state authority in order to be effective.

Second, both capitalism and nationalism privilege monoculture over diversity. The uniform trees, seeds, and crops of capitalist agriculture are analogous to the culturally homogeneous citizens of the idealized nation-state.[39] Yet both are uneven in that for all their seeming triumph, they continue to coexist with alternative ways of being and knowing in the world. Global cultures have been resisted, and not every site of production has yet been captured by the world-system. Contemporary struggles against monoculture, for example, inhere in attachments to biodiversity and to multicultural societies.

Third, and perhaps most important, capitalism and nationalism are combined in that neither exists in pure form, devoid of traces of earlier modes of life or conceptions of identity. Renan described "forgetting" as "a crucial factor in the creation of a nation."[40] The body of writings that Anthony Smith has called "modernist"[41] has forgotten many of the practices of "disavowal, displacement, exclusion, and cultural contestation"[42] at work in the constitution of modern nation-states. Also forgotten are the racial and religious traditions that still inform nationalist thinking about human diversity, nature, and origins. As Alejandro Portes once said, "Secular modernity lacks sufficient cultural depth to match the force of great national traditions."[43]

James Kellas has pointed out that "'God's People' is a favorite idea of nationalists."[44] Yet even those nationalisms that make no mention of a god (Christian or otherwise) treat the nation as sacred and demand sacrifice in its name. Nationalism is secular to the extent that religious difference is tolerated and conversion is not a condition of naturalization. But when it treats the immortalized nation as an entity worth dying for—as the ultimate object of individual loyalty—nationalism operates as a political religion.

Western models of the nation are *less secular* than they often appear, in part because the idea of the nation as a unilingual "family" of common descent derives from Christian scripture. When the Second Treasons Act of 1571 in England mentioned "nation," it still meant "no more than a family of kin."[45] The widening of the concept of nationhood to embrace all those in a given polity or territory may be traceable in part to the Authorized Version of the King James Bible. The Old Testament was borrowed from and modified in the course of the Protestant Reformation.[46] "By the eighteenth century," according to Slezkine,

> the rise of national states, national vernaculars, and national churches had resulted in the nationalization of Paradise (claims had been made that Adam and Eve spoke Flemish, French, and Swedish, among others), and then in the appearance of multiple autonomous paradises (all nations/languages had their own excellent ancestors).[47]

For Greenfeld, modernity is a product of nationalism—of the nationalist location of individual identity within a sovereign people—and not the other way around. By 1650 the term *nation* already meant "the sovereign people of England." It later acquired three other synonyms: *country, com-*

monwealth, and *empire.*[48] Neither nationalism nor modernity can thus be
understood without an analysis of how all those concepts—family, nation,
country, commonwealth, empire, and race—have overlapped in nationalist
thought and practice.

Western models are *more racial* than they often seem (and let it be
remembered that Protestant Britain and Catholic France have been models
of racial enmity toward *each other*), in part because the word *race* entered
the English language in 1508 as a synonym for family lineage. English-
language Bibles of the period were consistent with other writings in their use
of the term *nation* as interchangeable with *tribe* (a people connected by kinship and language), and with *race.*[49] Race (like nation) has come to be associated since then with culture, time, and geopolitical space. But its earliest
attachment to family, nation, and fixed human difference has not been severed. It has been commercially reproduced in publications such as government documents, children's stories, travelers' tales from distant lands, and
popular books, newspapers, and magazines.

Accounts that find the origins of the national idea in modernity have
sprouted only since the decolonization of European empires and the onset of
the Cold War, not since the dawn of the modern age. The following section
shows that Enlightenment principles, revolutionary ideals, and vernacular
languages have not always been treated as central to the national idea in the
West. Nor has binary classification always been the norm.

NATIONALISM AND MODERNITY

To treat nations as modern is often to presume that they did not exist (indeed
were not even conceived) prior to a recent and historically discrete period.
Leaving aside for the moment the question of whether modernity is simply
an epoch (as opposed to a series of attitudes and orientations toward the
world), it is important to know when the modern age—and thus nationalism—is supposed to have begun. The answer is by no means obvious,
depending as it does on whether the time before modernity is described as
ancient, medieval, feudal, or traditional. But as in the work of Michel
Foucault (which concerns itself with such novelties as "modern rituals of
execution"),[50] the literature on nations and nationalism tends to locate
modernity's birthday somewhere around the end of the eighteenth century.
Thanks largely to the fame of Anderson's *Imagined Communities,* the notion
that the national idea "was born in an age in which Enlightenment and
Revolution were destroying the legitimacy of the divinely ordered, hierarchical dynastic realm" continues to circulate.[51]

Yet according to Greenfeld, "The emergence of nationalism predated
the development of every significant component of modernization."[52] Self-

consciously indebted to Max Weber,[53] Greenfeld has claimed that "it is possible to locate the emergence of national sentiment in England in the first third of the sixteenth century." While that sentiment initially took a benign cultural form (a Chaucerian revival), it was simultaneously manifested in anti-alien feeling (a riot against foreign artisans in 1517 in London) and in diatribes against agents of the Holy Roman Empire.[54]

Marc Shell's *Children of the Earth* also shows that a vision of an English nation-state was manifest in the writings of Henry VIII's daughter Elizabeth.[55] The conceptual apparatus of nationalism could not have depended on modern institutions, because it already existed in written form, in what Shell has called "the political fictions of premodern familial nationalism."[56]

Those whom Greenfeld has described as "the founding fathers of the discipline of sociology"—intellectuals whose life's work it was "to account for the emergence of modern society"—did not treat the national idea as peculiarly modern either.[57] In his analysis and critique of a period of human history defined (for him at least) by the development of "modern private property," Karl Marx describes the preceding era as either "feudal" or as the Middle Ages. Written in the mid–nineteenth century, Marx and Engels's "The German Ideology" located the conditions of "this new phase" in power relations that were global in scope. Increased trade and communications between hitherto isolated towns, in combination with a rapid rise in manufacturing, brought "the various nations . . . into a competitive relationship" with each other for the first time. Previously "inoffensive exchange" was replaced by struggles for trade, which were "fought out in wars."

Commercial struggle was apparently fueled by "the colonization of the newly discovered countries" that began "with the discovery of America and the sea-route to the East Indies" in 1492. Between the middle of the seventeenth and the end of the eighteenth century, "the nation dominant in sea trade and colonial power" (England) had secured for itself "a relative world market" as well as "freedom of competition inside the nation" and "the science of mechanics perfected by Newton." Thus was England, for Marx, the most advanced of the "civilized nations." Although soon joined by others, it was England that led in the development of a modern state, modern capital, a modern world market, modern and large industrial cities, modern peoples, and modern society.[58]

Given his attempt to explain why "a definite *mode of life*"[59] instantiated by England emerged out of the disintegration of feudalism, it seems fair to describe Marx as a theorist of modernity. It is noteworthy then that when Marx wrote of "modern nations" he contrasted them to "the ancients," not to feudal institutions.[60] By describing Phoenicians "in primitive history" as a nation,[61] Marx clearly did not consider nation to be a modern concept.

More obviously modern (and significant) for Marx was "civil society," an eighteenth-century and bourgeois conception that "has as its premises and basis the simple family and the multiple, the so-called tribe."[62] According to contemporary Marxists such as Nigel Harris, Marx had little to say about nationalism because he considered it a passing phase and less significant, in the long run, than transnational proletarian solidarity.[63] But the "simple family" has been a core element in nationalist renderings of identity, and other themes central to Marx's discussions of state and civil society—such as sovereignty and democracy—have figured prominently in more recent accounts of nationalism. A consideration of Marx's analyses of "bourgeois ideology" sheds important light on the religious foundations of modern political concepts.

In terms reminiscent of Anderson, Marx bemoaned the fact that in the state, "man is the imaginary member of an imaginary sovereignty, divested of his real, individual life, and infused with an unreal universality."[64] For Marx the novel political idea (and ideal) fostered by bourgeois intellectuals was political democracy; it was first realized in states emancipated from the imperial power of the Catholic Church. Yet Marx's essay "On the Jewish Question" contains an important insight into the purported secularity of the modern "political state."

Marx argued that the "secular maxim" underpinning political democracy was an existing religious principle: the Christian ideal of man as "a sovereign being, a supreme being." Marx insisted that "the perfected Christian state" is the atheistic democratic state, the one that has effectively displaced religion onto civil society and "not the so-called *Christian* state which acknowledges Christianity as its basis." A Christian understanding of sovereignty was for Marx the spiritual foundation of modern political society. It enabled the state to occupy the same spiritual place that heaven (for Christians) occupies in relation to earth.[65]

Marx's work calls into question any presumption of a firm boundary between nationalism and religion, because it highlights the indebtedness of secular political principles—like democracy—to Christian conceptions of identity. The Christian ideal of human sovereignty that Marx alluded to owes more to the Protestant Reformation than to the teachings of Jesus Christ himself. But such a principle is modern only if modernity is pushed back into the sixteenth century, into the temporal domain referred to by Marx as the Middle Ages.

What then of a Marxian relationship between capitalism and nationalism? Dominant ideas are always those through which a ruling class expresses its interests as the general interest, according to Marx.[66] It could be inferred from this that the national idea has come to dominate global political life thanks to the "conceptive ideologists" (Marx's term) at work for transnational capital.[67] The problem with this formulation is that as capitalism has become globalized it has become less unified; national boundaries may serve the interests of some capitalists while being antithetical to the needs of others. And particularly in its more virulently racist formulations, nationalism has been practiced by the ideologues of organized labor.

Capitalism could have had more to do with nationalism in the nineteenth century than it does at the end of the twentieth. Following Marx, Lenin posited that "one of the modern requirements of capitalism is undoubtedly the greatest possible national uniformity of the population, for nationality and language identity are an important factor making for the complete conquest of the home market and for complete freedom of economic intercourse." Yet Lenin went on to insist that "the national composition of the population" is "*one* of the very important economic factors, *but not the sole and not* the most important factor" (his emphasis). What capitalism most needed to function, for Lenin, was the free movement of labor between villages and towns. Since the consequence of labor mobility was the appearance in urban locations of "mixed populations," homogeneity was not a prerequisite of production.[68]

The centrality of *global* movement to nationalism (as well as to capitalism) will be considered later in the chapter. But first, a brief reference to Weber's work on "modern culture" is in order. Unlike Marx, Weber believed that "capitalism and capitalistic enterprises" have existed throughout human history—"in China, India, Babylon, Egypt, Mediterranean antiquity, and the Middle Ages, as well as in modern times."[69] What for Weber was peculiarly Western and modern was a form of capitalist organization typified by four principal features: "the rational capitalist organization of (formally) free labor"; "the separation of business from the household"; "rational bookkeeping"; and "our legal separation of corporate from personal property."[70]

Theoretical differences between Marx and Weber are less significant for present purposes than their shared assessments of modernity. Both considered modern capitalism to be fundamentally "dependent on the peculiarities of modern science."[71] Both analyzed the spiritual basis of modern life; the principle of individual sovereignty was the spirit of civil society for Marx, whereas for Weber, Calvin's conception of the calling was the spirit of capitalism. And each of them bemoaned the human costs of modern capitalist production, a system that for Weber ran on the subordination of man to economic acquisition.

The "reversal of what we should call the natural relationship" of man to money[72] could be effected, Weber felt, only with the overthrow of a supposedly natural trait that he designated "traditionalism." The "idyllic state" in which non-Calvinist man supposedly lived was destroyed for Weber once "the old leisurely and comfortable attitude toward life gave way to a hard frugality."[73] Fanciful indeed may have been Weber's rendition of man's "natural" disposition. But it seems clear that he (like Marx) deemed modern man to be an impoverished version of a human being.

Weber was more obviously a theorist of nationalism in the modern age than were either Marx or Lenin. In one of his essays, Weber defined a nation as "a community which normally tends to produce a state of its own."[74] Asking how national sentiment is produced, and under what conditions, Weber considered the influence of "times of external danger" (war); of "differences among anthropological types" (race); of "tradition"; of "aesthetic aversions" that are "social in nature"; and of "a common language."[75]

In keeping with Lenin and also more recent theorists like Anderson, Weber attached some significance to the binding power of language. But in contrast to Anderson, Weber did not attribute the displacement of Latin and the emergence of national languages to conditions associated with capitalism. "Pecuniary and capitalist interests are anchored in the maintenance and cultivation of the popular language," according to Weber, but they did not engender it in the first place. He attributed the emergence of vernacular languages to "courtly and chivalrous lyric" poetry addressed to women, and the steady progression of those languages to "the influence of the broadening administrative tasks of state *and church*" (my emphasis).[76]

Weber did not consider nationalism to be dependent on the circulation of a common language, on the needs of capitalism, or on anything else that he considered to be peculiarly modern. The conditions that fed nationalism for Weber were those associated with imperial rule from Rome. He argued as follows:

> The conciliar, and at the same time nationalist, reaction against the universalism of the papacy in the waning Middle Ages had its origin, to a great extent, in the interests of the intellectuals who wished to see the prebends of their country reserved for themselves and not occupied by strangers via Rome. After all the name *natio* as a legal concept for an organized community is found first at the universities and at the reform councils of the church. At that time, however, the linkage to the national language *per se* was lacking; this linkage, for the reasons stated, *is specifically modern* [my emphasis].[77]

Marx and Weber's thought suggests four key points about the modernist approach to nations and nationalism. First, modern capitalism's capacity to spread the popularity of nationalist thought through commercially produced books, periodicals, and daily newspapers has been confused with the ability to invent it. Dissemination is not the same as creation. Second, social institutions such as the church have been as important a site of nationalist activity and influence as the state. Third, it is only the linkage of a shared language to national identity that is specifically modern, not the national idea itself. That idea was already apparent in the "waning Middle Ages," where it functioned in opposition to "strangers via Rome" as well as to foreign artisans (who were mainly Jewish). And fourth, the roots of the modernist approach are not in early modern thinking but in modernization theory, a literature whose genesis was conditioned by decolonization and the onset of the Cold War.

DECOLONIZATION AND THE REINVENTION OF THE MODERN

We do not claim to have invented the idea of the modern man. . . . The modern man's character, as it emerges from our study, may be summed up under four major headings. He is an informed participant citizen; he has a marked sense of personal efficacy; he is highly independent and autonomous in his relations to traditional sources of influence . . . and he is ready for new experiences and ideas. . . . The more modern men [are] shaped by the modernizing institutions we have identified, namely, the school, the newspaper, and the factory.

—Inkeles and Smith, 1974[78]

Modern Nation-States and Traditional Societies

Nationalism is peculiarly a product of or a response to the distinctive forces which have gone into the shaping of the modern world. Those forces are inherently and inevitably "democratic."   *—Rupert Emerson, 1960*[79]

John Locke wrote in 1698 of the "several Nations of the Americans" supposedly living in a savage state of nature.[80] Karl Marx wrote of "civilized nations" composed of "advanced peoples." In his essay "On Imperialism in India," Marx contrasted them to the "semi-barbarian, semi-civilized communities" that supposedly existed in "Hindostan" before "English steam and English free trade" destroyed them.[81]

While they do not equate nations with Western modernity, the works of Locke and Marx reflect and reinforce "a chain of ideas vital to the colonialist enterprise."[82] On the one side of the imperial divide was often said to stand—in the words of David Ricardo—"the universal society of nations throughout the civilized world."[83] On the other side was imagined a repository of all things backward, savage, primitive, barbaric, childlike, and heathen.

The binary opposition between civilized and barbaric largely disappeared with the breakup of European empires. The dichotomy of advanced/primitive did not long survive decolonization either, although

David McClelland could still contrast "modern nations" to "primitive tribes" in a book published in 1968.[84] What took their place in modernization theories of state-building and national development was the now familiar distinction between modern nation-states and traditional societies.

The most influential theorists of modernization—such as McClelland and Seymour Martin Lipset—have claimed an intellectual debt to Weber.[85] Yet the construction of tradition is not built on Weber's concept of traditionalism. That concept referred to a particular attitude toward money, not toward all social values and the treatment of others. Traditionalism, by the same token, was not antithetical to democracy or to the progressive forces of the Enlightenment. It was hostile only to a "peculiar ethic" that Weber thought derivative of Calvinism:

> The *summum bonum* of this ethic, the earning of more and more money, combined with the strict avoidance of all spontaneous enjoyment of life, is above all completely devoid of any eudaemonistic, not to say hedonistic, admixture. It is thought of so purely as an end in itself, that from the point of view of the happiness of, or utility to, the single individual, it appears entirely transcendental and absolutely irrational.[86]

"Tradition" hails not from Weber but from the pattern-variables of Talcott Parsons.[87] Parsons's 1951 distinctions between achievement and ascription, universalism and particularism, and specificity and diffuseness have been described in the following terms by Lipset:

> A society's value system may emphasize that a person in his orientation to others treats them in terms of their abilities and performances (achievement) or in terms of inherited qualities (ascription); applies a general standard (universalism) or responds to some personal attribute or relationship (particularism); deals with them in terms of the specific positions which they happen to occupy (specificity) or in general terms as individual members of the collectivity (diffuseness).[88]

Classification of decolonizing societies as traditional and the once imperial states as modern was soon commonplace. Modernization became a synonym for development, and the theoretical task was to explain the process of transition from the former ideal type of society to the latter. According to Daniel Lerner, for example, a traditional society passes into the modern world once it acquires five key traits: (1) a degree of self-sustaining growth in the economy; (2) a measure of political participation; (3) a diffusion of secular-rational norms in the culture; (4) an increase in physical and social mobility; and (5) a corresponding transformation in personality to equip individuals to function effectively in a modern social order.[89]

In the terms of Lerner or Parsons, a social system conditioned by religious principles, by "inherited qualities" such as skin color or sex, by family ties, and by collective identities (such as those based in race, gender, or nationality) deserves classification as traditional. Religion, race, gender, family, and nation have all underpinned the construction of what Smith in 1971 called "another stereotype of modernity, the nation-state of Western Europe and America."[90] The extent to which actual men in ideal type situations are independent of "traditional sources of influence" is thus debatable. And yet the majority of peoples in the former colonies are the ones supposedly "tied to the rigid, diffuse, and ascriptive patterns of tradition."[91]

Theories of nationalism in the 1960s were inseparable from those of modernization. Nationalism in newly independent states has been linked by Weber's followers to the conditions and functioning of a modernizing society, even though Weber himself drew attention to anti-imperialist struggle. Nationalism supposedly offered a novel sense of community as a way to cope with the social disintegration of traditional societies, while simultaneously asking for acceptance of rapid and painful change in the name of the greater good.

The most common approach to nationalism was a "functionalist perspective" that starts, according to Smith in his early work, "from the suggestions in Rousseau, draws heavily on Durkheim's analysis of complex society, and ends by echoing Weber." The notion of nationalism as a "secular religion" emerged from Durkheim's analysis of the French Revolution and informed the work of some but not all of the functionalists. Nationalism was equated by David Apter and others with the manipulation of religion for political ends, or defined as a form of "political religion" that invested the new state and its laws with sacred qualities.[92]

If that older insight into the connectedness of religion and nationalism (one found in Marx and Weber as well as in Durkheim and Rousseau) has been lost, it is thanks in part to the influence of Smith himself. Insisting that "between traditional religion and nationalism there is a decisive break," Smith argued in the early 1970s for thinking of nationalism as a secular ideology "*alongside* religion" (his emphasis).[93]

The following chapter addresses in more detail why the notion of nationalism as ideology is problematic. The failing of the functionalist perspective is not that it drew on Durkheim but that—as with the particular readings of Weber—it did not draw enough. Somehow the nationalism at work in the "totalitarian" new states of Africa and Asia was not traced to the circulation of French (or British) nationalist thought. As Smith has explained it:

> The sources of these new religions are to be sought in the 'needs' of the new nations: the need to build a polity, the need to transcend 'primordial' ties of ethnicity, language and religion, to reconstitute a strong central authority, to develop economic rationality among a traditionally-minded citizenry; above all, the need for rapid material development. These needs

drive men to sacrifice themselves to realise the ends of the society; their commitment parallels the sense of vocation and the urge for frugality and self-discipline of the early Puritans.[94]

Not all modernization theorists joined nationalism to need. The "mass society" school considered nationalism an expression of "organized insecurity" and found its appeal in promises to control change—another important insight.[95] But what these older writings share—with each other and with more recent modernist works—is an emphasis on disintegration, breakdown, and decisive breaks with "traditional sources of influence." Modernity is conceived as a revolutionary epoch characterized by a specifically modern set of ideas and practices. A fundamental rupture in ways of thinking about God, man, nature, and authority is attributed to public schools, newspapers, and factories. And the theoretical gaze is on nation-states isolated from their global context, instead of on a network of power relations linking imperial centers to the rest of the world.

Despite Inkeles and Smith's reinvention of the modern "man," it would not be fair to say that modernization theory as a whole ignored women. McClelland, for example, argued that a successful approach to development "would be to promote the rights of women," on the grounds that progressive mothers are more likely to raise young men with an "entrepreneurial drive."[96] But the assumption that modern nation-states are by definition gender-neutral is one shared with the modernists. As Smith's later work has noted, they consider "that a single criterion, the inclusion of the masses and women, is decisive for determining the emergence and presence of the nation."[97] None of the major theorists of nationalism have paid much attention to the question of why nations are gendered in particular ways at different times—often, but not always, as "motherlands."[98]

Nationalism values the autonomous and rational man, but only to a point. Nations may be conceived as any living thing with special traits or the capacity to flourish in a particular place. Nations have been imagined as human bodies, both male and female; as animals such as dogs; as plants, trees, or flowers; and as immortal souls.

I have argued elsewhere that the possibility for modern man to replace God as sovereign being in the world was contained within Christian thought; it did not constitute a decisive break from it:

> This is because the boundary between God and man was historically fragile in two senses: on the one hand, God has often been endowed with human characteristics, as when Christians speak of Jesus as "God's son"; on the other hand, Jesus himself has generally been considered "both God and man," that is, a God in human form. From this perspective, modernity is less an era which has proclaimed the "death of God" *per se* but rather the death of "God the father" and the supremacy of Jesus his son.[99]

"God the father" has been mimicked if overthrown by nationalist practices and narratives. Nationalism lays claim to the fruits of divinity identified in the Old Testament. Adam and Eve were ejected from Eden after eating from the tree of the knowledge of good and evil, and before they had a chance to eat from the tree of immortality. Individuals may claim to know the difference between good fellow nationals and evil aliens, but only nationalists can legitimately demand the sacrifice of human life as a means to collective immortality.

The concept of race has received more attention than the concept of gender in modernization theory. Rupert Emerson described African nationalism as racial in light of the appeal of *négritude*,[100] a concept that Léopold Sédar Senghor defined as cultural affirmation and not as racial attachment.[101] Racial identity in the modern West, by contrast, has been equated with notions of biological distinctiveness (blood, skin color, stature, and presumed genetic traits) and treated as separate from historical and cultural constructions of nationhood.[102]

Whatever the geopolitical emphasis of the study, race is presumed to have had the same referents throughout history and is not acknowledged—as Renan recognized in 1882—to be "something which is made and unmade."[103] And neither the older nor the more recent literature has shown how nationalism in Africa or Asia has drawn on the "chain of ideas" about race that helped to sustain imperialism.

Kwame Anthony Appiah has argued that pan-Africanist philosophy, at least as coopted by African nationalism, is underpinned by the "distorted rationality" of imported racial thinking. While Appiah has discussed the "illusions of race" accepted by Alexander Crummell and W. E. B. Du Bois,[104] V. Y. Mudimbe has analyzed the discourses of missionaries, anthropologists, and African literary figures and politicians. Mudimbe has shown how all of them—even the most explicitly Afrocentric—depend on racial categories and conceptual systems drawn from a Western epistemological order.[105]

Balibar has suggested that the racial nationalism emergent from colonial situations "would not constitute itself as the ideology of a 'new' nation if the official nationalism against which it were reacting were not profoundly racist."[106] The argument is consistent with Partha Chatterjee's thesis that nationalism in European colonies was derivative of imperial nationalism. It assumed an essential difference between a colonial world imagined as backward, and a post-Enlightenment West assumed to be more advanced. In calling for a synthesis of Western rationalism and Eastern spirituality, some "eastern" nationalists have challenged constructions of inferiority. But acceptance of a rational/spiritual dichotomy as historical fact is for Chatterjee indicative of failure to escape from colonial markers of difference.[107]

Western Nations and Ethnic Nations

> We can term this non-Western model an "ethnic" conception
> of the nation. Its distinguishing feature is its emphasis on a
> community of birth and native culture.
> —*Anthony Smith, 1991*[108]

> One of the richest and most civilized parts of Europe has
> returned to the barbarism of the late Middle Ages. . . . Ethnic
> nationalism was the invention of the German intelligentsia
> during the period of the Napoleonic invasion of the German
> princedoms, between 1792 and 1813.
> —*Michael Ignatieff, 1993*[109]

> Ethnicity: Heathendom, heathen superstition.
> —*The Oxford English Dictionary*

German historians Friedrich Meinecke and Hans Kohn have been faulted for
holding "the nationalist belief that nations have existed from time immemo-
rial, though often in prolonged slumber."[110] Yet their equally contentious
practices of boundary construction and classification remain very much
alive, in conventional distinctions between models called political/cultural,
subjective/objective, or (more recently) civic/ethnic.[111] According to
Greenfeld, for example, global dissemination of the national idea has result-
ed in "two radically different forms of the phenomenon" or "two branches
of nationalism . . . grounded in different values."[112]

Writing at the turn of the twentieth century, Meinecke suggested a basic
difference between the *political* nations he found in England, France, and
the United States and the *cultural* nations of Italy, central Europe, and east-
central Europe. Race was absent from both. Political nationalism was said to
make national membership contingent upon loyalty to common institutions
and state-given rights to citizenship, while cultural nationalism attaches it to
social traits such as language, religion, and customs. The political nation
was supposedly built from individual subscription (from people choosing
their own national identity), and the cultural nation from collective inheritance (where the preexisting traits of the national community define the individual born into it, not the other way around).[113]

Western nations such as England or Britain, France, and the United
States are supposedly constituted through common attachment to territory,
way of life, and history, not through collective traits. The modern "political
state" (as Marx called it) is one that extends civil rights to its citizens and
"maintains that the nation should be composed of all those—regardless of

race, color, creed, gender, language, or ethnicity—who subscribe to the nation's political creed."[114] William Pfaff, among others, has insisted that "the only possible answers to the question of what it is to be French, or British, today are cultural and political, not ethnic."[115]

Western nations are possibly analogous to families, but according to Michael Waltzer, they are also like neighborhoods without borders or like social clubs of diverse membership.[116] Citizenship is then akin to a national membership card, one supposedly handed out as a reward for loyalty and not on the basis of unchosen criteria such as race.

The Western model remains an ideal type, because every nationalism has combined political and cultural elements in diverse ways. The idea of an "ethnic" nationalism that strips individuals of choice is even more novel than the notion of "traditional" societies. Conditioned by new global norms of self-determination and racial equality (the International Convention on the Elimination of All Forms of Racial Discrimination, for example, took place in 1969 after four years of planning), the concept of ethnicity is a code for racialized differences among people presumed to be of the same race.

The term *race* has no stable meaning, as the following chapter shows in more detail. But what is common to those conceptions picked up by nationalist thought over time (race as lineage, race as type, and race as subspecies) is not skin color in particular or even physical type more generally. It is the association of race with natural difference—with the shared characteristics of social groups that cannot be chosen or shed. In historical debates about the nature of man, difference explained as the product of forces beyond an individual's control (such immovable forces as divine will, ancestry, environment, climate, animal instinct, cranial capacity, or genetic makeup) has been understood as racial.

Nationalism may invent, ignore, or dissolve racial boundaries, which are never natural and always socially constructed. But nationalism is racial when it treats permanent difference (especially difference found within the borders of state territory) as alien, threatening, and a problem to be solved. The famed tolerance of Western societies is no exception, because that which must be tolerated has already been constructed as unfamiliar, foreign, and less developed. Liberal humanism has been practiced as well, but only when prospects for assimilation or integration are not threatened by numbers. Only then do once racialized minorities (who have been "white" as well as "black") cease to be represented through metaphors of dirt, disease, evil, and plague. National inclusion is contingent upon racial sameness.

Different models have been associated with different stages of political development. Kohn distinguished in the 1940s between western European and east-central European types of nation. He argued that the former (in which he also placed the United States) depended upon the coincidence if not prior emergence of a strong administrative state. The latter was therefore more likely to be endorsed by nationalist movements in "backward" societies.[117]

Michael Ignatieff made a similar assumption a half-century later, when he stated that "nationalism has often been a revolt against modernity, a defense of the backwardness of economically beleaguered or declining classes and regions."[118] Also reminiscent of Kohn, Pfaff in 1992 described "radical difference" from "nationhood of the Western, secular, and ethnically plural kind" as typical of societies that "have yet to demonstrate their ability to live by a secular political standard." The "ethnic" model was traced by Pfaff only to "the new nations that came out of the collapse of Austria-Hungary and the Ottoman Empire."[119]

Among an earlier generation of modernization theorists, Emerson questioned whether Kohn's schema could explain state-based nationalism in Asia.[120] And yet the possibility that each nation-state might be home to a combination of hybrid national types, that the roots of nationalism in the colonies might be in the nationalism of their imperial powers, and that nationalist thought has racialized aliens remains largely unexplored.

In a 1960 article about "nation builders" in Africa, Emerson did acknowledge that "the European powers have been engaged in a process which has a great bearing on the formation of nations." But colonial administrators were apparently responsible only for "the establishment of a number of separate and independent states," not for the nationalist thought that Chatterjee would argue drove demands for statehood. Instead of investigating how "Western-oriented leaders" were Western in their orientation to the nation, Emerson claimed that "Latin America and the Middle East furnish unhappy models which are already having their imitators elsewhere." He also likened the "actual situation of the new states" in Africa to "the disaster of Nazism."[121]

However disastrous Nazism may have been, it emerged out of the historical context of German nationalism in particular and of European nationalism more generally. The idea of the nation "as a social organism functioning according to its own disposition, like a natural being," has been credited to the Romantic nationalism of Germans such as Johann Gottlieb Fichte.[122] "The Volk was the decisive ethnic twist given to the French idea of *la nation*," according to Ignatieff.[123] But if a nation/Volk distinction soon ceased to correspond to the territorial boundaries of France and Germany, then the nationalism of peoples under imperial subjection everywhere cannot be neatly separated from the nationalism of the colonizers. Nor can "ethnic" nationalism be blamed on the unmediated influence of the Bad White German.[124]

Shmuel Almog has argued that the Romantics rejected consensual or

"social contract" principles of community espoused by modern political theorists and endorsed instead a reversion to "the organic concepts of the
ancient and medieval periods."[125] Over time, "this model would tend to typify nationalism in general, leaving little room for open-mindedness" toward
Jews, in particular.[126]

The status of Jews in seventeenth-century France was anomalous; they
were neither foreigners (*aubains*) nor citizens of the kingdom (*régnicoles*).
To gain the opportunity of becoming naturalized as Frenchmen, Jews had
first, paradoxically, to be classified as foreign. Peter Sahlins has explained it
as follows:

> During the course of the eighteenth century, this anomalous status was
> transformed as the Jews came to be considered foreigners. Indeed, it was
> the apologists, royal officers, and fiscal agents of the French monarchy,
> impelled both by anti-Semitism and fiscal greed, who increasingly classi-
> fied the Jews as foreigners, thus unwittingly creating the conditions for the
> possibility of their becoming citizens. . . . The monarchy was forced to
> grant letters of naturalization to Jews during the last decade of the ancien
> regime, making them citizens after having labeled them foreigners.[127]

The legal emancipation of Jewish "foreigners" took place throughout
Europe in the 1860s, at a time when "the liberal and radical camp" were urg-
ing Jews to modify their religion and customs.[128] Jewish minorities were
obliged "to identify with the people among which they lived, to the point of
merging seamlessly into the nation."[129] But this was too much for those
attracted to the novel idea of the Jews as a Semitic race with immutable
characteristics (the term *anti-Semitism* did not appear in Europe until the
1870s). The emancipation of Jews was branded as treason and Jews themselves were considered natural aliens and enemies of the state. Almog has
noted that "antisemitic groups enjoyed considerable parliamentary success
in the 1880s in Germany and Austria and were highly influential in France,
particularly following the Dreyfus Affair in the last decade of the century."[130]

France evidently wants to forget the historical context of its own World
War II practices, such as the conversion of an apartment complex outside
Paris into the Drancy concentration camp. According to Tzvetan Todorov,
"The French—with, of course, notable exceptions—prefer to think that
everything was the fault of the Germans and that Vichy was guilty only of
being weak."[131] These factors alone do not explain why 25,000 French-born
Jews (known as Israelites) were deported to camps in Poland along with
50,000 immigrant Jews. Nor do they explain why deportation at the time
was blamed on the victims—who were said to be a threat to French employment, peace, and identity—instead of on the Gestapo. France's humanist and

republican heritage may have "helped lessen the persecution of the Jews." But another tradition, one of "highly articulate antisemitism," justified the persecution that did take place.[132]

To acknowledge the centrality of race in constructing national identities and boundaries is to admit that Western nation-states are not inherently superior to the rest. If such acknowledgment is rare it is because colonial dichotomies of civilized/barbaric and advanced/primitive have not been transcended; they have only been relabeled as modern/traditional or Western/ethnic. Race-based nationalism that cannot be denied (Jean-Louis Le Pen in France, neo-Nazis in Germany, the British National Party, and so on) has been diagnosed as a "moral cancer" and blamed on political "wimps" who fail to prescribe early treatment.[133] This illustrates Peter Fitzpatrick's point that racism in countries with "innocent" legal systems is routinely cast as "something aberrant, a particular episode that disturbs the normal course."[134]

Ignatieff's analysis of "the new nationalism" at work around the world makes clear the importance in all nationalisms of race, religion, and gender. "European racism" is identified as "a form of white ethnic nationalism," while nationalism itself is "the dream that a whole nation could be like a congregation; singing the same hymns, listening to the same gospel, sharing the same emotions, linked not only to each other but to the dead buried beneath their feet." Nationalism is a gendered concept, for Ignatieff. "It seems obvious" to him "that the state's order is the order of the father, and that nationalism is the rebellion of the sons."[135]

Despite these provocative insights, *Blood and Belonging* ends by reasserting the civic/ethnic dichotomy with which it begins. And while modernization theory is eschewed, the explanation for nationalist sentiment and violence is no more than a combination of Anderson (the centrality of language to identity) and a crude Hobbesian realism. "Thomas Hobbes would have understood Yugoslavia," according to Ignatieff,[136] because nationalism is a product of the fear and insecurity that occur in a state of nature:

> When the Soviet empire and its satellite regimes collapsed, the nation-state structures of the region also collapsed, leaving hundreds of ethnic groups at the mercy of each other. Faced with a situation of political and economic chaos, people want to know whom to trust, and whom to call their own. Ethnic nationalism provided an answer that was intuitively obvious: Only trust those of your own blood.[137]

If the answer is obvious, the question of how people with the same physical traits can know their "own blood" is not. Struggle between Serbian and Croatian nationalists, for example, is described as "a war where the enemies went to school together, worked in the same haulage company, and now talk on the CB every night, laughing, taunting, telling jokes."[138] The protagonists clearly spoke the same language, so differences of kin and kind could not be self-evident after decades of communist rule.

It is not the object of this book to explain nationalism in the "new states" of Eastern Europe. But the notion of nationalism there as no more than the defense of preexisting groups, whose ancient mistrust is rooted in intuitively obvious differences, does not explain how allies have become enemies or neighbors transformed into racialized objects of mass rape and extermination. The collapse of state structures may have bred insecurity and thus receptivity to nationalist messages. But nationalism was not invented by the young men with submachine guns encountered by Ignatieff on his travels. It was already in place, in the social and political institutions of the Soviet regime and the Yugoslavian state.

The sentiment that feeds much nationalist violence, in Brackette Williams's words, is that "someone else's roots are growing in the national/ethnic soil, distorting the particular form of human nature that ought to be sprouting there."[139] It is all too easy to treat such sentiment as peculiar to the "wounded, therefore aggressive, nationalisms of Eastern Europe and the Mediterranean."[140] But as Jean Baudrillard has stated, Bosnia is only the "new frontier" of a Europe that is trying to remake itself through "ethnic purification."[141] If Le Pen has largely disappeared from the political scene in France, it is only because his ideas resonate with, and have been appropriated by, the institutions of the European Community. Tougher asylum laws, troop patrols, and passport checks are political signs that "Western Europeans are turning against the strangers in their midst."[142]

"Bashing foreigners" in a context of economic reconstruction and endemic unemployment only reinforces racist and antiforeign policies, as Martin Woollacott has argued.[143] But the impulse to bash is an effect of *global* conditions and the reinscription of certain groups as foreign. It needs to be analyzed in historical and global context, not simply blamed on malignant cells, lack of political development, or the absence of state authority.

GLOBAL POLITICS AND THE AUTHORITY OF TRADITION

The early African novel produced under [colonial] circumstances, took its themes and moral preoccupation from the bible. . . . I also incorporated a biblical element—the parable—because many literates would have read the bible. People would be familiar with these features and I hoped these would help root the novel within a known tradition.

—*Ngugi Wa Thiong'o, 1986*[144]

Global Reach and National Boundaries

> In the space of the world-economy . . . the division between
> subhumans and super-humans is a structural but violently
> unstable one. Previously, the notion of humanity was merely
> an abstraction. But, to the question, "What is Man?" which—
> however aberrant its forms may appear to us—is insistently
> present in racist thought, there is today no response in which
> this split is not at work.   —Etienne Balibar, 1991[145]

Marx once said that "world conditions" are a source of dominant ideas.[146] Nationalism is not possible without an idea of the nation; this is what Greenfeld meant by the claim that "the only foundation of nationalism as such . . . is an idea."[147] But nationalism is no less founded on a second idea—that of the alien.

The classical alien of the Western world, the one expelled en masse from England, France, Spain, and Portugal in the late Middle Ages, is the "wandering Jew." The familial nationalism of that era was conditioned by three overlapping factors: traditional Christian hostility toward Judaism; the European discovery of Africa and America in 1492; and the Inter Cetera Bull of Pope Alexander VI, which called in 1493 for the propagation of the Christian empire in these newly discovered territories.[148]

"Europe's most assiduous producers and consumers of travel accounts were the Germans," according to Slezkine.[149] The immediate need to reconcile travelers' tales of people in distant lands with the biblical story of creation gave rise to the theory of polygenesis. According to Michael Banton, the idea that "Adam was the ancestor of the Jews alone, and that other peoples' nature and history could be traced back to other ancestors . . . was first advanced by Paracelsus in 1520."[150] Polygenesis may have contributed to "the convergence of emergent nationalism and Jew-hatred at several historical junctures that essentially preceded the emancipation of the Jews" in nineteenth-century Europe.[151]

Polygenesis certainly contributed to the typological school of racial science, one founded by Georges Cuvier in 1800. It is noteworthy, however, that typologists such as Josiah Nott ignored Jews and argued that the Bible and natural history proved the existence of three distinct species of the genus man. The three were identified as Caucasian, Mongolian, and Ethiopian (in contemporary parlance, white, Asian, and black) and traced back to the three sons of Noah (Shem, Japheth, and Ham).[152] Their differences were then classified and measured in accordance with the scientific norms of the time.

The global reach of the Catholic Church (but not that of the East India Company) was challenged in seventeenth-century England by political dissidents such as John Locke. Richard Ashcraft has pointed out that the "radicals" sought to wield reason "as a critical weapon against the ritualistic practices of Catholicism or the Anglican church."[153] But early modern political thought—which was also nationalist thought—was grounded in readings of Christian scripture and did not depend on secular reasoning alone.[154] Opposition to the absolute authority of the king was also joined to support for overseas dominion, or commonwealth, in Locke's *Two Treatises of Government*.

The world conditions associated with empire and dissolution (be that empire Holy Roman, Hapsburg, Ottoman, British, Soviet, or some other), with war (especially World Wars I and II), and with capitalist expansion (particularly labor migration and industrial development) have been productive of both national identity and alien difference. The "global" in global politics is given by forces that transgress and contest boundaries—by movement, transmission, and flows.

However indirect its rule, empire requires the transportation of imperial administrators into the colonial situation. The colonist who accepts such a situation "will surely be transformed into a conservative, reactionary, or even a colonial fascist," according to Albert Memmi.[155] Perhaps not required, but certainly in evidence in European colonies, have been missionaries, settlers, merchants, financiers, adventurers, and convicts, at least some of whom (along with imperial administrators) have traveled from one colonial situation to another. Nationalism worldwide owes as much to the circulation of overlapping racial and religious scriptures (including Christian opposition to Judaism) as it does to anything specifically modern.

Spies, terror, war, and other forms of global political violence are increasingly represented in visual display. The speed of movement across state borders is as characteristic of such activities in the late modern age as is their "video game" quality.[156] But while the rapidity with which such phenomena shift location may be new, their mobile character is not. Standing armies do not stand and fearful citizens do not sit. The former march and the latter seek refuge.

Transnational capital operates through the ever more rapid circulation of money between world stock and currency markets; via the transportation of goods and services across dispersed points in a global network; by the shifting of production processes from one site in the global economy to another; and through the migration of labor to areas of capitalist activity. Whether the issue at hand is refugee flight, humanitarian relief operations, development programs, drug trafficking, United Nations peacekeeping, the spread of AIDS, diplomatic negotiations, or some other less newsworthy item, global life does not keep still.

Nationalist practices are both cause and effect of global politics. Efforts to manage, contain, and capture global forces often fail, leading to "sovereignty at bay" predictions of the demise of state power. Such efforts appeal often to the needs, wishes, and interests of a nation whose sovereign boundaries must be defended at any cost, a nation supposedly rooted culturally in time and space. Globalization is always a challenge to national boundaries.

And yet it is one of the paradoxes of nationalism that without global relations of power, the manufacture of alien difference would be much more difficult. Novel nationalisms are most often apparent in times of global change, not just when "traditional" societies or state structures disintegrate. They emerge to challenge existing inventions of the nation even as they leave untouched those elements that have become common sense. The latest version may rise to dominance and become routine, especially if it can claim the stamp of scientific authority. But the preceding ones do not automatically disappear, which means that competing nationalisms within one state are likely to be a source of political contestation and struggle.

Nationalism and the Global Scriptures

Like the African novel, nation-states have been engendered under colonial and not merely capitalist circumstances. Interwoven narratives of race, nation, and family were disseminated first in imperial countries, then transported to colonial settings where "the printing press, the publishing houses and the educational context . . . were controlled by the missionaries and the colonial administration."[157]

It is not the case that the "willed merger of nation and dynastic empire" in "official nationalism" only developed "*after,* and *in reaction to,* the popular national movements proliferating in Europe since the 1820s."[158] Sudipta Sen has argued that the concept of the household became a strong metaphor for the nation-state in the eighteenth century.[159] Locke's metaphor of the propertied household in his *Two Treatises of Government*—one composed in aristocratic fashion of parents, children, and servants—contributed as least as much to imperial nationhood as did "popular linguistic-nationalisms."[160] The reification of the household gave to those nationalisms their language of power. The nation and state were figured allegorically in the nineteenth century as parental guardians (not as one autonomous man), the colonized were the children, and colonial administrators were the civil or public servants.

The narratives that sold the national idea in the modern age did so by turning back to traditions of thought about identity that were shaped by European discovery and the global reach of Christianity. One such tradition was (and remains) Hellenic republicanism: "Already in the fifth century B.C. Plato had gone so far as to argue that the people of the ideal republic should think themselves member siblings of one family."[161] Of greater enduring significance are the overlapping traditions of biblical theology (carried into colonial settings with missionaries and settlers) and racial theory (which has found inspiration in sources as diverse as Christian scripture, travelers' accounts of America and Africa, and the writings of modern scientists).

As does nationalism, these traditions treat the landed (or more generally propertied) family as the primary source of human identity. They all contain imaginary tales of original creation that situate humankind within the context of a domestic household and natural world. And they all bound the kinship group in time and space and define it in relation to the divine, the unfamiliar, and the bestial.

Nationalism is not unlike the Holy Bible because it is also a performative scripture. The concept of nation is found in both. Familiar to readers of the Bible, for instance, would be the story of how the families of Noah's three sons repopulated the earth after the Great Flood destroyed everyone else. From these three family lineages, according to the book of Genesis, "the population of the isles of the nations was spread about in their lands, each according to its tongue, according to their families, by their nations."[162]

Both nationalism and the Bible are a combination of old and new "testaments," comprising multiple chapters written by different authors. Each scripture contains parables—fictitious narratives or allegorical tales of spiritual and moral significance—and stories of creation and redemption. Nationalism defines the kinship group by identifying strangers (know thine enemy). It treats the immortality of the collective body and soul as the highest human ideal (develop and defend the nation; to thine own kin be true; lay down your life for your country). And it offers multifaceted justifications for the behavior and practices of the nation in terms that vary from one narrative to the next but that couch racial and religious precepts in the language of moral respectability.[163]

Nationalist scriptures always contain a story of how the nation was founded, usually but not always in opposition to some form of tyranny. In the national genesis tale, the newborn nation is either cloaked in the allegorical mantle of a human baby or treated as a mature human just emerged from a historic slumber. Such stories are fictitious because although nations are always brought into being somehow, they are neither born nor awakened like people. Nationalist discourse invents nations in moments of anxiety attendant upon shifting global power relations; it does not arouse them fully formed from a deep sleep. Birth, by the same token, entails a moment of emergence and also an act of separation; the umbilical cord joining mother and child is severed and the latter is contained for the remainder of its life within the boundaries of its own skin. The boundaries that constitute the national and the alien are imaginary, by contrast, and scarcely ever contiguous with the borders of the so-called nation-state. National separation is never a completed action but a political ideal.

Marginality and Hybridity

An argument made by Mudimbe and echoed by Appiah is relevant to the above points about nationalism. Mudimbe has analyzed the invention of

Africa that occurred during the era of European discovery (beginning in 1492) and its subsequent colonization. According to Mudimbe, "The novel text which emerges from these expeditions is not fundamentally original" because it "follows a path prescribed by a tradition." All discourses "have not only sociohistoric origins but also epistemological contexts."[164] What can be imagined or thought about is bound to be constrained (even if silently or unconsciously) by the epistemological order within which new thinking emerges. No discourse, in that sense, can be original or completely autonomous because the elements of a former episteme are always to be found within it. In Appiah's words, "The idea of a discourse as free from the constraints of the authority of tradition is an extraordinarily modern conception in Europe."[165]

Mudimbe has described *marginality* as an effect of colonialism, but the term does not refer to an outer limit or to distance from a central core. Marginality is the condition of the present; it "designates the intermediate space between the so-called African tradition and the projected modernity of colonialism." Marginality "reveals the strong tension between a modernity that often is an illusion of development, and a tradition that sometimes reflects a poor image of a mythical past." As a temporal space in which both past and future reside, marginality is a "locus of paradoxes."[166]

"Radical separations between past and present" typify modern conceptions of time, according to Anderson. Leaving for the next chapter the question of whether *evolutionary* time is premised on such a "radical separation," it is not only in Africa that nations are constituted in marginality. National time displays the traces of a medieval or messianic conception of time, one defined by Anderson as "a simultaneity of past and future in an instantaneous present."[167] Marginality (in Mudimbe's terms) is the condition of the national present, a time where nationalist narratives deploy myths of the past and visions of the future in efforts to manage current anxieties and rapid change.

Modern nation-states are not that modern. They are hybrids, the products of a complex interplay of attitudes and orientations toward man, God, nature, and authority that span historical time and global space. There is no such thing as a pure "type," national or otherwise. As Senghor once said, "So we, too, are objectively half-castes."[168]

THE REMAINING CHAPTERS

The remainder of this book develops and illustrates the broad themes highlighted above. Chapter 2 discusses the meanings and practices of nationalism, those scriptural performances through which boundaries between nationals and aliens have been created and maintained. The first part of the chapter pays particular attention to mimicry of religious scriptures, especially of those Old Testament books that have been borrowed from and modified since the time of the Protestant Reformation.

The second part of the chapter analyzes changing conceptions of race over time, paying particular attention to associations of racial identity with culture, time, and geopolitical space. The discussion reinforces the argument that overlapping racial and religious traditions must be taken into account when explaining the power of nationalism in the present, even where such traditions are unconscious and their historical contingency has been forgotten.

The practices and narratives examined in Chapter 2 have not been operative in all places at all times. Nor are they all to be found in the behavior and objectives of ideologically driven movements for statehood. Contextual case studies that place competing nationalisms within social institutions and global relations of power are a vital supplement to any such generalized discussion. By the same token, those scriptural performances most indebted to Christian narratives of race and religion have been circulated around the globe. Dichotomous classification of nationalisms as Western/ethnic, old/new, advanced/backward is a problematic procedure that reinscribes nationalist divisions.

Chapters 3, 4, and 5 take up the challenge to examine nationalist practices in different contexts. South Africa, Britain, and Australia were chosen as much for their interconnectedness and similarities as for their obvious differences. Each has been a part of the British Empire; each has been both colonizer and colonized; and each dominant nation within has been defined (in addition to Britishness) in relation to aliens from Europe, Africa, and Asia. Each case defies classification, albeit in different ways, as either Western or "ethnic."

Numerous books and articles have been written on each of the cases examined, so the limits of the investigation must be acknowledged from the outset. The major limitation is that the full panoply of competing nationalisms cannot be addressed. In the chapter on Britain, there is no sustained engagement with the subnationalisms of England, Ireland, Scotland, and Wales;[169] nor is there discussion of Afro-Caribbean, Asian, or Black nationalisms.[170] The chapter on "white Australia" discusses Aboriginal and Asian peoples as they have been scripted by others; their own inscriptions of identity and difference are not the focus.[171] South Africa is discussed in light of competing "white" nationalisms and the new "rainbow" variety, not with regard to Black, Asian, and Colored nationalisms.[172]

The above limitations may be regrettable, but they are not arbitrary. Linkages between race (or ethnicity) and nationalism are frequently attributed to black nationalisms in the United States, Britain, and Africa, or else assumed to emerge from political contestations that pit an oppressed black group against a white racist power structure.[173] All too often, as Williams has argued, "white" is treated in such analyses as an unmarked category, and whiteness is reproduced and essentialized instead of unpacked and debunked. A preferred alternative, for Williams, is to set race within a global context and to subject the naturalness of *all* racial categories to critical scrutiny.[174] That is what these chapters attempt to do.

Every human collectivity—be it race, nation, ethnic group, or tribe—is a social construction and not a divine or natural phenomenon. For all that families and clans can be made to appear the most primary of human attachments, there is no one type of family (such as the nuclear family) that is more primary or natural than any other. Chapter 6 does not intend to predict the future of nationalism nor to settle the question of whether it is better to be for or against the nation. Instead it returns to the question of how national identities and boundaries are conditioned by global change. The cessation of the Cold War and the collapse of certain state structures are not the only relevant issues. The conclusion shows that actual families and households are increasingly subject to the forces of globalization against which nationalism operates, and suggests that change may be occurring in ways that threaten to complicate nationalist appeals to cultural rootedness in time and space.

NOTES

1. Locke, *Two Treatises of Government,* 286.
2. The classic statement within the genre remains the book of that title by Vernon, *Sovereignty at Bay.*
3. On state-building see Tilly, *The Formation of National States in Western Europe.* The literature on national development is discussed in more detail later in this chapter.
4. Hobsbawm, *Nations and Nationalism Since 1780: Programme, Myth, Reality,* 3.
5. See, for example, Ashley, "Untying the Sovereign State: A Double Reading of the Anarchy Problematique"; Doty, *Imperial Encounters: The Politics of Representation in North/South Relations;* Shapiro and Alker, *Challenging Boundaries;* Walker, *Inside/Outside: International Relations as Political Theory;* and Weber, *Simulating Sovereignty: Intervention, the State and Symbolic Exchange.*
6. Macmillan and Linklater, *Boundaries in Question: New Directions in International Relations,* 12.
7. Smith, *Theories of Nationalism,* 51.
8. Balibar in Balibar and Wallerstein, *Race, Nation, Class: Ambiguous Identities,* 47.
9. Balibar in Balibar and Wallerstein, *Race, Nation, Class,* 43.
10. Gilroy, *Small Acts: Thoughts on the Politics of Black Cultures,* 155.
11. Balibar in Balibar and Wallerstein, *Race, Nation, Class,* 53.
12. Mudimbe, *The Invention of Africa: Gnosis, Philosophy, and the Order of Knowledge,* 37.

13. Gellner, *Encounters with Nationalism,* 46.

14. Kristeva, *Nations Without Nationalism,* 1.

15. McNeill, *Poly-ethnicity and National Unity in World History,* chapter 2.

16. See the chapter "Beyond National Identity?" in Smith, *National Identity,* 143–177.

17. Gellner, *Encounters with Nationalism,* 38.

18. See the chapter "The Renaissance of Nationalism?" in Alter, *Nationalism,* 125–152.

19. Hobsbawm, *Nations and Nationalism Since 1780,* 9–10.

20. As Kellas has argued, "There is no integrated theory of the politics of nationalism which, while taking account of the many theories relating to the subject, focuses especially on the political dimension and produces an integrated theoretical analysis." Rooted as it is in sociobiology, his own "integrated theory of the politics of nationalism and ethnicity" is bound to be considered problematic by many. See Kellas, *The Politics of Nationalism and Ethnicity,* 1–2.

21. Hobsbawm, *Nations and Nationalism Since 1780,* 5; Renan, "What Is a Nation?"

22. Deutsch, *Nationalism and Social Communication: An Inquiry into the Foundations of Nationality,* 13.

23. Gellner, *Nations and Nationalism,* 7.

24. For Benedict Anderson, "The idea of a sociological organism moving calendrically through homogeneous, empty time is a precise analogue of the idea of the nation, which is also conceived as a solid community moving steadily down (or up) history." See Anderson, *Imagined Communities: Reflections on the Origin and Spread of Nationalism,* 24–26.

25. See, for example, Kellas, *The Politics of Nationalism and Ethnicity;* Lijphart, *Democracy in Plural Societies: A Comparative Exploration;* Lijphart and Grofman, *Choosing an Electoral System: Issues and Alternatives;* and Horowitz, *Ethnic Groups in Conflict.*

26. According to Balibar, nationalism is a concept that is difficult to define because it never functions alone. It is joined always (in addition to such terms as *patriotism, populism,* and *chauvinism*) to *nation* and *racism.* See Balibar in Balibar and Wallerstein, *Race, Nation, Class,* 46.

27. One of the most detailed and, in many ways, important recent studies of nationalism is that of Liah Greenfeld. Greenfeld's major contribution is to call into question the presumed dependence of nationalism on modernization. Yet for all its creativity, the five-country historical study (of England, France, Russia, Germany, and the United States) sets out to answer the same set of "origin" questions that inform the classic texts. As she states at the beginning, "The specific questions which this book addresses are why and how nationalism emerged, why and how it was transformed in the process of transfer from one society to another, and why and how different forms of national identity and consciousness became translated into institutional practices and patterns of culture." See Greenfeld, *Nationalism: Five Roads to Modernity,* 3.

28. Ignatieff, *Blood and Belonging: Journeys into the New Nationalism,* 10.

29. Greenfeld, *Nationalism,* 3.

30. Anderson, *Imagined Communities,* 145.

31. Slezkine, "Naturalists Versus Nations: Eighteenth-Century Russian Scholars Confront Ethnic Diversity," 186.

32. Anderson, *Imagined Communities,* 11.

33. Anderson, *Imagined Communities,* 17–18.

34. Gellner, *Nations and Nationalism*, 39.

35. See the chapter "From Kinship to Ethnicity" in Gellner, *Encounters with Nationalism*, 34–46.

36. Gellner, *Nations and Nationalism*, 7.

37. See, for example, Wallerstein, "The Present State of the Debate on World Inequality."

38. Weber, *The Protestant Ethic and the Spirit of Capitalism*, 54–62.

39. I am indebted to the writings of Vandana Shiva for this insight. See Shiva, *Monocultures of the Mind: Perspectives on Biodiversity and Biotechnology.*

40. Renan, "What Is a Nation?" 11.

41. See Smith, *National Identity*, 44.

42. Bhabha, *Nation and Narration*, 5.

43. Portes, "On the Sociology of National Development: Theories and Issues," 188.

44. Kellas, *The Politics of Nationalism and Ethnicity*, 25.

45. Greenfeld, *Nationalism*, 38.

46. Greenfeld, *Nationalism*, 52–53.

47. Slezkine, "Naturalists Versus Nations," 186.

48. Greenfeld, *Nationalism*, 3, 18, 31.

49. Greenfeld, *Nationalism*, 52.

50. See, for example, Foucault, *Discipline and Punish: The Birth of the Prison*, 8–11.

51. Anderson, *Imagined Communities*, 7.

52. Greenfeld, *Nationalism*, 21.

53. While professing to have been influenced by all of "the founding fathers of the discipline of sociology," Greenfeld indicates that "it is Weber's thought that I find the most congenial." See Greenfeld, *Nationalism*, 17.

54. Greenfeld, *Nationalism*, 42.

55. Shell, *Children of the Earth: Literature, Politics, and Nationhood.*

56. Shell, *Children of the Earth*, 23.

57. Greenfeld, *Nationalism*, 17.

58. I have used the term *modern* only where Marx himself used it. All quotes and references are from Marx, "The German Ideology: Part I."

59. Marx, "The German Ideology," 150. Emphasis in the original.

60. Marx, "The German Ideology," 186.

61. Marx, "The German Ideology," 180.

62. Marx, "The Germany Ideology," 163.

63. Harris, *National Liberation*, 40.

64. Marx, "On the Jewish Question," 34.

65. Marx, "On the Jewish Question," 34–39.

66. Marx, "The German Ideology," 172–173.

67. Marx, "The German Ideology," 173.

68. Lenin, "Critical Remarks on the National Question," 48–50.

69. Weber, *The Protestant Ethic*, 19.

70. Weber, *The Protestant Ethic*, 21–22.

71. Weber, *The Protestant Ethic*, 24.

72. Weber, *The Protestant Ethic*, 53.

73. Weber, *The Protestant Ethic*, 68.

74. Weber, "The Nation," 176.

75. Weber, "The Nation," 176–177.

76. Weber, "The Nation," 179.

77. Weber, "The Nation," 179.

78. Inkeles and Smith, "Becoming Modern," 161.

79. Emerson, "Nationalism and Political Development," 19.

80. Locke, *Two Treatises of Government*, 338.

81. Marx, "On Imperialism in India," 657.

82. Torgovnick, *Gone Primitive: Savage Intellects, Modern Lives*, 99.

83. Ricardo, "On Foreign Trade," 75.

84. One essay from that book was republished as McClelland, "The Achievement Motive in Economic Growth." See also McClelland, *The Achieving Society*.

85. According to McClelland, he "had always been greatly impressed by the very perceptive analysis of the connection between Protestantism and the spirit of capitalism made by the great German sociologist, Max Weber." See McClelland, "The Achievement Motive in Economic Growth," 143. Lipset has argued that "the general Weberian approach has been applied to many of the contemporary underdeveloped countries." See Lipset, "Values, Education, and Entrepreneurship," 41.

86. Weber, *The Protestant Ethic*, 53.

87. Parsons, *The Social System*.

88. Lipset, "Values, Education, and Entrepreneurship," 41.

89. Lerner, *The Passing of Traditional Society*.

90. Smith, *Theories of Nationalism*, 50.

91. Almond and Powell, *Comparative Politics: A Developmental Approach*, 72.

92. Smith, *Theories of Nationalism*, 47–49.

93. Smith, *Theories of Nationalism*, 57, 54.

94. Smith, *Theories of Nationalism*, 49.

95. Smith, *Theories of Nationalism*, 57–59.

96. According to McClelland, "If the sons are to have high *n* Achievement, the mothers must first be reached." See McClelland, "The Achievement Motive in Economic Growth," 155.

97. Smith, *National Identity*, 44.

98. For a feminist critique of the "mainstream" literature on nations and nationalism, see Racioppi and O'Sullivan See, "Nationalism Engendered: A Critique of Approaches to Nationalism."

99. Manzo, "Modernist Discourse and the Crisis of Development Theory," 7.

100. Emerson, *From Empire to Nation: The Rise to Self-Assertion of Asian and African Peoples*, 154–156.

101. Senghor, "The Struggle for Negritude," 96–97.

102. See in general the chapter "Patriotism and Racism" in Anderson, *Imagined Communities*, 143–152. See also Kellas, *The Politics of Nationalism and Ethnicity*, 5.

103. Renan, "What Is a Nation?" 15.

104. Appiah, *In My Father's House: Africa in the Philosophy of Culture*.

105. Mudimbe, *The Invention of Africa*.

106. Balibar in Balibar and Wallerstein, *Race, Nation, Class*, 53.

107. Chatterjee, *Nationalist Thought and the Colonial World: A Derivative Discourse?*

108. Smith, *National Identity*, 11.

109. Ignatieff, *Blood and Belonging*, 47, 85.

110. Smith, *National Identity*, 43.

111. See, for example, Alter, *Nationalism,* 14–15; Ignatieff, *Blood and Belonging,* 6–8; and Kellas, *The Politics of Nationalism and Ethnicity,* 52.

112. Greenfeld, *Nationalism,* 9.

113. Meinecke's *Weltburgertrum und Nationalstaat* (first published in German in 1907) has been published in English as *Cosmopolitanism and the National State.*

114. Ignatieff, *Blood and Belonging,* 6.

115. William Pfaff, "Reflections: The Absence of Empire," *The New Yorker,* August 10, 1992, 60.

116. "We can think of countries as neighborhoods, clubs, and families." See Waltzer, "The Distribution of Membership," 6.

117. Kohn, *The Idea of Nationalism.*

118. Ignatieff, *Blood and Belonging,* 154.

119. Pfaff, "Reflections," 59–62.

120. Emerson, *From Empire to Nation,* 432 (footnote 9).

121. Emerson, "Nationalism and Political Development," 16, 22–23.

122. Almog, *Nationalism and Antisemitism in Modern Europe 1815–1945,* 7.

123. Ignatieff, *Blood and Belonging,* 85.

124. Ignatieff has argued that "all the peoples of nineteenth century Europe under imperial subjection—the Poles and Baltic peoples under the Russian yoke, the Serbs under Turkish rule, the Croats under the Habsburgs—looked to the German ideal of ethnic nationalism when articulating their right to self-determination." See Ignatieff, *Blood and Belonging,* 7.

125. Almog, *Nationalism and Antisemitism,* xiii.

126. Almog, *Nationalism and Antisemitism,* 10.

127. Sahlins, "Fictions of a Catholic France: The Naturalization of Foreigners, 1685–1787," 97.

128. Almog, *Nationalism and Antisemitism,* xiv–xv.

129. Almog, *Nationalism and Antisemitism,* 2.

130. Almog, *Nationalism and Antisemitism,* xviii.

131. Todorov, "Xenocide: Antisemitism à la Française," 157.

132. Todorov, "Xenocide," 156.

133. See, for example, the article by Luc Rosenzweig, "Moral Cancer Eats at Germany's Heart." This was first published in *Le Monde* on July 24, 1993, and republished in *The Guardian Weekly,* August 8, 1993, 14.

134. Fitzpatrick, "Racism and the Innocence of Law," 252.

135. Ignatieff, *Blood and Belonging,* 8, 127, 247.

136. Ignatieff, *Blood and Belonging,* 23. See also the discussion of "the state of nature" and "the war of all against all," 42.

137. Ignatieff, *Blood and Belonging,* 9.

138. Ignatieff, *Blood and Belonging,* 46.

139. Williams, "The Impact of the Precepts of Nationalism on the Concept of Culture: Making Grasshoppers of Naked Apes," 144.

140. Kristeva, *Nations Without Nationalism* 47.

141. Jean Baudrillard, "Pas de Pitié pour Sarajevo," *Libération,* January 7, 1994, 6–7 (translation from the French is mine).

142. John Darnton, "Western Europe Is Ending Its Welcome to Immigrants," *The New York Times,* August 10, 1993, A1, A8.

143. Martin Woollacott, "Bashing Foreigners Won't Work," *The Guardian Weekly,* March 22, 1992, 7.

144. Ngugi, *Decolonizing the Mind: The Politics of Language in African Literature,* 69, 78.

145. Balibar in Balibar and Wallerstein, *Race, Nation, Class,* 44.

146. Marx, "The German Ideology," 173.

147. Greenfeld, *Nationalism,* 3.

148. At the time of writing, the Inter Cetera Bull had not been formally revoked by the Catholic Church. On the 500th anniversary of the bull, a meeting of Aboriginal peoples held at Julayinbul in the north of the Australian continent issued a statement calling on the pope to end "the Age of Subjugation." My thanks to Johanna Sutherland for bringing the bull and this meeting to my attention.

149. Slezkine, "Naturalists Versus Nations," 171.

150. Banton, *Racial Theories,* 1.

151. Almog, *Nationalism and Antisemitism,* 2.

152. Nott, *Types of Mankind: Or Ethnological Researches Based Upon the Ancient Monuments, Paintings, Sculptures, and Crania of Races and Upon Their Natural Geographical, Philological, and Biblical History.*

153. Ashcraft, *Revolutionary Politics and Locke's Two Treatises of Government,* 54.

154. See Mitchell, *Not by Reason Alone: Religion, History, and Identity in Early Modern Political Thought.*

155. Memmi, *The Colonizer and the Colonized,* 55.

156. See Der Derian, *Antidiplomacy: Spies, Terror, Speed, and War.*

157. Ngugi, *Decolonizing the Mind,* 69.

158. Anderson, *Imagined Communities,* 86.

159. Sen, "The Patriarchal Economy of Imperialism: On Domesticity and Dominion in British-India."

160. Anderson, *Imagined Communities,* 109.

161. Shell, *Children of the Earth,* 12.

162. All biblical quotations are from the *Revised Standard Version of the Holy Bible.* See Genesis 10, verse 5.

163. On this point see Goldberg, "Modernity, Race, and Morality."

164. Mudimbe, *The Invention of Africa,* 13, 16, ix.

165. Appiah, *In My Father's House,* 92.

166. Mudimbe, *The Invention of Africa,* 4–5.

167. Anderson, *Imagined Communities,* 24.

168. Senghor, "We Are All Cultural Half-Castes," 75.

169. See Crick, *National Identities: the Constitution of the United Kingdom.*

170. See Gilroy, *Small Acts.*

171. See Pettman, *Living in the Margins: Racism, Sexism, and Feminism in Australia.*

172. See Manzo, *Domination, Resistance, and Social Change in South Africa: The Local Effects of Global Power.*

173. See, for example, Kellas, *The Politics of Nationalism and Ethnicity,* 98–105.

174. Williams, "Dick and Jane and 'Just Us.'"

2

Spiritual and Racial Families: Nationalism as Scripture

Man is everything in the formation of this sacred thing which is called a people. Nothing purely material suffices for it. A nation is a spiritual principle, the outcome of the profound complications of history; it is a spiritual family not a group determined by the shape of the earth.

—*Ernest Renan, 1882*[1]

BOUNDING EDEN: IDENTITY THROUGH DIFFERENCE

The negative or 'anti'-character of nationalism in a colonial setting is simple enough to explain, but it is by no means unique to colonialism. Everywhere the national "we" has been to a considerable degree defined by contrast to the alien and opposing "they."   —*Rupert Emerson, 1960*[2]

National creation has been a topic of some debate in the study of nations and nationalism. Having made the above point, Emerson went on to claim that the role of nationalists everywhere (except, apparently, in Africa) "is not that of creating the nation but of rousing it to consciousness."[3] Smith has largely concurred, arguing that "by comparison with non-Western cases, the rise of Western nations owed much less to national*ism* and a movement to create a 'nation where none existed.'"[4]

The "nations before nationalism" position must explain how nations are brought into being if not through nationalist practices. Smith's theory is that they emerged initially as an unintended consequence of bureaucratic incorporation by aristocratic *ethnies* (his term for ethnic groups). But that merely raises the question of why the ethnie as opposed to the nation should be treated (in Emerson's words) as "something which is there as a great historical fact."[5]

Those who do not want to emulate sociobiology and explain ethnic or national identity as a function of instincts[6] take the position that nationalism

37

creates nations *everywhere.* According to Gellner, for example, "It is nationalism which engenders nations, and not the other way around."[7] Hobsbawm, too, has argued that "nations do not make states and nationalisms but the other way around."[8]

The issue of creation is complicated by the multiplicity of meanings that attach to the concept of nationalism. For different authors the term signifies an ideologically driven form of behavior or type of movement;[9] a theory of political legitimacy;[10] a state of mind or a style of thought;[11] a narrative performance;[12] and a process of boundary creation and/or maintenance.[13] The first two meanings associate nationalism with the workings of the modern state; nationalists are those who seek to exercise state power, to form independent states where none existed before, or to legitimize existing institutions. Nationalism is the hyphen that joins nation to state; it is a modern movement for statehood and legitimacy. Nationalism presumably becomes redundant once its mission is accomplished, to be replaced by diplomacy and other forms of institutionalized statecraft.

Nationalism could not exist without the twin concepts of national and alien. Nationalism can and does exist where demands for statehood are not in evidence. But nationalism is not merely an ideology or state of mind. Homi Bhabha's notion of nationalism as a narrative performance and Daniele Conversi's discussion of boundary creation and maintenance both suggest that nationalism is also active, productive, and repetitious.

Nationalism involves a range of dispersed practices through which boundaries are created and maintained. Nationalism is a scriptural performance, one that constitutes national identity in opposition to alien difference. The question of whether the nation creates nationalism or vice versa is unanswerable from this perspective, just as the question of whether "we" precede "they" does not permit of an answer. Nationalism, nations, and aliens are not autonomous entities that can exist independently of one other. As Geoffrey Bennington has put it, "The idea of the nation is inseparable from its narration; that narration attempts, interminably, to constitute identity against difference, inside against outside."[14]

The nation, by the same token, is not a unified force that dies or goes to sleep, to be reborn or roused to consciousness at a later date. Peter Alter's description of the nation as "a goal rather than an actuality"[15] is more accurate. Boundaries can be made to appear timeless and beyond question. But precisely because national boundaries are constructed and always contestable, the reproduction of the national and the alien requires constant practice. It occurs continuously in a range of social institutions such as schools and media, and in daily routines associated with "policing, suspicion, and crossing (or refusal of entry)."[16]

Nationalism entails the policing of access to territory by agents of state authority. Immigration laws and their implementation, border patrols, and the apprehension of "illegal aliens" are nationalist practices masquerading as modern statecraft. At the same time, the space of the nation rarely coincides with lines on a map. Imperial realms have been imagined as one large national household. And within the boundaries of sovereign nation-states, "the racial-cultural identity of the 'true nationals' . . . is inferred from (and assured by) its opposite," the "false nationals" and aliens in residence.[17] The suspicious surveillance of "problem communities" has become another routine element of nationalist practice.

David Campbell has described national boundaries as "shifting horizons marked by flux and ambiguity."[18] Flux and ambiguity are most apparent in the wake of global transformation. When the future appears uncertain or the interests of dominant classes have changed, the present is cast as unnatural and the past rewritten to suit contemporary conditions. Nations can always be remade, by novel narratives that redefine identity and shift the boundaries between national and alien.

Subsequent chapters will show that the boundaries of "white" nations have been altered in ways that call into question secular/spiritual and racial/ethnic distinctions. The remainder of this chapter looks at the various ways in which nationals and aliens have been engendered in nationalism. Part one focuses on those practices that have circulated globally and are not specific to any one nationalism, either within or across state boundaries. Part two analyzes the affinities between racial theory and nationalist thought over time.

NATIONALISM IN PRACTICE

Genesis and Exodus: Stories of Creation and Redemption

And the Lord said to Moses, "Go in, tell Pharaoh king of Egypt to let the people of Israel go out of his land. . . . I will set apart the land of Goshen, where my people dwell, so that no swarms of flies shall be there; that you may know that I am the Lord in the midst of the earth.
                    —*Old Testament (Exodus 6, verses 10 and 22)*

And so today we recall the birth of the Ashanti nation through Okomfo Anokye and Osei Tutu and the symbolism entrenched in the Golden Stool; the valiant wars against the British, the banishment of Nana Prempeh the First to the Seychelle Islands; the temporary disintegration of the nation and its subsequent reunification.   —*Kwame Nkrumah, 1953*[19]

Nations are typically invented through allegorical stories about birth or awakening. In the former case nations are invested with godlike founding fathers, those who brought the nation into being when they either planted their feet in alien soil or stood up in opposition to some form of oppression and tyranny. Public statues are the *corpus mysticum* of the nation, according to Adam Lerner; they "circulate the heroes of the past, who exist in the national afterlife, through the streets and among the living."[20]

Allan Boesak has suggested that the Exodus theme of escape from oppression underpins black theology in the United States, liberation theology in Asia and Latin America, and Black Consciousness philosophy in South Africa.[21] When slaveholders in the United States treated passages on obedience to masters as central to the Bible, "the entire Christian legacy had to be remade" by the slaves. According to Garry Wills, "parts of Scripture that came to vivid life in their [slave] experience were ancient Israel's Egyptian captivity and Babylonian exile. . . . There have always been black preachers and believers ready to use the Christian professions of the masters against them."[22]

The "allure of redemption myths" has been evident in South Africa, where "the Exodus narrative and its New Testament analogues have achieved a hold on the imaginings of Afrikaans and African nationalism alike."[23] At different times and in the service of different nationalisms, the Afrikaner nation has stood for the oppressed Israelites (in the mythology of the Great Trek away from British imperialism) and the oppressive Egyptians (in black nationalist opposition to apartheid). The British nation has stood for both as well, although in a somewhat different sense. Britons were the people of Israel in the Protestant story of the Puritan Rebellion (against the papal "pharaoh"); more recently they have been the Egyptians held in thrall by a fear of internal aliens.

Wherever Christianity has been used as an instrument of social control, the Bible has been refashioned as a weapon of rebellion. Redemption myths are appealing because the people of Israel can stand for any nation that has "groaned under their bondage and cried out for help" (Exodus 2, verse 23), regardless of whether or not the ancient Israelites were possessed of a national consciousness. Of key significance is that God rewarded with land those who had suffered collectively in his name. In nationalism, disproportionate benefits enjoyed by certain groups within a state may be justified with the same logic. The alleged suffering endured by the forefathers of these groups for the sake of national deliverance is held up as the reason for their privileged place in the national present.[24]

In the case of awakening, nations are said to have been aroused to consciousness when their members instinctively thought or acted as one, for example by pulling together in the presence of danger. Campbell has shown that "danger is not an objective condition" because it does not exist "independently of those to whom it may become a threat."[25] Whatever is supposedly dangerous to the nation as a whole must be represented as nondiscriminatory, as something that threatens all if it threatens any.

Nations may be portrayed as innocent victims of negligent politicians or forces beyond their control. The most attractive motifs are those that invoke social diseases (like cancer), or natural disasters (like flooding). The imagery of aliens as a few malignant cells inside a body politic is most effective where numbers are small and people settled; it is used most often against racialized minorities and other "resident aliens." A flood is the sum total of undifferentiated drops of water that move in the same direction; refugees who transgress territorial boundaries are more likely to become "floods" than "tumors."

For a nation to be "awakened" it must have been asleep to danger and thus deserving of some censure for failing to avert invasion, attack, swamping, flooding, or swarming. In this regard, the other side of the Exodus tale—God's treatment of Egypt as opposed to Egypt's treatment of Israel— has echoes in nationalism as well.

The more that the "descendants of Israel" were oppressed, "the more that they multiplied and the more they spread abroad" (Exodus 1, verse 12). Until the Egyptians woke up and realized that the best way to cope with their fear of numbers was to send the people of Israel away, God visited a series of plagues upon the pharaoh's "house." First he turned the Nile into a river of blood and killed all the fish. Then he sent plagues of frogs, gnats, and flies; he settled a fine dust over all the land, and boils and sores over man and beast. These punishments for sin were followed by rains of hail and fire, by a "dense swarm of locusts," by thick darkness, and finally—when all else failed—by the hand of death upon all of the firstborn of Egypt. Only then were the Egyptians, paradoxically, able to rid themselves of their "dread" of an oppressed people.

Whether it does so through birth or awakening, nationalism engenders nations in a context of relations of power that transcend or precede state boundaries—relations that inhere in empire, the expansion of capitalism, and war. International relations are not the extent of global politics but their effect.

Death and Development: Immortality Through Sacrifice

> One loves in proportion to the sacrifices to which one has consented, and in proportion to the ills that one has suffered. . . . A nation is therefore a large-scale solidarity, constituted by the feeling of the sacrifices that one has made in the past and of those that one is prepared to make in the future.
>
> —*Ernest Renan, 1882*[26]

To balance the budget, the government has relied greatly on Nigerians' willingness to make sacrifices, as a result of which projected revenues are much higher than in 1985.
—*West Africa, 1986*[27]

In the absence of actual fighting, annual days of remembrance are occasions for the nation to give thanks to its surviving veterans of war. These "holy days" also serve the pedagogical function of teaching the young what their nation is supposed to stand for (or at least against).

A more fixed reminder of wartime sacrifice and heroism is a nation's war memorials, which immortalize collective identity for the national unborn. These often resemble temples or churches when not representing the nation as soldiers, generals, weeping women, or secular deities. A notable exception is the Vietnam War memorial in the United States. This smooth black wall contains, in even typeface, the names of all the uniformed dead; as such it symbolizes perfectly the boundary-producing and standardizing practices of nationalism. It is also devoid of mystical or heroic allusions, which probably explains why (in the wake of lengthy protests from certain sectors of the U.S. public) the wall has been supplemented by a trinity of bronze male soldiers.

As a later section will demonstrate, exclusion of the foreign is often legitimated with the sociobiological claim that "kin" are programmed to defend themselves from those of a different kind. Such narratives often redeploy the language of invasion when the country is no longer at war and work to effect unity by reinscribing difference as a threat.

Nationalism is not necessarily a language of hatred, at least not outside of wartime. When not appealing to the scientifically respectable doctrine of racial instinct, the negative emotions it whips up could just as easily be fear, suspicion, or contempt. But conversely, nationalism *does* aspire to be an ethic of love.

Sacrifice is the ultimate ethical principle of Christianity. To sacrifice self and family (or self *for* family) is to prove one's faith in God as well as love of Jesus Christ and one's fellow man. God (with the help of the Virgin Mary) sacrificed his only son for humankind; Christ sacrificed his own life so that others might live; Abraham agreed to sacrifice his only son, Isaac; Christ's disciples began a tradition of martyrdom to the faith; and Christians everywhere have been taught that "greater love hath no man than this—that he laid down his life for his friends." As the ultimate icon of national sacrifice and suffering, the war memorial has become the modern analogue of the crucifix in predominantly Christian societies.

Christianity is not the only religion to ever forge unity in redemptive suffering or to find in sacrificial death the key to immortal life. But as Jean Elstain has argued, sacrifice in modern warfare is a practice that continues rather than undermines the Christian tradition of martyrdom. For the continued life of an often feminized nation and masculinized state, female citizens are called upon to sacrifice their male kin (like Mary), and men are expected to sacrifice their own bodies (like Christ) in time of war. Reflecting the will to community and to a universal ethic of love, wartime sacrifice is for Elstain integral to modern understandings of sovereignty.[28]

Because of the extent to which modern nations have been engendered in death and suffering, Bruce Kapferer has described nationalism as a religious order. The "secular" nationalism of Australia and the "religious" nationalism of Sri Lanka were both spawned within a context of British colonialism. Each constructs identity through different myths and legends. The central motif of Australia's creation narrative, according to Kapferer, is the defeat of the "diggers" at Gallipoli in World War I. Yet this legend "derives some of the force behind its argument from its elaboration within the historical and cultural world of Western Christianity quite as much as Sinhalese nationalism gains its power within a Buddhist historical world." It is not in organized religion but in "the flames of the destruction of war" that the religious order of Australian nationalism flourishes.[29]

Australia is not unique. Reminiscent of Marx's discussion of religion as the spirit of civil society, Wills has suggested that "it would be a very religious nation that produced the first secular state."[30] The U.S. pledge of allegiance (where the hand is typically placed over the heart) has been described by Wills as an "act of homage."[31] At certain times (such as during the Irish Catholic presidency of John F. Kennedy), the evangelical tradition has existed in tension with "a secularizing religion of the state that had its own rites and sacred symbols (touch football, PT-109 tie clips), even its own religious order (the Peace Corps)."[32] The idea of a U.S. mission in the world has been given less theological expression since the 1960s. But as Wills has pointed out, "When wartime calls for sacrifice, American duty becomes again a divine imperative."[33]

Warfare is a time when the nation is called upon to kill as well as to die—to inflict suffering and not merely to experience it. Christianized nations are not the only ones to ever initiate wars, and all wars are a perversion of Christ's message to "love thy neighbor as thyself." That is why a tradition of "conscientious objection" has always coexisted with "just war" theory. But the religious order of nationalism survives armistice and can operate without calls for the death of heretical traitors and infidel enemies. What matters is that individual sacrifice is the guarantor of collective immortal life and the ultimate expression of selfless love.

In the postcolonial states of the so-called Third World (and not only in Nigeria), sacrifice for liberation from imperialism has been superseded by demands for sacrifice in the name of national development. The notion of development as a false god runs in various guises through much of liberation theology, which considers idolatry far more of a problem for the modern age than atheism. The point has been made that in the New Testament, idolatry refers not so much to belief in non-Christian deities as to the worship of money, power, and pleasure. In its unfulfilled promise of these things to national subjects, development demands the sacrifice of human life in the same way that ancient gods once did.[34]

Development is not an inherently Christian concept, but neither is it a purely secular one devoid of religious imagery. Reminiscent of liberation theology, the Indian writer Vandana Shiva has described "maldevelopment" as a practice based on the sacredness of a modern way of life.[35] When Prime Minister Jawaharlal Nehru of India wanted high dams constructed after independence, he described them as "secular temples," not as purely technical instruments of economic growth.[36]

The Story of Eve: Sexuality and Disobedience

As mothers and housewives, women are in the vanguard of the new struggle for economic reconstruction and social progress. . . . The changes which are necessary in securing rural development . . . can only take place if the women themselves change their attitudes and practices and accept new ideas.
—*Tom Mboya, 1967*[37]

National *his*tory is often just that—the story of great men. The leaders of national liberation movements may be remembered as imprisoned men (for example, Nelson Mandela of the African National Congress [ANC]), even though women have been militant leaders in their own right (Winnie Mandela).

Women's exclusion from tales of national genesis and redemption has been challenged in subtle ways. The cover of Stephen Davis's history of the ANC, for example, foregrounds an older woman with raised fist leading a younger man with submachine gun.[38] More obvious challenges have been launched by feminist scholars such as Helen Irving. In asking questions about the role of founding "mothers" in Australian federation, Irving has rejected "the view that women were silent or absent while the nation was being built."[39]

It is not the case, though, that women are always ignored by nationalism, or that "national, racial, and ethnic categories are often ungendered."[40] As the speech by Mboya illustrates, women may be simultaneously venerated (as the nation's mothers or its chaste daughters) and mistrusted (in his case, as the carriers of "old" ideas). When linked to fashionable enemies, women with unfashionable attitudes and practices are transformed from an obstacle to progress into a danger to the nation. A classic example of this occurred in colonial New England, where Quaker women supposedly "had a ready network of external support from the devils directing the Indians in their campaign against the gospel community." The persecution of "witches" took place in a situation where the papacy—believed by reformers to be the ultimate diabolic force—was symbolized not as the Mother Church but as a Scarlet Woman or Whore of Babylon.[41] As for the devil himself, he was known in Puritan mythology as the Black Man.[42]

Anne McClintock has pointed out that women reproduce or subvert the boundaries of the nation "by accepting or refusing sexual intercourse or marriage with prescribed groups of men."[43] This means that nationalism often entails the policing of women's sexuality—for example, via legal prohibitions on interracial marriage.

The mythical "mother of everyone living" (Genesis 3, verse 20) is rarely mentioned in nationalist circles. Yet there is often a "story of Eve" quality in nationalism's treatment of both women and men (especially homosexual men). In the book of Genesis, Adam willingly obeyed God's command not to eat from "the tree of the knowledge of good and evil" until Eve—wanting to "be like God"—did so first. Confronted by their maker, Adam pointed the finger at his wife and she, in turn, blamed the subversive serpent ("the serpent beguiled me, and I ate"). Having been created human, the first couple acquired partial divinity through the serpent's seduction of the woman. Disobedience followed, and disobedience was the original sin.

Betrayal and repentance were to no avail. Upset that "the man has become like one of us," God exiled Adam from Paradise in order to prevent his access to the tree of immortality and complete godliness. God condemned Adam "to till the ground from which he had been taken" until death; he then "posted at the east of the garden of Eden the cherubs and the flaming blade of a sword that was turning itself continually to guard the way to the tree of life" (Genesis 3, verses 22–24). Eve was ultimately responsible for the production of a permanently policed boundary between Eden and the east, one that kept God immortal in opposition to finite humanity.

If John Locke is to be believed, "the Curse of God upon the Woman, for having been the first and forwardest in the Disobedience" was cited by his contemporaries as justification for absolute (male) monarchy. Locke pointed out in his first treatise of government that God punished Adam as well as Eve; he also reminded his political opponents that Adam's destiny was to be "a day laborer for his Life," not a king with all attendant "Privileges and Ease of Absolute Power."[44] In the second treatise, the concept of the familial household as an organizing metaphor for the colonial state was made quite explicit. There Locke argued for a shift from paternal power to *parental* power on the grounds that the "positive Law of God" (the Bible) vested authority over children in both parents in equal measure.[45]

Locke's nonconformism allowed for at least two political possibilities:

the extension of citizenship to females and the idea of empire as a "family" coruled by father and mother. The latter prefigures in turn the idea of the nation-state as a marriage partnership. But while Locke may have undermined conventional readings of the biblical Eve, "Eve" as a trope of disobedience and treachery did not disappear.

The Genesis theme of boundary production as necessitated by seduction and disobedience has been replicated in nationalist parables. The alien is as much the treacherous citizen as it is the foreign national, the social misfit who transgresses boundaries as well as the alien subversive. Efforts other than Locke's to undermine the authority of "the Kingdom of Darkness" ruled from Rome, such as Thomas Hobbes's seventeenth-century *Leviathan,* drew upon copious biblical references in arguing for allegiance to "Christian sovereigns."[46] As Campbell's work had demonstrated, *Leviathan* is a nationalist classic of boundary production because it constitutes the obedient citizen as a rational individual, the all-powerful state as a "Mortall God," and all others as strangely foreign. The strategies of otherness at work in the text, Campbell argues, remain central to more recent constitutions of national identity in the United States.[47]

The Mark of Cain: Fugitives and Wanderers

> Little foxes that destroy our vineyards—are these not the perverse Hebrews who dwell among us? Even though these Jews may be small compared with our great and esteemed nation, yet with their tongues and their sharp teeth they can chop down a tree and eat it, branches, leaves and all. These are the kinds of bad deeds these Hebrews inherited from their forefather—"a plain man, dwelling in tents" [Genesis 25:27].
> —*Anonymous Pole, 1830*[48]

The Bible has been mined at different times for nationalist messages with racial themes. The most popular parables discovered therein are accounts of family treachery that make no explicit mention of race. Their racial meaning is thus coded and inheres in associations of race with both family lineage and permanent difference.

The "mark of Cain" story—which describes God's punishment for the murder of Abel—appears in the fourth chapter of the book of Genesis. Cain is condemned to become "a fugitive and a wanderer" and forced to take up residence "in the land of Nod, east of Eden." He is marked for unrewarded labor and not with a physical stain ("when you till the ground, it shall no longer yield to you its strength"). The nature of the *protective* mark that God puts upon Cain "lest any who came upon him should kill him" is not specified. The significance of the story is therefore not that Cain becomes a different color but that he is condemned to a different way of life, one lived beyond the eastern boundaries of the land of Eden.

Movement is a threat to national boundaries; any peoples who "wander" can be identified with Cain, just as anyone disobedient or vulnerable to subversion may be scripted as Eve. One of Cain's descendants was Jabal, the "founder of those who dwell in tents and have livestock" (Genesis 4, verse 20). The English adventurer Richard Jobson—who read biblical messages about black men's sexuality into the book of Genesis—would have known of Jabal when he likened the nomadic, cattle-raising Fulbe people of Gambia to "our country beasts."[49]

Citing an argument made by Lawrence Rose,[50] Laurence Thomas has described "the wandering Jew" as "a part of the folk-lore of Western culture."[51] The success of the myth is said to derive from its association of homelessness with wickedness: "Each individual Jew lay under a curse from which to redeem himself and his race, a curse symbolizing inherited ethnic guilt."[52] The Jews' capacity to survive agony and servitude could then be adduced as evidence of divine punishment, a reading that stands in tension with the concept of redemptive suffering found in Exodus.

Modern anti-Semitism often divests itself of theological justifications for Jew hatred, even as it has "absorbed certain elements from antiquity, particularly from the struggle of the Church against Judaism."[53] Negative character traits attributed to Jews everywhere in the late nineteenth century remained those of the classical alien: in-group loyalty and hostility toward others; parasitism and greed; shallow intellectualism; and subversiveness and arrogance.[54] Jewishness was further associated with corruption, disease, sexual mutilation, and seduction in nineteenth-century England.[55]

Some of the negative stereotypes just mentioned may be a function of anti-Semitism in particular and not of racism more generally. As Frantz Fanon once said, "The Negro symbolizes the biological danger; the Jew, the intellectual danger."[56] But stereotypes circulate, and any group of people viewed as permanently different from a national ideal can be treated as analogous to another racialized group. Nineteenth-century race science did not invent the interpretation of human difference as race. What novel disciplines such as anthropometry (the measurement of skulls and brain weights) did was to throw a mantle of scientific respectability over "the analogies between anthropoid apes, lower races, women, criminal types, lower classes, and the child."[57]

According to Thomas, "The notion of an inherently evil people is peculiarly a religious one, whereas the notion of an evil person *simpliciter* is not, nor is the notion of an intellectually inferior people."[58] But evilness and inferiority are not mutually exclusive (just as Jew hatred and anti-Semitism are not). Despite being "separated by the sexual question," the Jew and the

Negro have had one point in common, in Fanon's view: "Both of us stand for Evil."[59]

The Curse of Ham:
Culture and Race, Blackness and Lifestyle

The torch of Lady Liberty symbolizes our freedom and represents our heritage, the compact with our parents, our grandparents, and our ancestors. It is that lady who gives us our great and special place in the world.

—Ronald Reagan, 1989[60]

It is here [at Normandy] that a certain way of life prevailed over the single true enemy, Nazism.

—François Mitterrand, 1994[61]

Renan described a nation as a daily plebiscite, a continual reaffirmation in the present of the collective desire to continue a common life.[62] According to Greenfeld, the idea of each nation as unique has become a more important tenet of nationalism than popular (democratic) sovereignty.[63] Nationalism celebrates and defends the singularity of culture. "National culture" describes the production in official languages of nationalized art— poetry, film, novels, plays, and songs, as well as paintings. But "national culture" also embraces the supposedly "ethnic" notions of collective inheritance, destiny, and a shared way of life.

Linguistic diversity has been central to cultural nationalism. It has been read, first of all, as an expression of God's will for humankind as a whole. This reflects nationalist use of the Tower of Babel story in the Old Testament, where God scatters "the sons of men" around the world and confuses their language (Genesis 11, verses 5–9). Second, in Anderson's secular reading of "national print-languages," they have been politically important as ways to communicate images of antiquity and to challenge sacred communities integrated by Latin.[64] Here the very use of particular languages may have political meaning, conveying cultural resistance to imposed languages of power. And finally, the German nationalist Johann Gottfried von Herder spoke of a nation's "folk spirit," one reflected for him in the unique idioms of a national language. In this third sense, language is valued less as a mode of communication or resistance and more as a carrier—in Ngugi's words—"of a people's experience in history."[65]

Marx considered capitalism to be a mode of life. Weber wrote of capitalism as an element of "modern culture." For Lenin, "It is under the guise of national culture . . . that the Black-Hundreds and the clericals, and also the bourgeoisie of *all* nations, are doing their dirty and reactionary work."[66]

Over time the concept of "national interest" has been placed in the service of a historically contingent mode of production. Challenges to capitalism (or in communist states, to communism) have been contained by alliances of the "civilized" against a shared enemy, and by state-based policing of alien subversives.

Yet the idea of the nation is not an invention of the capitalist age, and nationalism is not always the handmaiden of capitalist interests. Capitalism is the mode of production of a globalized economy; as a global way of life it is too dispersed and shared to be the unique province of any one nation. By the same token, capitalist classes within states are less unified than divided in matters of lifestyle and social values. The objective of nationalism, as Balibar had remarked, is "not to expose the historical and social heterogeneity of the 'people,' but to exhibit their essential unity."[67]

Modes of life do not settle within national boundaries. And for all that certain nations may claim to be the founders of sovereignty, freedom, or democracy, there is no single nation that owns the patent on them. Nothing is unique to a nation except its own symbols of universal principles. That is why loyalty to the nation is often gleaned from attachment to flags (the ultimate symbol of identity in sovereign space), to statues and monuments (which symbolize national time and immortality), to government buildings (the "houses" of democratic freedoms), and to patriotic songs (the anthems of official languages).

"National culture" has been derived from racial character. According to Balibar, theoretical racism treats race as synonymous with culture and as the nation's historical backbone. Nationalism may seek to return dispersed "relatives" to the national family by force or by invitation. But in the name of national survival and strength, nationalism will demand racial/cultural sameness. It will place beyond the boundaries of the nation all those who have been marked as racially different.[68]

The practice of associating blackness with degeneracy, sin, madness, disease, dirt, and working-class occupations is long-standing in Christian societies. One need look no further than the fairy tales of the brothers Grimm, which were billed as *Tales for Young and Old* and not as children's fables. In a story entitled "The White Bride and the Black Bride," God cursed two women who angered him by turning them "as black as night and as ugly as sin."[69] As a South African judge once said to Steve Biko, "You use 'black,' which really connotes dark forces over the centuries."[70]

Hereditary slavery has been scripted as a biblical curse. Like the story of Cain, the "curse of Ham" tale in the book of Genesis is an injunction to respect paternal authority. Ham was one of the three sons of Noah. When he discovered his father lying naked in a drunken stupor, Ham announced the fact to the other two. Without looking at him, Shem and Japheth "walked backward and covered the nakedness of their father." In anger at his youngest son, Noah cursed Ham's son Canaan (not Ham himself) and condemned him to be the slave of Shem and Japheth. To the seventeenth-century traveler Jobson, large penises and sexual appetites were the legacy of Ham's punishment for seeing his father's nakedness.[71]

Practices such as Jobson's—whereby the black male has been "turned into a penis" and objectified on a global scale—were of particular interest to Fanon.[72] In Fanon's philosophy, racial mythology in colonial situations was not the novel result of a desire to justify oppression (an argument made by Albert Memmi, for example).[73] He rooted it instead in a "collective unconscious" that was culturally acquired, "the sum of prejudices, myths, collective attitudes of a given group."[74]

Whatever his purpose in the colonies, "in Europe the Negro has one function: that of symbolizing the lower emotions, the baser inclinations, the dark side of the soul."[75] Through the projection of his own immoral impulses and shameful desires onto an encountered black world, "the European has tried to repudiate this uncivilized self" and absolve "every civilized and civilizing country" of sin.[76] For Fanon, "the Negro is not. Any more than the white man."[77] Each category is a mythical invention not dependent on actual physical contact.

Racial constructions of black people as bestial in character and lifestyle have drawn from a classical tradition of European travel writing as well as from Christian constructions of blackness. The ancient Roman scholar Pliny, for example, titillated readers with the following account of beings living in Africa:

> [They] have no articulate voice, but only utter a kind of squeaking noise, and thus they are utterly destitute of all means of communication by language. The Garamantes have no institution of marriage among them, and live in promiscuous concubinage with their women. The Augylae worship no deities but the gods of the infernal. The Gamphasantes . . . go naked and are unacquainted with war. . . . The Atlantes, if we believe what is said, have lost all characteristics of humanity; for there is no mode of distinguishing each other by names . . . nor are they visited with dreams like the rest of mortals.[78]

The physical traits of Africans were one marker of lost humanity for Pliny, but deviance from comprehensible social norms and good manners was just as significant. Monstrous features were sometimes attributed to Africans by his contemporaries; Herodotus, for example, described Africans as "dog-eared men" with "eyes in their breasts."[79] Like contemporary UFO abduction stories, such tales were presented to their readers as a genre of authorship based on actual experience. As Luise White has suggested, such stories illuminate the social values and beliefs of the writer, even if they are false. For whether or not depictions of aliens ring true, they tell us "not about aliens, but about ourselves."[80]

Recurring contact with peoples expected to be strange and exotic did not immediately end the tales of discovered monstrosity. But they began to coexist with a contrasting vision that was equally illuminating (and fanciful). To portray an African in the fifteenth century, according to Mudimbe, a painter would simply copy a Greek statue and color it black.[81] In the same era, Captain John Smith wrote that "the naturall Inhabitants of Virginia" were "of a color browne when they are of any age, but they are borne white."[82] An early engraving, "Natives of Botany Bay," in what was to become Australia, was "based more on the conventional classical ideal of the noble savage" than on a more realistic illustration of Aborigines.[83]

The power of the myth of Eve as "the mother of everyone living" meant that human beings were seen as essentially of one type until racial typology invented two more races. People discovered in Africa and America after 1492 were not necessarily recognized as human, any more than alien abductors (who are reportedly gray, not green, in color) are now seen as such.[84] The point is that believing is seeing; travelers who expected to find descendants of Adam and Eve scattered throughout the world noted physical similarities and not—as occurred again later—traits shared with various animals.

Blackness remained but one marker of cultural difference as the modern age approached. As J. M. Coetzee has pointed out in his discussion of seventeenth-century travelogues, European explorers and imperial agents placed their discoveries within an inherited epistemological framework that comprised no less than nineteen conceptual categories. Physical appearance was one such category, but it was always accompanied by some combination of the rest, by reference to such factors as recreations, customs, religion, language, and character.[85]

The "nascent anthropology" of the travelogue (as David Theo Goldberg has called it), was "the means by which the wider public was teaching itself to read." A cultural boundary between "a common European 'we' that coalesced in the 1450s" and a non-European "they" was reinscribed in stories that "played a key role in the commercial survival of the printing press a century later." This literature also "popularized the interpretation of race in terms of ancestral relatedness."[86] Whether or not Africans were indelibly black was open to some interpretation, for the ancient Greek tradition attributed the fixed characteristics of a people to their environment, not to divine will or to a shared gene pool. But either way, the conceptual overlaps between race, culture, nation, and family were already apparent at the dawn of the modern age.

Emergent disciplines of biology and anthropology were responsible for the classification of physical and cultural differences—hence Weber's description of races as "anthropological types."[87] "The catalog of national characters emerged in lock-step with the classification of races," as Goldberg has pointed out,"[88] so that cultural markers of difference stood for both. To know the race of a person was to claim to know the collective character of the nation to which that person supposedly belonged.

Since "historically specific forms of cultural connectedness and solidarity" are so often equated with race thinking, Goldberg has described cultural difference as a "mask of race." Racial identity need not appeal to biological unity. Jews now understand themselves as a race, according to Goldberg, in reference to their "shared traditions" and not to physical type.[89] By this logic, African American culture is the product of a slave heritage, an African ancestry, and a common experience of oppression. It is not a racial phenomenon simply because "black" Americans (who may have blue eyes and fair skin) claim it as their own; it is racial because it is specific to that group and cannot be freely chosen by those outside its boundaries.

"National culture" operates as a mask of race as well. This happens when social traditions are rendered the outgrowth of historical experiences in a specific place; as such they can be emulated but never fully acquired by foreigners. Culture that is national is as natural to that people as its native flowers and plants. Analogies between strong nations and matter that thrives in local soil go back to the Swedish (eighteenth-century) natural philosophy of Carl Linnaeus[90] and are not uncommon. They are aided by relations between political economy and natural science and by the division of all living things—not just of human beings—into species and families.

Sometimes "cultural passers can be integrated into the national community but they are not to be confused with the national community."[91] "Racial fanaticists," as Weber once noted, tend to be especially hostile toward oppressed groups who adopt the same way of life and social aspirations as themselves. Such hostility was for Weber "social in nature" and conditioned by relations of power: "I have heard but one explanation for it: The Negroes have been slaves; the Indians have not."[92]

Unconditional invitations to racialized minorities to become "full members of a new community" by acquiring citizenship—as happened in decolonizing Kenya—are not unheard of. But even then the "immigrant community" invited by Tom Mboya to become Kenyan was presumed to already enjoy a Kenyan way of life by virtue of its historic relationship to the land. Citizenship was offered only to those British settlers already "in the same Kenya boat," not to any person willing to leap aboard.[93]

Described by François Mitterrand as the "single true enemy" of "a certain way of life," Nazism was responsible for the deaths of the 6 million Jews whose memories have been kept alive and of the untold numbers of Gypsies, homosexuals, Afro-Germans, and others who tend to be forgotten.[94] Nazi Germany is an example of what happens when nationalism answers its own call for the "purification of the body of the nation" from "alien," "hereditarily ill," or "asocial" elements with extermination.[95] But if the impulse to genocide is atypical in the annals of nationalism, the logic of representation that informed it is not.

Personifying the Nation: Social Bodies and Collective Souls

Naked woman, black woman

Clothed with your color which is life, with your form which is beauty!

In your shadow I have grown up; the gentleness of your hands was laid over my eyes

And now, high up on the sun-baked pass, at the heart of summer, at the heart of noon, I come upon you, my Promised Land,

And your beauty strikes me to the heart like the flash of an eagle.

—*Léopold Senghor, 1935–1940*[96]

There is a religious war going on in this country for the soul of America. It is a cultural war as critical to the kind of nation we shall be as the Cold War itself, for this war is for the soul of America. —*Pat Buchanan, 1992*[97]

"Nationality," Renan said, "has a sentimental side to it; it is both soul and body at once."[98] The earliest body metaphors date back to antiquity, where they "operated in structural terms of the linkages between the head, organs, and limbs." Later, "the phrase *corpus politicum* gained renewed currency and was used extensively in the conservative response to the protest literature prevalent in England after 1350."[99] The medieval idea of the church as the *corpus mysticum* of Christ became interwoven in the late Middle Ages with that of the Roman Church as a *sacrum imperium.* Since then the Catholic Church has been represented most often as a female (either the Mother Church or Whore of Babylon) and its nuns (who wear gold wedding rings) as the Brides of Christ. The national people have been personified in similarly conjugal fashion as "a 'female' identity to which the head (the 'male' ruler) is married."[100]

Nationalism still invests its object with anthropomorphous qualities of gender, personality, health, and soul. Williams has suggested that "in nationalist ideologies, European and non-European, national and subnational, it is the female who comes to stand for the spirit of the nation, the site of its reproduction."[101] This is often, but not always, the case. Nations may be female or male, weak or strong, autonomous or dependent, fully grown or newly born, healthy or sick. Images of the national body are always contextual. They reflect the national self back upon its constituent parts, while situating the nation in relation to aliens who may or may not be human as well.

Body metaphors take different forms. In one configuration the body is an idealized vision of whatever nationalism worships—marriage, fertility, health, sanity, cleanliness, purity, efficiency, and order have been common traits. All that is base, lower, and offensive in society is projected (as in racial mythology) onto the body of the alien.

In some cases it is sufficient to represent the nation as its absolute and heroic leader. On the 1652 cover of Hobbes's *Leviathan,* for example, the body of a king with drawn sword and scepter was filled with miniature persons facing his head. More recently the face of Kwame Nkrumah appeared directly below the word *Ghana* on the cover of his 1957 autobiography.[102] But when negative traits are encoded as nonhuman threats—especially as those that spread if left unattended—there is a corresponding injunction to cure, treat, cleanse, or eliminate the danger. This is the logic that genocide takes to an extreme.

Nationalism also projects traits associated with weakness, dependence, and vulnerability onto the national body and their opposite onto a tyrannical yet still human adversary. These convey a constructed vision of how the nation now is or once was, not how it should be. They can work (like the first) as justifications for hostility and resistance to the foreign.

Anti-imperialist or neocolonial struggles typically deploy metaphors of rape when speaking of the national past; theirs is a female nation or "motherland" that was once penetrated unwillingly by outside forces but has now found the means to fight back. When "her" capacity to resist oppression is rendered dependent upon the war-fighting capacity of young men, the nation's female attributes may be abandoned and its personality read as the militaristic qualities of camaraderie, bravery, and honor. Once an ungendered child or a young woman, the nation is transformed into an adolescent boy.

Imperialist and/or sovereign nation-states are often symbolized by strong, mature women—for example by Marianne or Joan of Arc for France, Britannia for Britain, Liberty for the United States—when they are not represented as men. But in eighteenth-century England, Britannia was "pictured frequently as set upon, raped, and otherwise attacked by French and other foreign cultural intrusions."[103] More recently in France, metaphors of rape and sodomy have become familiar modes of expression for anti-immigrant sentiment. As François Landon has pointed out in his analysis of Le Pen, the political threat of foreign invasion is figured as the rape of the nation by syphilis-bearing immigrants who dishonor "our wives, our daughters, our sons."[104]

I have argued before that colonial relations of power were sustained

by a parent/child metaphor, one that did not disappear with decolonization:

> For the three main branches of developmentalism the parent/child
> metaphor portrayed First World states as healthy adults and those in the
> Third World as healthy children. With the "development of underdevelop-
> ment" literature, however, the image of the "satellites" is not really that of
> children . . . rather it is that of adults whose growth has been "stunted."
> . . . The image of Third World states in the "growth with dependence" mod-
> els is that of young adults, who although almost as grown-up as their "par-
> ents" remain totally dependent upon them for money and know-how.[105]

Body metaphors are appealing because they suggest unity and a common purpose. More often than not they disguise internal hierarchy, for
"when the collectivity is seen in unitary terms, it tends to assume the character of a collective individual possessed of a single will, and someone is
bound to be its interpreter."[106] Body metaphors may be inherently authoritarian, regardless of what form the national body is given. But they are not
inherently genocidal. It makes a difference to the treatment of aliens whether
they are scripted as another body with recognizably human (if negative)
attributes, or as a nonhuman force that threatens human life. An overbearing
parent or an underdeveloped child is a less murderous image than that of a
cancerous tumor.

Like Seeks Like: Humankind and Animal Instinct

> The biological nation . . . is a social group containing at least
> two mature males which holds as an exclusive possession a
> continuous area of space, which isolates itself from others of its
> kind through outward antagonism, and which through its
> defence of its social territory achieves leadership, cooperation
> and a capacity for concerted action.
> —*Robert Ardrey, 1967*[107]

> It's inevitable that we [Ukrainians] first feel the need to mark
> our territory, as a dog stakes out his territory. To unite we must
> first separate. We have to find our own space.
> —*Volodymyr Chernyak, 1992*[108]

Animal metaphors of kin and kind have coexisted in nationalism along with
body metaphors. The Bible records the creation of all living things, not
merely of humans, and a central problem for religious thought since then,
according to Banton, has been how to "discern God's design or to sort out
the diversity of living forms."[109] Racial thought has pondered the nature of

species and philosophical thought the nature of man. Both have grappled with related questions that also inform nationalist thought about identity and difference. What kind or species of animal is man? How many different *types* of species are there, and can they change? And what distinguishes human species (man) from animal species (beast)? All of these questions can presuppose human animals on both sides of the national/alien divide, the first two more so than the third.

In Christianity, the ultimate marker of bestiality is the absence of a soul. A soul is by nature invisible, so its absence must be inferred from the presence of something else—such as different characters and lifestyles. In the nationalism of Elizabethan England, this fed into the notion that "whoever is not of [our] sect, [we] account him as a beast that hath no soul."[110]

The inscription of aliens as beasts does not automatically justify their torture, annihilation, or exclusion from human community. Christianity allows for two different positions on animals and kinship, according to Shell: "(1) Animals are akin to humans; that is, they are our brothers, hence to be thought of and treated as if they were members of our tribe or species. In this view, we are not the "keepers" of animals but their equals. . . . (2) Animals are extraspecies and extratribal beings, and hence, like all essentially nonhuman things, are outside the 'covenant.'"[111]

The first of the two positions just mentioned seems to demand kindness toward animals rather than cruelty. According to Shell, though, it often leads not to the elevation of animals to human status but their relegation to the realm of exploitable things. Since medieval times in particular, "if one is not essentially akin to a Christian, one is not humankind, and, as an animal, one has no legal right to be treated kindly: One is exploitable along with vegetables and stones."[112]

The use of animals without rights has taken many forms. Oxen, asses, and horses have been worked as farm instruments. Goats have been trained to suckle human children. Cows have been used for food and drink and also to innoculate human beings with animal diseases.[113] "Wild" animals such as lions, tigers, and wolves have been treated as savage beasts and either shot for sport or placed in cages. "Domestic" animals like dogs, cats, and rabbits have become family pets. A host of different animals—from mice to monkeys—have been used in scientific experiments.

Animal metaphors in nationalism may be benign, as when a national sports team names itself the Lions, Eagles, Springboks, or Wallabies. But aliens without national rights have been exploited in exactly the same ways as animals without human rights—as tools, nurse-mothers, sport objects, pets, and experimental subjects. Aliens have been equated with disease and with the sexual habits of dogs and rabbits. It is the concept of species that allows for easy analogies between humankind and animalkind. What matters in nationalism is not the analogy per se, but how the production of species difference is deployed.

The first part of Hobbes's *Leviathan,* titled "Of Man," was a philosophical attempt to differentiate men as eligible members of a commonwealth from beasts as social outcasts. Those faculties shared by man and beast were identified by Hobbes as understanding, prudence, sense, and imagination. Only man, according to Hobbes, knew absurdity, curiosity, and speech, for while a dog could understand his master's call, only the human master could speak to the dog.[114] The faculty in which "a man did excel all *other* animals" (my emphasis) was the faculty of reason. By reason Hobbes meant "that when [man] conceived any thing whatsoever, he was apt to inquire the consequences of it, and what effects he could do with it."[115]

Man was an animal in Hobbes's formulation, even if some animals were beasts and others not. Beasts were by definition outside of Hobbes's body politic. The political problem was what to do with those animals that were *capable* of reason but had not yet acquired it. Hobbes suggested that "children, fools, and madmen that have no use of reason, may be personated by guardians, or curators." Anyone that broke the rules of commonwealth and threatened the security of others, by contrast, deserved "the destruction of his nature by violence."[116]

The right of self-preservation as justification for reciprocal violence and slaughter is found in Locke as well. The treatment of "wild Savage Beasts with whom Men can have no Society or Security" was to be quite different from that meted out to underdeveloped humans. Those who declare war against all humankind "may be destroyed as a Lyon or a Tyger." Children, by contrast, must be educated, "because the ignorance and infirmities of Childhood stand in need of restraint and correction; which is a visible exercise of Rule, and a kind of dominion."[117]

It is possible to see from Locke how parent/child metaphors have sustained imperial relations of power through the principle of guardianship. But if colonized peoples and racialized minorities have been "children," they have also been "apes"—creatures from which "higher" races have supposedly evolved more quickly than "lower" ones. Again, to treat a human as analogous to an ape is not to presume a difference in kind or to mandate ill treatment. Desmond Morris, for example, has described apes as man's "nearest relatives."[118] But evolutionary models of man have metamorphosed into ethology and sociobiology, Darwinian derivatives that use the concept of instincts to explain away the constructed nature of political boundaries.

According to Paul Shaw and Yuwa Wong, "Studies involving the behavior of social insects and nonhuman animals" should lead us to expect "zero cooperation or blatant aggression to be directed towards strangers." In their "inclusive fitness" model (or "kin selection theory"), "all individuals will be

subject to care who are sufficiently genetically related. . . . Genetic relatedness would [thus] be greatest with members of one's own lineage and one's
own kin or 'ethnic' group."[119]

Like souls, genes are invisible to the naked eye. Relatedness and
strangeness must be inferred from something else, such as physical similarity. But "similarity-creation" in humans is the work of scientific knowledge,
not of animal instincts.[120] Even in literal families there can be no absolute
certainty of consanguineous kinship, for as Shell has noted, "The Siamese
twin is the only person who knows for sure who his or her kinperson is."[121]

In nominal kinship systems such as nations, the probability that "we
cannot really tell whether a being is our kind or not our kind, our kin or not
our kin"[122] is even greater. As Joshua Goldstein has pointed out, "The difficulties of applying a kinship-based theory of war to a world that has been
divided into genetically-mixed nation-states for centuries" are occluded in
the new Darwinism. Whatever the conscious intentions of individual authors
may be, this explains why "the rapid rise of sociobiology is seen by some as
a conservative political move."[123]

Martin Barker has argued that in contemporary Britain, "it is the use of
the concept of instincts that gives the new racism the appearance of scientific validity."[124] The "survival of the fittest" over time—whether it be the
survival of the entire group (for the ethologists) or of individual members
(for sociobiologists such as Shaw and Wong)—supposedly requires the
aggressive defense of territory from outsiders. Hostility toward strangers
and the marking off of territory is supposedly characteristic of all animals,
human and nonhuman. Thus is racism constituted as a genetic trait and racial
separation the key to in-group success.

THE MASKS OF RACE: CULTURE, SPACE, AND TIME

> Upon what criterion . . . should one base this national right?
> . . . Several confidently assert that it is derived from race. . . .
> It is a population's race which remains firm and fixed. This is a
> very great error. . . . Race is something which is made and
> unmade.   —*Ernest Renan, 1882*[125]

Renan argued that nations should be constituted by affective sentiment
(which can change) and not be based on whatever is presumed to remain
fixed. But he made no pretense that they actually were: "Nowadays . . . race
is confused with nation and a sovereignty analogous to that of really existing peoples is attributed to ethnographic or, rather linguistic groups."[126]
Renan blamed the confusion on the emergent discipline of anthropology,
which used the term *race* as synonymous with family, to indicate a blood

relationship. If nations were defined by common descent, "the noblest countries"—England, France, and Italy—could not be nations because these were places "of essentially mixed blood."[127]

The problem that Renan faced in detaching race from nation was that the practice was so widespread. Joseph Chamberlain, for example, proclaimed as British secretary of state for the colonies in 1895 that "the British race is the greatest governing race that the world has ever seen."[128] Even those who recognized the "mixed blood" of their own populations equated the formation of new races (from racial mixing) with the formation of new nations.

France's Arthur de Gobineau is best remembered for his studies of cranial capacity in different races. According to Banton, Gobineau assumed that all races were the product of prior miscegenation; the Persian race no longer existed in a scientific sense any more than did the French race. Of all the peoples of France, the French were identified as the one in which the original type (or race) was least evident. Yet for Gobineau the consequence of this mixing was the constitution of new races with distinctive cultures: "It is even this obliteration which we accept, in physique and in culture, as being our own type. It is the same with the Persians."[129]

The suggestion that new nations are synonymous with new races was made even more explicit by Karl Vogt in Germany. In the mid-1800s, Vogt predicted the formation of an American race out of the racial mixing of immigrant groups:

> The Anglo-Saxon race is itself a mongrel race, produced by Celts, Saxons, Normans and Danes, a raceless chaos without any fixed type; and the descendants of this raceless multitude have in America so much intermixed with Frenchmen, Germans, Dutch, and Irish, as to have given rise to another raceless chaos, which is kept up by continued immigration. We can readily believe that from this chaos a new race is gradually forming.[130]

Banton has suggested that race was often confused with nation because the meaning of the term *race* began to shift in the nineteenth century. This made it easier for European nationalism to cast national sentiment as an expression of race.[131]

Two views of human diversity—race as lineage and race as type—were in contention in the 1850s. Following the publication in 1859 of Charles Darwin's book *On the Origin of Species by Natural Selection: Or the Preservation of Favored Races in the Struggle for Life,* a view of races as evolving subspecies began to emerge. But application of Darwin's animal transmutation theory to man was slow in coming, in part because Darwin's fear of censure by the Anglican Church led him to omit any reference to humans until the very last page. By the time his *Descent of Man* was published, Darwin's ideas had been coopted and three competing meanings of

race—which probably intersected in ways unimagined by their creators—
were circulating simultaneously. All were available to nationalism and have
since been "passed along, inherited, reproduced, and transformed to suit prevailing conditions."[132]

It is necessary to look closely at the three competing meanings—race as
lineage, race as type, and race as subspecies—in order to understand their
continued hold on nationalist conceptions of culture, space, and time.

Communities of Common Descent:
Culture and the National Family

> Races, like families, are the organisms and ordinances of God;
> and race feeling, like family feeling, is of divine origin. The
> extinction of race feeling is just as possible as the extinction of
> family feeling. Indeed, a race *is* a family.
> —*Alexander Crummell, 1860s*[133]

"All that believe the Bible," wrote John Locke, "must necessarily derive
themselves from Noah."[134] Family membership is purportedly given by
shared ancestry; one common parent is sufficient but two makes for a closer relationship. If all of humanity is traced back only to the family lineages
of Noah's three sons and not to one original pair, then the idea of fixed racial
difference can be read into the Bible. Those who wanted to challenge the
monogenesis view of race in the sixteenth century could divide the scriptural creation story into two time periods—before the Flood and after the
Flood—and promote polygenesis instead. From the surviving families of
Shem, Ham, and Japheth were three races supposedly born.

If sixteenth-century Europeans lacked a racial consciousness, as many
scholars believe, then it was probably because they had no easy means of
racial identification; Shem's descendants could not be spotted across a
crowded room. Banton argues that a substantial literature in the seventeenth
and eighteenth centuries about Africans and other non-Europeans did not
contain the word *race*. What made Africans culturally different, according
to Anthony Barker's reading of that literature, was their hostile environment; Africans were neither natural slaves nor especially well equipped to
work elsewhere.[135] When the agitation about slavery began, only a few of
the proslavery writers asserted that Africans were naturally inferior.
According to Banton, "The detailed information which many of them provided came from a context of mistrust and ethnocentric contempt and not
from assumptions about racial inferiority."[136]

The view that Africans were not considered racially inferior would be
contested by Christian Delacampagne, who has argued that inferior status
and ill treatment were justified on grounds of degenerate "nature." Even if

Barker is correct and most writers did in fact blame the African environment and not biology for cultural inferiority, there *is* a sense in which that inferiority could be explained in the racial terms of the time. As Delacampagne has pointed out, premodern racism could invoke the curse supposedly inflicted on Ham's descendants to justify European slavery.[137] Enslaved peoples were scripted as latter-day Canaanites.

Whether it was God or the environment that was to blame, the understanding of Africans as culturally inferior to Europeans meant that they could not be considered members of nations that defined themselves in cultural terms. The rival explanations offered different answers, though, to the question of whether blacks could ever be deemed worthy of national inclusion. If the environment were to blame, then black culture could be improved either by improving the African environment (a "white man's burden" type of argument) or by removing Africans from their environment (a justification for slavery). God's curse, on the other hand, was devoid of an expiration date; Ham's descendants were doomed to permanent exclusion.

A new phase in the history of racial thought, according to Banton, was inaugurated in 1800 by Georges Cuvier. Cuvier treated each race as a separate species, although he "could accept that all men were descended from Adam."[138] Cuvier identified only three types: Caucasian (also known as white), Mongolian (also Oriental or Asian), and Ethiopian (Negro or black). For Cuvier's friend Charles Hamilton Smith, the key distinction between the types was a matter of hair, not skin color or cranium: "For Smith the three types were the woolly-haired or Negro; beardless or Mongolian; and bearded or Caucasian."[139] Each of these was further subdivided on geographic, linguistic, and physical grounds.

The persistence of trichotomous classification established a continuity in racial thought. The older understanding of race as lineage did not disappear in any case but adapted itself to the newly emerging one. The assumption that individuals of similar race both look alike and possess common ancestors is attributed by Banton to anthropology.[140] Its acceptance explains why the metaphor of the family remains central to the way people talk about members of their own race. The continued assumption that races are people united by common descent also enables the nationalization of racial identity.

Two features of Cuvier's conception of racial difference were particularly important, the second more novel than the first. He claimed that the different types could be hierarchically arranged, with Caucasians at the top and Ethiopians at the bottom. He also suggested that "differences in culture and mental quality were produced by differences in physique."[141]

The concept of race as type circulated widely in the United States, where it offered an alternative to biblical justifications for slavery. Published in New York in 1833, a pamphlet by Richard Colfax asserted the permanent inferiority of enslaved Africans. Despite their "proximity to refined nations," Negroes had supposedly "never even *attempted* to raise themselves above their present equivocal station in the great zoological chain."[142] For Colfax, cultural inferiority could not be environmental if the environment of the slaves changed (they were no longer in Africa) but the slaves themselves did not. Their inferiority must therefore be "natural."

In summary, both race as lineage and race as type attempted to explain physical and cultural difference.[143] The continuation of both understandings is evident when race is conflated with physical similarity, common descent, and common culture. It is a brew that can only intensify the connection of race to nation.

Geographic Racism: Race, Climate, and Territory

Concerning this Division of the World, That some say it was by lot, and others that Noah sail'd round the Mediterranean in Ten Years, and divided the World into Asia, Africa and Europe, Portions for his three Sons. America then, it seems, was left to be his that could catch it.   —*John Locke, 1698*[144]

Although it may have assumed that people of common descent live in the same place, the race as lineage conception was less spacial than either race as type or race as subspecies. Those who favored the latter two meanings argued that there were certain areas where different races not only *did* live but *ought* to live. In this way, race theory reinforced the Tower of Babel story in the book of Genesis.

In typological thinking, each race was like a native plant: best suited to a particular climate and zone of the earth.[145] Inherited characters were a function of different environments, not of genetic material, and indigenous people would always have a natural advantage over settler races from elsewhere.[146] According to Banton, racial typology constituted an international school of thought that shared three key assumptions:

1. Variations in the constitution and behavior of individuals are the expression of differences between underlying types of a relatively permanent kind, each of which is suited to a particular continent or zoological province.
2. Social categories in the long-run reflect and are aligned with the natural categories that produced them.
3. Individuals belonging to a particular racial type display an innate antagonism towards individuals belonging to other types, the degree of antagonism depending upon the relationship between the two types.[147]

The novelty of Darwinian theory—the idea of races as subspecies of the genus man—came from the notion that human races evolve and multiply by means of natural selection. Nature and climate did not impose a limit, for Darwin, on either species change and development or on the possibility of transplantation. Organisms with features best adapted to particular environments would thrive there and pass the required traits to their offspring. Features that did not help an organism to survive were expected to gradually die out. But the organism itself need not become extinct. It could simply transmute into something else.

According to Banton, "The change-over to a Darwinian mode of explanation was neither simple nor straightforward."[148] The idea of man as a human animal was not, after all, a novel one: "The key question was whether he was just an animal."[149] The notion of the survival of the fittest—first promulgated by modern eugenicists and reworked in sociobiology—is certainly a misreading of Darwin, who theorized more the preservation of the most adaptable feature. But even if Darwin himself was not a social Darwinist, his writings aided the confusion of race with nation that so appalled Renan.

In 1866, Darwin described "geographical races, or subspecies" as "local forms completely fixed and isolated." A geographic race or subspecies was one that had evolved in isolation; with the passage of sufficient time and development it would prove incapable of breeding with other branches of the same parent stock. In nationalism any suggestion that autonomy is required for progress is appealing to those who believe in isolation of their own racial stock against the dangers of interbreeding.

Also in Darwin's work, the number of human races was not fixed at three (or five, as in the work of Samuel Morton).[150] Multiple races presupposed provinces that were smaller in size than entire continents. This enabled the idea of a "British race," a "French race," an "American race," and so on, whereby race coincided with political sovereignty rather than continental divide.

Journeys Through National History: Race and Time

There are two ways in which a sense of shared time is said to be constitutive of national identity. Many authors, following Renan, assume that the possession in common of a heroic past and great men—ownership based in many cases on mythical recreations or reinventions of history—provides the social capital upon which a national idea is based. Reminiscent of the Romantics, theorists such as Anderson have added that a nation also conceives of itself as an organic community moving steadily down (or up) history.[151] The sense of being at the same point on a historical journey is just as important to national identity as common ownership of the past.

Race as lineage aided mythologies of collective kinship. In England, for example, an ancestral myth was created that derived the chief virtues of the

English from their Anglo-Saxon forebears. Sir Walter Scott, according to Banton, promoted this idea in the best-selling novel *Ivanhoe* (published in 1820). Scott cast the resentment of Saxon peasants (whose hero was Robin Hood) toward their Norman rulers as a struggle between two races.[152] Presumably, only when the subject race achieved political sovereignty would its troubles be over.

Banton has further suggested that nothing did more to popularize the term *race* than Scott's historical romance, and that literary and historical narratives have contributed as much to the conflation of race with nation as speeches from public platforms.[153] The idea of imperial nations being composed of people of "superior racial stock" thus circulated in those very print languages that laid the basis for popular national consciousness.

Claims to the racial superiority of certain nations are less routine since decolonization than they were before. Races are more usually distinguished by cultural difference than by their place in a hierarchical "great chain of being." Yet the influence of past thinking continues to lurk, exhibiting itself in contemporary applications of evolutionary theory that place certain peoples further along the path of progress than others.

Lucius Outlaw has argued that evolutionary—as opposed to typological—thinking is now in some form the dominant intellectual framework for explanations of human and natural difference. Human groups are still ordered along an ascending scale, with a particular group's placement determined by its supposed development (or lack thereof) toward human perfectability: from "primitive" to "civilized" in the nineteenth century and from "underdeveloped" to "developed" in the twentieth. Such arguments are easily sustained and reproduced because evolution is still conceived as linear development along a single path that *all* peoples have to traverse.[154]

With its notion of "geographical races" placed along an ascending scale toward perfection (and the end of history), evolutionary theory has done nothing to undermine notions of national/racial superiority. But in an important sense it has also enabled the equation of race with nation. If those races supposedly lower down the evolutionary scale are not moving as fast as those higher up, they cannot be at the same point on the historical journey. By definition they cannot be imagined as members of the national community.

The progressivist conception of history, according to James Snead, developed a myth of the past whose now embarrassing aspects nonindustrialized cultures were seen to represent.[155] "Backward" cultures embodied the European past in the present, at the same time as the European present offered a vision of the future to the non-European Other. This is consistent with Johannes Fabian's argument that anthropologists have spatialized time. Dispersal in space has connoted sequence in history, and physical remoteness has been equated with temporal backwardness.

Labels that connote temporal distance need not have explicitly temporal references. Adjectives like *mythical, ritual,* or *tribal* have served the same function. Communication, for Fabian, is about the creation of shared time. The persistent tendency to place the referent of anthropology in the past is therefore antithetical to genuine communication and cross-cultural understanding.[156]

Temporal signifiers like uncivilized, backward, less developed, primitive, traditional, and now "ethnic" enable the coding of race in nonbiological terms. They also presuppose the national exclusion of those who represent the past in the present. South Africa's concept of "separate development" is but one example of a spacial and temporal distancing couched in the language of cultural and national difference. Exclusion need not be permanent if those further down the historical path are thought able to catch up. But the onward march of those at the front renders the prospects of simultaneous movement for all nonexistent.

In conclusion, race theory has historically equated race with culture, space, and time in such a way as to conflate race with nation. Race need not be discussed in purely biological terms because it has never been understood solely in that way. The failure to see how race has been coded in practices of boundary creation and maintenance between nationals and aliens is a failure to recognize the debt that nationalism continues to owe to racial thought.

NOTES

1. Renan, "What Is a Nation?" 18–19.
2. Emerson, "Nationalism and Political Development," 5–6.
3. Emerson, "Nationalism and Political Development," 16–17.
4. Smith, *National Identity,* 100.
5. Emerson, "Nationalism and Political Development," 16.
6. See, for example, the chapter entitled "Ethnicity and Human Nature" in Kellas, *The Politics of Nationalism and Ethnicity,* 8–19.
7. Gellner, *Nations and Nationalism,* 55.
8. Hobsbawm, *Nations and Nationalism Since 1780,* 10.
9. Peter Alter understands nationalism as "both an ideology and a political movement which holds the nation and the sovereign nation-state to be crucial indwelling values." See Alter, *Nationalism,* 6–8. In a similar vein, Kellas considers nationalism a phenomenon which "seeks to defend and promote the interests of the nation." See Kellas, *The Politics of Nationalism and Ethnicity,* 3. Smith defines nationalism as "an ideological movement for attaining and maintaining autonomy, unity and identity on behalf of a population deemed by some of its members to constitute an actual or potential 'nation.'" See Smith, *National Identity,* 73. Peter Worsley has suggested that the word *nationalism* is used to refer to three different types of movements: (1) those that seek to build, or consolidate, states on the basis of historical-cultural ties; (2) those that establish or seek to establish new states on

the basis of common citizenship or manufactured boundaries (such as those created by foreign colonial powers); and (3) "pan" movements that transcend state boundaries and appeal to wider cultural affiliations. See Worsley, *The Third World,* 69. John Breuilly, finally, uses the term *nationalism* "to refer to political movements seeking or exercising state power and justifying such action with nationalist arguments." See Breuilly, *Nationalism and the State,* 2.

10. The notion of nationalism as a political theory comes mainly from Gellner, who argues that the term signifies a political principle that holds that the state and the nation should be congruent. "Nationalism," for Gellner, "is a theory of political legitimacy." See *Nations and Nationalism,* 1. In *Nations and Nationalism Since 1780,* 9, Hosbawm also "[uses] the term 'nationalism' in the sense defined by Gellner."

11. Karl Deutsch defined nationalism as "a state of mind which gives 'national' messages, memories, and images a preferred status in social communication and a greater weight in the making of decisions." See his "Nation and World," 208. The description of nationalism as "a particular perspective or a style of thought" is in Greenfeld, *Nationalism,* 3–4.

12. Bhabha, "DissemiNation: Time, Narrative, and the Margins of the Modern Nation," 297.

13. Conversi, "Reassessing Current Theories of Nationalism: Nationalism as Boundary Maintenance and Creation."

14. Bennington, "Postal Politics and the Institution of the Nation," 132.

15. Alter, *Nationalism,* 21.

16. Bennington, "Postal Politics," 121.

17. Balibar, "Paradoxes of Universality," 285.

18. Campbell, *Writing Security: United States Foreign Policy and the Politics of Identity,* 78.

19. Reprinted in Nkrumah, *Ghana: The Autobiography of Kwame Nkrumah,* 198–199.

20. Lerner, "The Nineteenth-Century Monument and the Embodiment of National Time," 179–180.

21. Boesak, "Liberation Theology in South Africa."

22. Wills, *Under God: Religion and American Politics,* 197–198, 203.

23. Nixon, "Mandela, Messianism, and the Media," 48.

24. On this point see Williams, "The Impact of the Precepts of Nationalism," 181.

25. See the introductory chapter, "On Dangers and Their Interpretation," in Campbell, *Writing Security: United States Foreign Policy and the Politics of Identity.*

26. Renan, "What Is a Nation?" 19.

27. A special correspondent, "Spirit of Emergency," *West Africa,* January 13, 1986.

28. Elstain, "Sovereignty, Identity, Sacrifice."

29. Kapferer, *Legends of People, Myths of State: Violence, Intolerance, and Political Culture in Sri Lanka and Australia,* 2–6.

30. Wills, *Under God,* 353.

31. Wills, *Under God,* 81.

32. Wills, *Under God,* 116.

33. Wills, *Under God,* 208.

34. See Richard et al., *The Battle of the Gods.*

35. See Shiva, *Staying Alive: Women, Ecology, and Development,* 13.

36. Quoted in Morse and Berger, *Sardar Sarovar: The Report of the Independent Review,* 3.

37. From the chapter "Women's Role in National Development" in Mboya, *The Challenge of Nationhood,* 115–117.

38. Davis, *Apartheid's Rebels: Inside South Africa's Hidden War.*

39. Helen Irving, "Who Are the Founding Mothers? The Role of Women in Australian Federation."

40. Pettman, *Living in the Margins,* 2.

41. Wills, *Under God,* 141–142.

42. Wills, *Under God,* 75.

43. McClintock, "'No Longer in a Future Heaven': Women and Nationalism in South Africa," 105.

44. Locke, *Two Treatises of Government,* 208.

45. Locke, *Two Treatises of Government,* 345.

46. Hobbes, *Leviathan: Of the Matter, Forme and Power of a Commonwealth, Ecclesiasticall and Civil.*

47. See, for example, the chapter "Foreign Policy and Identity" in Campbell, *Writing Security.*

48. Quoted in Almog, *Nationalism and Antisemitism,* 20.

49. Jobson, *The Golden Trade,* 33.

50. Rose, *Revolutionary Antisemitism in Germany from Kant to Wagner.*

51. Thomas, "The Evolution of Anti-Semitism," 97.

52. The quotation is from Rose, but the page number of his book is not cited. See Thomas, "The Evolution of Anti-Semitism," 105.

53. Almog, *Nationalism and Antisemitism,* 5.

54. Almog, *Nationalism and Antisemitism,* 25.

55. Gilman, "'I'm Down on Whores': Race and Gender in Victorian London."

56. Fanon, *Black Skin, White Masks,* 165.

57. Stepan, "Race and Gender: The Role of Analogy in Science," 43.

58. Thomas, "The Evolution of Anti-Semitism," 106.

59. Fanon, *Black Skin, White Masks,* 180.

60. Ronald Reagan, "Remarks at the Presidential Ceremony for the Presidential Medal of Freedom," *Vital Speeches of the Day,* January 19, 1989.

61. Spoken to U.S. veterans of the allied invasion of Normandy, D-day fiftieth anniversary. Quoted in *The Daily Telegraph,* June 7, 1994, 4.

62. Renan, "What Is a Nation?" 19.

63. Greenfeld, *Nationalism,* 10.

64. Anderson, *Imagined Communities,* 18–19, 44–46.

65. Ngugi, *Decolonizing the Mind,* 13–15.

66. Lenin, "Critical Remarks on the National Question," 23.

67. Balibar, "Paradoxes of Universality," 285.

68. Balibar, "Paradoxes of Universality," 284.

69. The Brothers Grimm, *Grimms' Tales for Young and Old,* 461.

70. Quoted in Woods, *Biko,* 127.

71. Jobson, *The Golden Trade,* 52–54.

72. Fanon, *Black Skin, White Masks,* 170.

73. Memmi, *The Colonizer and the Colonized.*

74. Fanon, *Black Skin, White Masks,* 188.

75. Fanon, *Black Skin, White Masks,* 190.

76. Fanon, *Black Skin, White Masks,* 189–190.

77. Fanon, *Black Skin, White Masks,* 231.

78. Quoted in Miller, *Blank Darkness: Africanist Discourse in French,* 27.

79. Quoted in Miller, *Blank Darkness,* 27.

80. White, "Alien Nation: The Hidden Obsession of UFO Literature—Race in Space," 25.

81. Mudimbe, *The Invention of Africa,* 8.

82. Smith, "Of the Naturall Inhabitants of Virginia," 99.

83. White, *Inventing Australia,* 12.

84. White, "Alien Nation," 27.

85. Coetzee, *White Writing: On the Culture of Letters in South Africa,* 14.

86. Goldberg, *Racist Culture: Philosophy and the Politics of Meaning,* 63.

87. Weber, "The Nation," 177.

88. Goldberg, "Modernity, Race, and Morality," 210.

89. Goldberg, *Racist Culture,* 70–73.

90. See Koerner, "Linnaeus' Floral Transplants."

91. Williams, "The Impact of the Precepts of Nationalism on the Concept of Culture," 180–181.

92. Weber, "The Nation," 177.

93. See Mboya, *The Challenge of Nationhood,* 45–46.

94. On Afro-German victims of the Holocaust see Opitz, Oguntoye, and Schultz, *Showing Our Colors: Afro-German Women Speak Out.*

95. See, for example, Burleigh and Wippermann, *The Racial State: Germany 1933–1945.*

96. This is the first verse of Senghor's poem "Black Woman," published in the late 1930s in French as part of the series *Chants d'Ombre.* Reprinted in Reed and Wake, *Senghor: Prose and Poetry,* 105.

97. Pat Buchanan, "The Election Is About Who We Are." Speech delivered at the Republican National Convention, Houston, Texas, August 17, 1992. Quoted in *Vital Speeches of the Day,* August 17, 1992.

98. Renan, "What Is a Nation?" 18.

99. Campbell, *Writing Security,* 87–88.

100. Campbell, *Writing Security,* 91.

101. Williams, "The Impact of the Precepts of Nationalism," 174.

102. Nkrumah, *Ghana: The Autobiography of Kwame Nkrumah.*

103. Williams, "The Impact of the Precepts of Nationalism," 177.

104. François Landon, "Le Pen: Au nom de Jeanne et de la fesse," *L'Evénement du Jeudi,* November 22–28, 1990, 101–102 (translation from the French by Margaret Villers).

105. Manzo, "Modernist Discourse and the Crisis of Development Theory," 18–20.

106. Greenfeld, *Nationalism,* 11.

107. Ardrey, *The Territorial Imperative,* 191.

108. Quoted in Serge Schmemann, "Ukraine Facing the High Costs of Democracy," *The New York Times,* November 6, 1992, 10.

109. Banton, *Racial Theories,* 2.

110. Quoted in Shell, *Children of the Earth,* 171.

111. Shell, *Children of the Earth,* 164.

112. Shell, *Children of the Earth,* 165.

113. On goats and cows see Shell, *Children of the Earth,* 158–159.

114. Hobbes, *Leviathan,* 27.

115. Hobbes, *Leviathan,* 43.

116. Hobbes, *Leviathan,* 127, 123.

117. Locke, *Two Treatises of Government,* 315, 355.

118. See, for example, Morris, *Intimate Behavior.*

119. Shaw and Wong, "Ethnic Mobilization and the Seeds of Warfare: An Evolutionary Perspective," 6.

120. On this point see Stepan, "Race and Gender," 49.

121. Shell, *Children of the Earth,* 6.

122. Shell, *Children of the Earth,* 175.

123. Goldstein, "The Emperor's New Genes: Sociobiology and War," 39–40.

124. Barker, "Biology and the New Racism," 18.

125. Renan, "What Is a Nation?" 13–15.

126. Renan, "What Is a Nation?" 8.

127. Renan, "What Is a Nation?" 14–15.

128. Quoted in Banton, *Racial Theories,* 76.

129. Quoted in Banton, *Racial Theories,* 49.

130. Quoted in Banton, *Racial Theories,* 61.

131. Banton, *Racial Theories,* xiv.

132. Goldberg, "The Social Formation of Racist Discourse," 309.

133. Quoted in Appiah, *In My Father's House,* 17.

134. Locke, *Two Treatises of Government,* 283.

135. Barker, *The African Link: British Attitudes to the Negro in the Era of the Atlantic Slave Trade, 1550–1807.*

136. Banton, *Racial Theories,* 9.

137. Delacampagne, "Racism and the West: From Praxis to Logos," 86.

138. Banton, *Racial Theories,* 29.

139. Banton, *Racial Theories,* 53.

140. Banton, *Racial Theories,* 30.

141. Banton, *Racial Theories,* 28–30.

142. Banton, *Racial Theories,* 34.

143. Banton argues that both theories wanted to explain physical difference and cultural difference, but the presumption of cultural *inferiority,* not merely difference, was central to European thinking about Africans for centuries. See Banton, *Racial Theories,* 168.

144. Locke, *Two Treatises of Government,* 284.

145. Carl Linnaeus believed for some time that plants could be taught to adapt to hostile environments and climate zones but was forced to change his mind when coffee and tea would not grow in Scandinavia. See Koerner, "Linnaeus' Floral Transplants."

146. Banton, *Racial Theories,* 37.

147. Banton, *Racial Theories,* 38.

148. Banton, *Racial Theories,* 73.

149. Banton, *Racial Theories,* 30.

150. Morton's five races were defined as Caucasian, Mongolian, Malay, American, and Ethiopian. See Banton, *Racial Theories,* 35.

151. Anderson, *Imagined Communities,* 26.

152. Banton, *Racial Theories,* 13.

153. Banton, *Racial Theories,* 76.

154. Outlaw, "Toward a Critical Theory of 'Race,'" 66–67.

155. Snead, "European Pedigrees/African Contagions: Nationality, Narrative and Communality in Tutuola, Achebe, and Reed," 235.

156. See Fabian, *Time and the Other: How Anthropology Makes Its Object,* especially chapter 1.

3
Mimosas of the Veld:
White and Rainbow
Nations in South Africa

Each one of us is as intimately attached to the soil of this beau-
tiful country as are the famous jacaranda trees of Pretoria and
the mimosa trees of the bushveld . . . a rainbow nation at peace
with itself and the world.
                    —*President Nelson Mandela, May 10, 1994*[1]

Anthony Holiday has described South African politics as largely "the history of debates between inclusivist and exclusivist varieties of nationalism,
carried on within the confines of . . . the 'Whites-only' parliament in Cape
Town."[2] Debates have focused at different times on questions of territorial
possession, loyalty, language and religion, and collective suffering. National
identity has overlapped with and been conditioned by other identities, of
which European, Christian, African, White,[3] civilized, and anticommunist
have been the most significant.

To understand the changing nature of what Holiday has called "white
nationalism," it is necessary to situate state institutions (like the Whites-only
parliament) within a larger context of global power relations. The British
Empire, the Great Depression, African decolonization, two world wars, and
the Cold War between the United States and the Soviet Union have all
shaped national identities in South Africa.

Afrikaner nationalism is an umbrella term that subsumes within it a
complex array of "political" and "cultural" scriptures. Before the 1970s, the
exclusion from the nation of those classified by the post-1948 National Party
as African and Asian was not a matter of much public debate among those
classified as White. Until then, nationalist conflicts between free settlers
were cast as the "racial problem" to be solved. The only black[4] group to
recur consistently in these conflicts was the one classified after 1948 as
Colored.

The notion that nonblacks constitute a single nation—one referred to

71

variously as Afrikaner (also the family name of a group of wildflowers), South African, or White—has required the suppression of racial differences among them. Appeals to the shared origins, loyalties, or lifestyles of a homogenized race have tended to presuppose an alien threat. A supposedly "civilized" oasis within a sea of "barbarism," Whites have been exhorted to pull together to avert being "swamped" or "ploughed under." The Afrikaans expression *swart van die mense* (literally "black with people") also translates as "swarming with people."[5]

Organized resistance to apartheid has been an obvious cause of alarm, particularly when made to appear as the handmaiden of global communism. But all black people have been constructed as dangerous at different times, whether or not they have taken up arms against the state. Before apartheid crumbled as a legal structure, black people exercised a capacity to transgress boundaries between nationals and aliens. The production of a *swart gevaar* (black danger)[6] has thus been conditioned by several types of movements. These include the circulation of "immigrant" workers and their families between urban and rural areas; the migration of "illegal aliens" in and out of neighboring states and nominal homelands; and the circumvention of social segregation by various means.

The reliance on a black threat to unite Whites is only one of the ways in which Afrikaner nationalism has been both inclusive and exclusive. A contrasting vision of what it means to be an Afrikaner has kept "British imperialists" out of the nation while bringing Coloreds in. Here the shared language and Dutch Reformed Christianity of the two groups have been the binding factors, as well as the absence of loyalty to any other homeland than the one in South Africa. If there has not been more open resistance to the exclusion of Coloreds from political citizenship, it is because the so-called *bruin* (brown) Afrikaners have been considered less advanced than their "more pink than white" counterparts.[7]

The most restrictive nationalism of all omits everyone but *Boers*. Literally the term means farmers. When not used by black people as a derogatory term for all political conservatives, Boer encompasses only those who can claim descent from *Voortrekker* (pioneer) stock. The ancestral Voortrekkers were those who established republics in the interior of South Africa in a vain attempt to escape from the global reach of the British Empire. The biblical Exodus narrative has been read into the initial migrations by later generations in a nationalism that continues to engender the *Boervolk* (Afrikaner nation) through the death and suffering of its members.

Afrikaans-speaking South Africans have figured prominently in each of the above nationalisms, as well as in a broader South Africanism that has taken hold during the last couple of decades. Afrikaans speakers therefore defy easy classification as either a tribe or an ethnic group. Indeed, it is most often English speakers and so-called New Afrikaners who employ such categories when looking in Boer republics for the origins of apartheid. As I have argued elsewhere, the Boer myth of apartheid's origins "serves to locate responsibility for apartheid in the barbarous other, the Afrikaner, who in the course of his encounter with Africa becomes tribal, idiotic, the captive of irrational fears, and savage."[8]

Element of truth or not, the notion that apartheid was invented by a tribalized people "in a deep solitude"[9] treats distance from the Enlightenment as the key explanatory factor. But the influence of nationalist ideas imported from Europe, in conjunction with the circulation of racial and religious scriptures, have been far more significant.

Once constructed, boundaries between South Africa's various inhabitants have been routinely guarded. Here it is important to remember the special role that women may play in nationalism. The policing of women's sexuality in South Africa has been expressed historically in the form of prohibitions on sexual intercourse and marriage across the "color line." Nationalist fears of racial boundary crossing in urban areas have been the catalyst for the passage of such legislation.

Anne McClintock has argued that the "doctrine of crisis" that commemorates a nation of suffering women and children was "violently improvised in the shocked aftermath of the [Anglo-Boer] war."[10] In a similar vein, René De Villiers has pointed to competing nationalisms—one including all Whites and the other not—vying openly at three different times: after the Anglo-Boer War ended in 1902; before and during World War II; and before and after South Africa became a republic in 1961.[11] Both authors have shown how changing global power relations bring questions of national identity to the fore. Shifts in the placement of national boundaries (geographic and otherwise) have been most evident in South Africa at times of global upheaval.

Elements of national identity have been expressed and understood in racial terms, even between the two groups classified together as White. Different justifications for exclusion have circulated simultaneously, in ways that have not always added up to a unified, coherent scripture. The so-called Christian-nationalism of the 1930s, for example, was actually a composite of racial and religious elements concocted in various circles.

Justifications for the placement of boundaries have also changed in response to altered global circumstances. While some nationalists have been content to accept "pariah" status as the price to pay for self-determination, others have tried to find respectable analogues for their own behavior. They have not always succeeded—nor have they always failed. Efforts to equate the official policy of separate development with African decolonization were not without their supporters, either within or without the country.

How much that apartheid past should be remembered and how much actively forgotten is but one of the questions facing the manufacturers of "a rainbow nation." Also under active negotiation are matters associated with the reconfiguration of national space (homelands and land rights); with national culture (especially language policy, affirmative action, and the symbols of a shared way of life); and with national time (not only the mythologies and heroes of different groups but also the idea of development). Whether unity can be effected without the rallying cry of alien danger is not certain. Already there are signals that narratives of global potency since the end of the Cold War—in particular, calls to national defense against neo-Nazism and refugee "flooding"—are at work in South Africa as well.

The remainder of the chapter proceeds as follows. Part one illustrates how national identity has depended on territorial possession and spacial separation. The geographic boundaries of the South African national home have not remained fixed. Once confined to the Cape Colony, they expanded to incorporate other areas of settlement, only to be shrunk back to make way for so-called sovereign homelands. In each instance identity has been bound up with settled possession of, and identification with, a given territory. Those who "wander" have not been included within the nation. Only settlers of some variety have ever been South African nationals.

There is another sense in which South African nationalism has been about keeping still. Having staked their claim to a particular place, the nation's representatives have assumed the right to regulate movement for the sake of racial harmony, law and order, and/or national survival. Until recently, black South Africans violating such regulations were the only "illegal immigrants" of real concern to the South African state. With the collapse of apartheid, emphasis has shifted to those who embody the effects of destabilization in the southern African region, namely refugees from Mozambique.

It is now assumed that the so-called homelands will be reincorporated, even though resistance to automatic reincorporation continued right up to the first "all race" election of April 1994. Maps of South Africa are being redrawn, and what were once yellow areas within the boundaries of the Republic will (with the exception of "neighboring" Lesotho) be bleached white. It is also evident that the boundaries of the nine new provinces designed to replace the homelands will not allow for an easy correspondence with nominal identities.

Each region contains a mixture of areas that were separate under such apartheid laws as the Group Areas Act and the Promotion of Black Self-Government Act. There are also eleven official languages in South Africa now, not two (or nine). But negotiations over homelands boundaries have continued since the election, under the rubric of "self-determination" and "regional autonomy." The political debate is no longer—if it ever was—over whether South Africa should be a unitary nation-state or a federal nation-state. The question is whether South Africa should be a federal nation-state or a multinational federation.

The second part of the chapter analyzes shifting conceptions of cultural similarity and difference. When united as one, Whites have been exhorted to remember their shared customs and heritage. When separated as Afrikaners and non-Afrikaners, they have been reminded of their different languages, religions, and ways of life. In each case culture has correlated with race. So-called Europeans have all been members of the same race classified as White, while Afrikaners and non-Afrikaners have been described as distinct racial "types." That nonblacks could be racially the same (White) and racially different (Boer/Briton) at the same time highlights the dependence of nationalism on racial criteria, as well as the arbitrary and constructed nature of race itself.

Apartheid created multiple races within the black population of South Africa.[12] If each race is the bearer of a distinct culture, and shared culture is synonymous with national character, a logical move is to give each "nation" its own homeland. The conflation of race, nation, culture, and territory found its clearest expression in the National Party policy of separate development.

In a country with eleven official languages, no new racial classification scheme, and still contested national symbols, it is not clear whether a national culture can be found. That issue is considered in the concluding section of part two.

Finally, the chapter examines the role of time in the construction and reconstruction of national identity. Time as both a possession (the shared stock of common memories, myths, and heroes) and as a journey to perfection (the idea of development) is discussed. In the latter regard the reliance on a civilized/uncivilized dichotomy, one predicated on the idea of "natives" as backward in time, has been a central element in the exclusion of black people from the South African nation.

That dichotomy has also underpinned constructions of cultural difference, so the separation of culture from time is artificial. Yet different understandings of development have been implied in discussions of reform. The question of whether black South Africans were permanently "backward" informed debates between the United Party and the National Party in the 1940s. The extent to which national inclusion of the "underdeveloped" has conditioned efforts to reclassify South Africa as a developing country is also analyzed in the last part of the chapter.

NATIONAL HOUSES AND HOMELANDS

The friction is not between Dutch-speaking colonists and the colonial Englishman, but between the colonist in Africa and the Englishman 'at home'. . . . France, Holland, Germany, England each had a share in the origin of this People, and thus the name Afrikaner includes them all.
—General J. B. M. Hertzog, 1891[13]

English-speaking whites can be divided into South Africans
and South African British.
—*South African academic, 1988*[14]

The First Home: The Cape Territory

Established in 1652 as a refreshment station for the Dutch East India
Company, the Cape of Good Hope was never intended as a permanent
colony. Were it not for the actions of Jan Van Riebeeck, the employees who
staffed it might have been recalled to Holland and the station abandoned. It
was Van Riebeeck who issued licensed monopolies over a range of socio-
economic activities to a class of *burghers* (citizens) created from former
company employees.[15]

Sheila Patterson has described the year 1657—when nine burghers settled some twenty miles from the Cape settlement—as the "birth-year of the
Boer or Afrikaner nation."[16] The notion that the burghers thought of *themselves* as a nation (if that is indeed what Patterson implies) would be disput-
ed by those writers who consider Afrikaner (like European) nationalism a
nineteenth-century phenomenon. Nonetheless, it was from within the
burgher population that an Afrikaner identity, one predicated on territorial
attachment and a shared sense of economic injustice, first emerged.

The burghers soon resented what Marq De Villiers has described as
"a kind of state-controlled monopoly capitalism."[17] When commando
units appeared in 1705, the governor of the Cape ordered the arrest of the
leaders. It was at that point that a formal distinction was made between
company employees and the "people of that place." "*Ik ben een
Afrikaander!*" was supposedly yelled by one Hendrik Bibault at the local
sheriff.[18]

Stock farming beyond Cape Town brought the early settlers into contact
with the indigenous Khoikhoi peoples, with whom they traded first and
warred later. A group of farmers referred in 1706 to "that black brood living
among us," suggesting an absence of clear territorial divisions. Yet the
Khoikhoi, while seemingly also "people of that place," were called neither
European nor "Afrikaander" but Hottentot. They were said by the same
farmers to be possessed of the blood of Ham and thus descended from a different racial (biblically derived) lineage.[19] They were also considered
thieves and criminals because they took cattle supposedly stolen from them
by the settlers.

Treatment meted out to the indigenous San was much worse. Like the
Khoikhoi, the San were considered racially different and less than fully
human. But those without tradable commodities were shot down by hunting
parties, as if they were wild animals. Today the remainder of the so-called
Bushmen inhabit the independent states of Namibia (once the German
colony of Southwest Africa) and South Africa. A group of about 5,000 San

men who fought with a South African paramilitary unit called Koevoet were resettled in Namibia in 1994.[20]

By the 1830s, Cape legal scholars (some of whom studied law in Holland) and others were under pressure to justify colonial dispossession and extermination to antislavery and humanitarian movements in Europe. Respected figures such as Sir John Truter and J. de Vet stated that because Hottentots "led a wandering life," they were not "to be regarded as a nation." The argument rested on a distinction between *occupation* of land and *possession* of it, one indebted to the idea of nations as cultivators of privately owned property.[21] Whether inspiration came from the Bible or from Dutch law, the idea of fixed settlement was used to draw a boundary around Afrikaners and to separate them from both Europeans (company employees) and Hottentots (Khoikhoi).

According to Heribert Adam and and Hermann Giliomee, colonists were generally known as Afrikaners from the last quarter of the eighteenth century. A traveler named De Jong wrote of the Cape colonist in the 1790s that "he is proud of the name 'Africaan'; Citizen of the Cape he deems a title of honor." The "fatherland" was no longer the Netherlands, but the Cape Colony.[22]

With the conquest of the Cape by Britain (first in 1795 and then permanently after 1806), earlier colonists came under pressure to adopt the English language and British customs. Influential settlers such as Advocate Denyssen insisted that Afrikaners must retain their own "nationality." Adam and Giliomee have argued that national identity comprised two main elements. The first was cultural, namely shared language and Christianity. The second was the sense of advancement from the free black population, those whose ancestors had been brought to the colony as slaves.[23] Cultural uniqueness and racial superiority (manifested in the reference to ancestry) were thus central to Cape-based nationalism.

Another element is suggested by an editorial in the Dutch-language newspaper *De Zuid Afrikaan*. In 1835, it claimed that "it is an error we have frequently opposed, to suppose that as British subjects we are compelled to adopt a British nationality. A colonist of Dutch descent cannot become an Englishman, nor should he strive to become a Hollander."[24] At a time when race was still associated with common descent, *De Zuid Afrikaan* assumed that members of the Dutch "race" were not part of the British nation even though they were British subjects. Nor were they Hollanders, since they no longer considered Holland their home. Racial difference from other "civilized" nations was the third component of Afrikaner national identity.

British Imperialism and Expatriation

Analysts of Afrikaner nationalism have emphasized the important role played by British imperialism, or what Patterson has described as the "fumbling alienation and imperialistic leap-frog which characterized British colonial policy."[25] Disaffection with anglicization increased with the arrival of 5,000 British immigrants in 1820 and with the adoption of English as the official language in 1825. There was also discontent with "native" policy. An ordinance abolishing legal distinctions between the settler population and the Khoikhoi was promulgated in 1828, and a British Act of Parliament was passed in 1833 emancipating all slaves throughout the empire. A group of settlers thereupon decided to leave the Cape, and after a split in the ranks they established two new settlements. These were Potchefstroom (under A. H. Potgieter) and the Republic of Natal (under Andries Pretorius).

The Great Trek provided a set of founding fathers and ancestral myths for later generations of nationalists. Analogies have been drawn between the Trek and the departure of Israel from Egypt, not only in the speeches and writings of overt nationalists but in academic analyses of Afrikaner nationalism. The opening chapter of Patterson's *The Last Trek* is titled "Genesis, Exodus and Chronicles," while Chapter 1 of Vatcher's *White Laager* is called simply "Exodus."

Yet as André Du Toit and Hermann Giliomee have shown, the Voortrekkers did not think in those terms. Their spokesmen were not without Christian sensibilities. Piet Retief, for example, claimed that they left "with a firm reliance on an all-seeing, just, and merciful Being," and in order to escape from "vagrants, who are allowed to infest the country in every part." But the so-called pioneers described themselves as "emigrants" and "expatriates," and referred to the place they were leaving as the "motherland," the "paternal home," and the "beloved country." The supposed right of "free citizens" to "go where they like" was invoked as justification for the move, not the right to self-determination of a separate nation.[26]

Faced with the threat of British intervention, the Natal *Volksraad* (parliament) sought to justify its claim to a territory secured only after war with the Zulus in residence. A year after the 1838 Battle of Blood River, the collective suffering of those "driven away like bastard children from their paternal homes by strangers" was offered as evidence of their right to a "dearly-purchased and lawfully-acquired new country." The filling of Boschjesman's River with Zulu blood was forgotten and only that of "innocently and treacherously murdered relations and friends" remembered. Attachment to Natal as the place where blood had been spilled and the "bleached bones" of innocent kin lay buried was already replacing identification with the Cape.[27]

After British troops were withdrawn from Port Natal at the end of 1839, the Volksraad wrote to the Cape governor that "far from bringing destruction or corruption to the heathen peoples in these parts, we are instruments of God's will for the countering of the murder and violence among them." The "greater safety of the Cape Colony" and the "promotion of Christian civilization" throughout the region were joined to suffering as the rationale for political independence.[28]

Natal was annexed in the name of Her Majesty's government in 1843. In a catalog of complaints against British administration, Pretorius claimed in 1848 that "white African Boers" could not be expected to "reside in a country inhabited by so many colored people." A common identity with those who supposedly "allowed self-government and all privileges of liberty" to "the natives" in colonial reserves[29] thus seemed unlikely.

The national unity of Cape inhabitants and those expatriate communities formed after the initial departure was undermined by the further establishment of separate republics. The Transvaal (also known as the South African Republic) was annexed by Sir Theophilus Shepstone and a small British force in 1877. At the time, two parliamentary seats were held by English-speaking miners. Voting restrictions tightened after war broke out with the British Empire in 1880 (battles that President Paul Kruger's army actually won). But as Dunbar Moodie has pointed out, such restrictions applied to Afrikaans speakers from the Cape as well as to English-speaking *uitlanders* (aliens).[30]

British annexation of the Transvaal brought a different configuration of Afrikaner identity, one that replaced the idea of blood shed (collective suffering) with a more clearly racial notion of blood shared (descent from European stock). Jan Hofmeyr, editor of *De Zuid Afrikaan*, argued as follows:

> The annexation of the Transvaal has taught the people of South Africa that blood is thicker than water. It has filled the [Cape] Africanders, otherwise grovelling in the mud of materialism, with a national glow of sympathy for the brother across the Vaal, which we look upon as one of the most hopeful signs for the future.[31]

Hofmeyr defined a "brother" as "anyone who, having settled in this country, wishes to remain here to help promote our common interests and to live with the inhabitants as members of one family."[32] By invoking the common descent (race) of all settlers and casting them as members of an exclusively male family, Hofmeyr constructed an Afrikaner identity open to English-speaking men (but not, presumably, to Afrikaans-speaking women). In this he was opposed somewhat by S. J. Du Toit, founder in 1875 of the Society of True Afrikaners and the *Afrikaner Patriot* newspaper.

For Du Toit, the true Afrikaner was apparently someone of Dutch or Huguenot descent who spoke neither English nor Dutch but Afrikaans.[33] Yet membership of the Afrikaner Bond (founded by Du Toit in 1879) was not restricted in principle to such people. He described it as an organization in which all Africanders can feel themselves at home, and work together for the good of a united South Africa: in which no question of nationality will divide us, but in which all who recognize Africa as their fatherland will live together and work as brothers of a single house, though they be of English, Dutch, French or German descent, with the exclusion of all those who talk of England as their home or of Holland or Germany as their fatherland.[34]

The language issue was certainly salient for Du Toit, who agitated for official use of Afrikaans. But the above quote suggests how it was possible for the Farmers' Protection Association of Hofmeyr and Du Toit's Afrikaner Bond to amalgamate in 1883. In casting all male settlers as "brothers of a single house," Du Toit, like Hofmeyr, was collapsing racial boundaries between them. Residence in the same metaphorical household made possible both racial commonality and national identity.

The Anglo-Boer War and the South African Constitution

The objective of the amalgamated Afrikaner Bond was "the formation of a South African nationality by the fostering of true patriotism, as preparation for its final destiny: a United South Africa."[35] This was no easy task, especially after the Orange River Colony and the South African Republic joined forces in 1899 against another planned annexation of the latter by Britain.

The so-called Boer War took the lives of more than 26,000 women and children in British concentration camps. That war was a powerful stimulus to a national identity constituted (like the earlier nationalism in Natal) through collective suffering and British oppression. But at the time they became allies, the two republics were not "brotherlands." They were neighboring countries, united in opposition to a common enemy and not through a pregiven sense of a shared "folk spirit." As Henning Klopper (the first chairman of the Afrikaner Broederbond) expressed it, "We were two separate peoples. Although we were all Afrikaners, we had a different system to them, a different way of life almost."[36]

In 1910, the Union of South Africa was founded, a nation-state within the British Empire whose only national foundation was the constitution itself. British policy during the preceding constitutional debate was for an unqualified franchise for adult males of European descent, and a qualified franchise for educated, monogamous, and property-owning others. The rationale was that "Europeans could presume to be civilized,"[37] and thus entitled to an automatic say in how the "house" was run.

Excluded from eligibility to stand for Parliament (and, via the Land Act of 1913, from possession of most of the land) were three broad and overlapping categories of people. First, there were those whose forebears were brought to South Africa to labor, either as slaves (from the Dutch East Indies) or as indentured workers (from India). Second were "natives," those whose forebears seemed original to Africa and thus enjoyed the colonial "privilege" of access to reserved Crown land. And third were people like the Griqua, whose forebears were an admixture of everyone else's.

The injustice of exclusion has been much emphasized in the literature on South Africa. But a couple of related points are worth making about the official constitution of a European identity for South African citizens. First, it conflated race as lineage (descent) with race as type (skin color), as if those who shared a common descent were naturally of the same shade ("white"), and vice versa. Those who looked alike were presumed to possess common ancestors and to belong to the same race.

Second, the notion that common descent derived from *continent* of origin and not *country* of origin was prevalent but by no means universal at the time. During the Boer War, the British administrator Lord Milner is quoted as saying: "If I am also an imperialist, it is because the destiny of the English race . . . has been to strike fresh roots in distant parts of the world."[38] When General J. B. M. Hertzog accepted a position in Louis Botha's cabinet he pledged to "secure the cooperation of all South Africans, of whatever race, and . . . eliminate racialism from all political and national questions."[39] But "all South Africans" meant Whites only. The racial identity of the fully enfranchised was thus far from settled at Union.

Another unresolved issue was whether "true patriotism" had been fostered among all unqualified citizens. Again invoking the notion that Afrikaners had only one home, Hertzog called members of the opposition Unionist Party "foreign fortune seekers." The party's leader, Sir Thomas Smartt, declared his attachment to the British Empire in 1912, whereupon Hertzog responded that "Sir Thomas is not yet a true Afrikaner. Imperialism, in my view, is only good insofar as it is useful to South Africa."[40]

When Hertzog broke from the ruling South Africa Party (SAP) in 1914 to found the Nationalist Party, he continued to insist that "the European population of the Union . . . must be one People." At the same time, he claimed to prize their different languages, customs, religions, and morals.[41] The crucial distinction for Hertzog was between Afrikaners and "British imperialists," not between Afrikaans speakers and English speakers.

Decolonization and the South African Republic

After the Declaration of the Republic in 1961, a new Afrikaner nation was born—the Afrikaans and English-speaking Afrikaner. Compare the French and English-speaking Canadians.   *—South African politician, 1988*

In the pages of the Afrikaans-language journal *Koers in Die Krisis* (Direction in the Crisis), the evils of British imperialism were invoked again in the 1930s. Afrikaners were exhorted to take control of their economic destiny via a *Volkskapitalisme* (national capitalism),[42] and to fend off the "black threat" by becoming masters of their own domain.[43] Nationalist Party leader D. F. Malan argued that in the long run, a republic might be the only way to end "racial strife." He claimed to be in favor of *hereniging* (reunion), by which he meant "to bring together those who belong together." The advantage of a republic was that it would supposedly force English-speaking South Africans to choose between South Africa and Britain, to determine once and for all whether they possessed a genuine South African "civic sentiment."[44]

The (purified) National Party that came to power in 1948 vowed to break ties to the British Empire and instantiate a republic. But it was not until 1961 that the Republic of South Africa was founded. Coming as it did at the height of decolonization on the African continent, the second republican debate played less on the issue of patriotism and more on the necessity for collective survival.

As European powers began the process of relinquishing their African territories, Prime Minister Hendrik Verwoerd proposed to hold a referendum on the republican question. The preceding debate coincided with the creation of nominal homelands for those classified as African. Verwoerd claimed his government's policy was "not strange to the new direction in Africa,"[45] even though its products were more like colonial reserves than viable nation-states. He also argued that "until the Western nations realize more fully what is happening, we should at least combine and protect ourselves." The referendum was cast as a choice about national identity. *Not* voting for a republic, Verwoerd argued, meant continued disunity, while voting yes meant cooperating in "developing a united nation."[46] To save itself, the Afrikaner nation would have to push back its boundaries.

The yes vote carried with a narrow majority,[47] mainly because the two provinces most heavily settled by Afrikaans speakers—the Orange Free State and the Transvaal—swung the vote. Each race was to be a united nation, and each racial nation was to have its own homeland, except for those classified as Colored and Asian, who either did not warrant a homeland for some reason or were presumed to have one in India. As a Dutch Reformed minister explained it to me in 1988, "Indians have their own country and have no say in the Republic of South Africa—just as little as Australians would be deserving of a homeland if many of them came to live here."

Homelands by Design: Racial Separation and National Units

> There was a ferocious barbarian who resisted the intruding Christian civilization and caused the Afrikaner's blood to flow in streams . . . but God at the same time prevented the swamping of the young Afrikaner People in the sea of barbarism.
> —*D. F. Malan, 1942*[48]

The lesson we have learnt from history during the past 300 years is that these ethnic groups, the whites as well as the Bantu, sought their greatest fulfillment, their greatest happiness and the best mutual relations on the basis of separate and individual development.   —*M. C. de Wet Nel, 1959*[49]

The practice of constituting black South Africans as either "resident aliens" or "illegal immigrants" has over time been justified in various ways. The necessity to prevent "swamping," to respect God's will, to maintain racial harmony, to learn the lessons of history, and to recognize the right of national self-determination have all been offered. In each case nationalism has been Janus-faced, looking simultaneously to contain national treachery and alien subversion. Legitimacy has often been sought in the claim that races do best when kept apart, an argument drawn from racial typology and not one invented in South Africa.

Efforts to maintain national boundaries were particularly evident in the 1940s, when the labor of black men and women was wanted in wartime industry. In 1947, for example, Malan contrasted the option of apartheid to "national suicide." If nationals did not wake up to the dangers of racial mixing evident in urban areas, they risked collective drowning "in the black sea of South Africa's non-European population."[50] The same argument was used to defend apartheid in later decades. Having expressed regret for the necessity of apartheid, a Dutch Reformed minister told me in 1988 that "we whites will be swamped by a Black sea if there are no apartheid laws."

In the case of so-called Indians, Dan O'Meara has argued that Afrikaner traders relied on racist incitement to undermine them as competitors. The publication *Inspan* (exert) wrote in 1947 of the "vanguard of the Asiatic world" in Africa, claiming that it "threatens the existence of the whites and the continued survival of Western civilization."[51] A year later the National Party described South Africans of Indian descent as "a strange and foreign element which is not assimilable . . . they must be treated as an immigrant community." Repatriation was recommended in 1948 as the best response to the "Indian question."[52]

Efforts were made to cast separation as natural, even though the very evidence of intermingling to which nationalists kept pointing suggested otherwise. God's will, pain and suffering, ancestral intuition, and scientific discovery have all been used to undermine the appeal of racial mixing.

The renowned poet and theologian J. D. Du Toit delivered an address in 1944 entitled "The Religious Basis of Our Race Policy." Calling God the ordainer of national separation (the Tower of Babel parable), Du Toit argued that the Boers who left the Cape exemplified God's will. They were said to have ventured into the interior of a "barbarous" continent inhabited by the accursed sons of Ham. In collective suffering was the Boer nation conceived, a new "type" developed from the miraculous intermingling of European blood.[53]

Du Toit's suggestion that the Voortrekkers instinctively understood the necessity for racial separation had already appeared in the 1930s. The historical experiences and collective memory of Afrikaners were emphasized by Gustav Preller, who claimed that science merely confirmed what the Afrikaners' ancestors already knew:

> Science is only now gradually discovering the remarkable physiological differences between the brain of the white man of European descent and that of the Bantu—differences which are innate and constitute the measure of their respective intellectual capacities; but it is a striking fact that the Boers of a hundred years ago were aware of these natural differences.[54]

The notion of "natural differences" was used by Geoff Cronje and other nationalist intellectuals to support the idea of apartheid. Cronje (a professor of sociology) presented a South African literature on intelligence testing as proof that blacks were intellectually inferior to whites. Apartheid therefore amounted to a recognition that races had to develop separately in order for each to fulfill its unique destiny in accordance with its own abilities.[55]

Once in power, the National Party tried to discipline "sinners" and silence critics. In 1957, Prime Minister Verwoerd exhorted the nation to follow the example of its ancestors:

> If with admiration we look back at the way the forefathers by the purity of their lives left us a white nation, then we have to realize that it is our task also by a pure and decorous life to maintain a white nation here. Great is the pain and suffering of any family and any friend when this highest law has been infringed. But greater still is the pain and the damage to a nation when some of its children have sinned against its blood.[56]

Verwoerd's successor, B. J. Vorster, went as far as to claim that apartheid was "essentially the same policy my Voortrekker ancestors had in respect of this matter."[57] In defense of apartheid, Christian norms and values were linked to anticommunism and ancestry,[58] while racial purity was downplayed and emphasis given to cultural difference. The greater safety of "white civilization," in conjunction with the "development of national pride, self-respect and mutual respect vis-à-vis the different races of the country,"[59] became the official rationale for apartheid.

The 1959 Promotion of Black Self-Government Act declared that "the Black peoples of the Union of South Africa do not constitute a homogeneous people, but form separate national units on the basis of language and culture." It was certainly an original move, as McClintock has pointed out, to cast over "the wretched partition of the land the false glamor of independent 'nation' building."[60] Within the parameters of racial thought the move was quite logical, and not without its supporters in either the black population or other governments. But after decades of efforts by the National Party to equate opposition to its policies with communist subversion, separate development was abandoned. As the newspaper *Business Day* put it in 1993, "The Nationalist Government which created them now believes, in Mr. de Klerk's words, that it is advisable and desirable that the nominally independent states be reincorporated as soon as possible."[61]

Remapping South Africa:
Self-Determination and Regional Autonomy

The whites should also get a homeland, but along the coast. For example, in the Cape Province that has a long coastline.
—*South African academic, 1988*

The answers are possibly along a middle path between complete integration and segregation, a federation, although we mocked the old United Party in this regard.
—*Executive of the South African Broadcasting Corporation, 1988*

Alternatives to separate development were under active consideration before the birth of a new South Africa was announced on two separate occasions.[62] The option most favored by Afrikaans-speaking Whites in 1988 was "a federal state in which power is shared between White and non-White groups and areas so that no one group dominates." The least desirable option was a "unitary state with white-only power."[63] State President F. W. de Klerk insisted four years later that "every people having its own sovereign state with its own territory" was no longer "practically achievable" in South Africa. At the same time, he promised to place "the principle of self-determination in its varied manifestations" on the agenda of a multiparty forum for constitutional negotiations.[64]

De Klerk's supposed "idea of building a new nation out of disparate nations" was rejected by the Conservative Party. Claiming to speak in 1991 "on behalf of the majority of the white nation," its leader, Andries Treurnicht, argued that "South Africa's thirteen peoples and racial groups are not one nation and never will be." Treurnicht rejected "domination by any other nation and its allies" and insisted on the "right to govern ourselves and to protect our value system."[65] He also demanded that "our claim to land is recognized."[66]

While the Conservative Party heaped demands once made to British colonial administrators on the National Party government, others set out to

found their own *volkstaat* (national state). There are three imagined volk-
staats in South Africa. One is in the town of Morgenzon in the Eastern
Transvaal. Bought in 1982 by the Oranje Werkers—a group led by Hendrik
Verwoerd's son Hendrik—Morgenzon contains a White population of 400
and a black population of 6,000.[67] Verwoerd's grandson is unlikely to ever
live in the imagined volkstaat of his literal father. At an African National
Congress rally in 1993, Wilhelm Verwoerd described himself as the symbol
of a new generation, not just the grandson of a symbol.[68]

There is also Orania, a small desert town in the northern Cape province.
This was paid for in 1990 by the Afrikaner Volkswag, an organization led by
Hendrik Verwoerd's son-in-law Carel Boshoff. Orania is envisaged as the
embryo of a larger state, one rivaled since 1993 by the plans of the Cape
Republic Party.[69] A year after its purchase, only fourteen families had
trekked to Orania.[70]

The third homeland is currently no more than a computer-generated
map. Endorsed by the newly formed Afrikaner Volksfront (AVF) in July
1993, the plans were described as "historically viable" by the AVF's chairman, General Constand Viljoen.[71] Reminiscent of apartheid design (and to
some, of a swastika), the starlike homeland created by architect Koos
Reyneke comprises "the old Boer Republics, less all the areas where other
ethnic groups are in the majority. Less the gold mines."[72]

The AVF formed to demand recognition of "the right to self-determination." The binding factor, according to Viljoen, was "the threat to the
Afrikaner people from a unitary state."[73] From the beginning, a political
problem has been how to convince opponents that "resident aliens" would
not be forcibly removed from a volkstaat. But the conceptual boundaries of
the "volk" itself were contested within the AVF. As *The Weekly Mail* pointed out, Viljoen "includes coloreds among Afrikaners. The general's relative
moderation has alarmed the hard right, who called a meeting to consider
whether the generals are actually state agents sent to neutralize the right."[74]

The threat of unitary statehood was not strong enough to hold together
what *The Sunday Times* described as an "uncomfortable coalition of conservatives, volkstaaters, generals, and neo-fascists."[75] Viljoen resigned in
March 1994 following an AVF rift over whether to participate in the upcoming elections, and took up leadership of a newly registered Freedom Front.
The Afrikaner Weerstandsbeweging (AWB) responded with insults of biblical and anticommunist inspiration. According to the AWB, Viljoen was "a
political Judas goat sent by the Broederbond/ANC/NP/Communist Party
alliance to lead us to the slaughter."[76] By then the Volksfront was part of a
larger coalition called the Freedom Alliance, one that included the leaders of
two black homelands slated for reincorporation.

BophuthaTswana's President Lucas Mangope could have been speaking
for all black South Africans in January 1994 when he stated that he would

not "willingly revert back to a system where we will be oppressed by a far away government," the only change being "the skin color of the people at the top."[77] Mangope's demise proved to be a telling indictment of the mythology of "separate national units" in homelands such as "Bop." It also illustrated how the larger system of apartheid was tumbled, as well as the absence of meaningful sovereignty in any of the nominal homelands.

Mangope had openly defied one of the mandates of the Transitional Executive Council (TEC), established in December 1993 to prevent the National Party from using its institutional power to unfair advantage in the upcoming elections. The TEC was to ensure free political activity and campaigning in all areas of South Africa. The problem was that its jurisdiction extended only to its own participants—and Mangope refused to join the TEC.

"Bop" residents took matters into their own hands in March 1994. According to *The Sunday Times,* "The millions of ordinary black folk who destroyed apartheid" brought down Mangope's regime through strikes, riots, and preparations for a march on Pretoria to demand reincorporation.[78] After threatening to force the issue if the crisis were not resolved, TEC representatives (accompanied by South Africa's minister of foreign affairs and an army general) "personally informed President Mangope . . . that his presidency was no longer recognized by the South African government and the TEC, and that in the circumstances he could not continue as head of the Government of BophuthaTswana."[79]

The third leg of the Freedom Alliance was Gatsha Buthelezi's Inkatha Freedom Party (IFP). It is noteworthy that none of the plans for a volkstaat have included the former Republic of Natal, a reminder of how motivated by the political present is remembrance of historic homelands. Buthelezi insisted in 1992 on the right of Zulus to "exercise their sovereignty" through a referendum on the "Constitution of the State of KwaZulu/Natal."[80]

As the chief minister of a homeland designed by the National Party, Buthelezi was always a paradoxical figure. He claimed to speak for all of the descendants of Shaka and Dingaan in southern Africa, while his political power base was largely among the "KwaZulus" of the so-called Bantustan. The resolution of that paradox since the destruction of apartheid has involved demands for the exercise of sovereignty in the whole of Natal. Buthelezi has counted on some strange bedfellows—political allies whose ancestors fought his own at the Battle of Blood River. But he also drew Zulu King Goodwill Zwelithini into the Freedom Alliance in the run-up to the elections.

Zwelithini told supporters in July 1993 that agreement must be reached on "a new constitutional dispensation which pleases KwaZulu." KwaZulu/ Natal seemed at the time to mean the "whole of Natal," according to *The Star* newspaper.[81] Seven months later, the Freedom Alliance reiterated

demands for a volkstaat council, for two ballot papers in the elections, for
exclusive regional powers (such as taxation rights) that cannot be changed
by a central government, and for a name change from Natal to KwaZulu/
Natal. In a meeting with F. W. de Klerk, Zwelithini simultaneously demanded the restoration of a Zulu kingdom that supposedly existed before British
colonialism.[82]

Against all the odds, the IFP campaigned for the first "all race" elections. Buthelezi subsequently became minister for home affairs, and many
of the Freedom Alliance's demands are either under negotiation or already
met. Candidates were presented to voters on two separate ballots, one
national and one for each region. KwaZulu/Natal (KZN) became one of
South Africa's nine new provinces, its capital to be either Ulundi or
Maritzburg. A "commission on the demarcation/delimitation of regions" has
been charged with the task—in the words of *The Natal Mercury*—of dividing the country "into natural centers of regional authority, which should
have maximum autonomy over their own affairs."[83] The first official meeting of the Volkstaat Council was held in June 1994, a reward (according to
President Mandela a year later) to those who had restrained their followers
from violent opposition to majority rule.[84]

The one preelection demand unlikely to be met is for a Zulu kingdom.
A televised fistfight between Buthelezi and Zwelithini in September 1994
seemed to signal the end of joint demands for a "historically viable"
Zululand.[85]

New Rights and Repatriation

The geographic boundary separating the Republic of South Africa from
Mozambique has never been impenetrable. On a visit to the border in 1988
I found it demarcated by an electrified fence. On the South African side a
warning sign in four languages (the words were *gevaar, danger, nghosi,* and
perigo) was topped by a skull and crossbones. Small encampments of soldiers in the uniform of the South African Defence Force (SADF) guarded the
fence.

The soldiers acknowledged no other purpose than the apprehension of
the dozens of Mozambicans cutting through the fence on a daily basis. "So
much for the Marxist paradise on the other side," was one wry comment. But
it is debatable how much Marxism was to blame for the situation. The same
soldier identified the nearest hospital as the initial destination for most of the
Mozambicans, who may or may not have been headed for mining areas
where thousands of their fellow countrymen have historically labored. Some
appeared to have stepped on land mines planted by the Frelimo government
to discourage flight. Others had been maimed and injured by Renamo, a

rebel movement supported by the South African government after the decolonization of Portuguese colonies in 1975. The border in the late 1980s was the effect of years of destabilization of the southern African region by a range of political forces.

Transmigration from Mozambique—whether of mineworkers or refugees—is thus not a recent phenomenon. But with the dismantling of so-called influx control laws, regulations on movement have been redirected. For those whose rights to literal homes and land were once heavily circumscribed, the interim government has an ambitious housing policy (one central to the Reconstruction and Development Plan)[86] and a commitment to land repossession (the Restitution of Land Rights Bill).[87] For those illegally crossing the borders with neighboring states, the same government has a policy of repatriation.

An agreement signed in September 1993 enables the voluntary repatriation of Mozambican refugees under the auspices of the United Nations High Commissioner.[88] This was followed within a month by a bilateral, diplomatic agreement on repatriation.[89] President Mandela's first state visit in 1994 was to Mozambique, an initiative linked by *The Star* to that country's "historic suffering at the hand of South Africa and its peculiarly problematic ties with some of South Africa's biggest crime headaches."[90] The Joint Defence and Security Committee, designed to combat such "headaches" as cattle rustling, drug and gun smuggling, and organized car theft, emerged from negotiations between South Africa and Mozambique in 1993.[91]

In October 1993, South African police were reported as saying, "There are more than a million illegal immigrants on the Reef, and they are losing the battle to stem the flow." Although *The Star* implied that "most of the aliens" were fleeing war and drought in Mozambique and Zimbabwe,[92] so many people in traditional areas of mining activity could have reflected economic reconstruction and the closure of marginal mines.[93] Indeed, the immigration policy announced by Home Affairs Minister Mangosuthu Buthelezi in August 1994 explicitly prohibits entry to unskilled and semiskilled workers. It seems destined to favor those applying in increasing numbers from Asia and Eastern Europe[94] at the expense of the 81,000 Mozambicans deported from South Africa in 1993.[95]

Warning signs of danger have been hung over the activities of right-wing citizens as well as Mozambicans. The newspaper *Business Day* urged General Viljoen before the elections to "accept that the neo-Nazi ultra right—a tiny, if dangerous, minority—cannot be accommodated."[96] The interim government has seemed willing since then to accommodate demands for a volkstaat. But President Mandela has also said that "it would be unrealistic for Government not to expect danger from the right wing" and has hinted at greater efforts to disarm opponents.[97] Unfashionable attitudes and practices have always attracted nationalist attention, and in this regard the "new" South Africa is no exception.

CUSTOMS, CIVILIZATION, AND CHARACTER

Culture and Civilization

Bloody battles arose continually among them . . . accompanied by all the atrocities by which barbarous peoples so sorrowfully distinguish themselves from those who are civilized. . . . . Such was the general state of the natives who occupied this country at the establishment of our settlement.
—*Advocate J. de Wet, 1838*[98]

English and Afrikaans speakers have cultural and value systems which are in agreement. We are one nation.
—*South African businessman, 1988*

Adam and Giliomee have described early settlers as "cultural chauvinists who looked down upon the 'heathen,' 'primitive,' or 'barbarous' indigenous people of the colonies in which they settled."[99] Those in Cape Town seemed to think they were "more enlightened" than the "yokels and rustics" who established new republics.[100] But immoral impulses and shameful traits were more often projected onto "natives."

Whether or not the civilized/uncivilized dichotomy was understood as a *racial* distinction is open to some dispute. Adam and Giliomee have called it "debatable" that consciousness of race existed in the Cape Colony.[101] J. A. Loubser has stated that "early Europeans did not entertain race-consciousness."[102] And in their analysis of Afrikaner political thought to 1850, Du Toit and Giliomee have claimed to find no real evidence of racial thinking. Settlers apparently blamed the African environment and social conditions for the "backward state of civilization" of the indigenous peoples.[103]

It is important to remember that race still meant common descent in the seventeenth century. Even if most writers blamed Africa and not biology for cultural inferiority, J. M. Coetzee has argued that Hottentots were not thought to be "in the line of descent that leads from Adam via a life of toil to civilized man."[104] The indigenous people were assumed to descend from Ham, and according to the 1706 "farmers' lament" quoted by Adam and Giliomee, "there is no trusting the blood of Ham, especially as the black people are constantly being favored and pushed forward."[105]

Notions of permanent difference spread with increasing colonization.

Coetzee has shown that the "Hottentot character" was contructed as primarily idle. Those who were neither Khoikhoi nor San were called Caffers or Negroes, but since they also "wandered," they were scripted as essentially the same. In a letter to the editor of *De Zuid Afrikaan* in 1838, for example, farmer A. J. Louw spoke of "innate rapacity, savage disposition, indolence and natural propensity toward a wandering life, peculiar inclination to strong liquor, jealous covetousness to the property of their fellow creatures, faithless refractory character, and unfitness for military duty." What was wanted, apparently, was "proper laws to check the ungovernable passions inherent to uncivilized beings."[106]

There *was,* then, a consciousness of racial differences (and inferiority) in the seventeenth century. The argument was not that "Ham's children" had smaller brains and thus lesser intellectual capacities. That "scientific" claim came later, in the 1930s, from nationalists like Gustav Preller. What was assumed instead was that the culture of black people (their behavior, character, modes of living, and so on) was inherited from their cursed ancestors. Christian missionaries complicated this view by assuming that any living creature with a soul could be taught to reason and thus advance along the path of historical progress. But the presumption that race determines culture did not disappear. It remained available for mobilization later, in the service of apartheid and of an exclusive brand of Afrikaner nationalism.

Folk Spirit and Volk Language

The English speakers do not make the same effort to speak Afrikaans as the Afrikaans speakers do.
—*Executive of the South African Broadcasting Corporation, 1988*

As previous discussion demonstrated, the question of whether English-speaking South Africans were Afrikaners or "British imperialists" complicated efforts at unity. Boundaries were strengthened by Afrikaans-language tales of suffering and death during the Great Trek and the Anglo-Boer War, stories that seemed to provide their readers with a unique language, literature, and history. McClintock has described the "language movement" of the early twentieth century as the work of "a class of cultural brokers and image makers" dedicated to the "new, invented community of the *volk.*"[107]

The Vrouemonument was unveiled in 1913 in commemoration of those who died in British concentration camps. This memorialized permanently an identity based in collective suffering. A frieze of the monument shows several women clustered around the body of a single dying child. They are the symbolic mothers of the infant nation, grieving for its death at the hands of British imperialism.

In August 1914, World War I broke out, and the Union Parliament voted to support Britain. That decision sparked an armed rebellion in the Transvaal in 1915, while Afrikaans speakers in the Cape eagerly volunteered to join the British forces.[108] Such political divisions so soon after Union were troubling to those striving for the national unity of South African citizens. At an official ceremony in December 1916, for example, Prime Minister Botha pleaded for the unity of the Afrikaner people, a category in which he specifically included English-speaking South Africans. Church ministers who spoke at the same ceremony echoed Botha's message.[109]

There were still competing scriptures, from those who emphasized the unique culture of speakers of Afrikaans. Among them were ministers of the Nederduits Gereformeerde Kerk (NGK), the largest of the three Dutch Reformed churches in South Africa. The church's self-professed role, according to Moodie, was to "teach the people to see the hand of God in their history" via Afrikaans-language education. In a 1920 address, theologian William Nicol described mother-tongue education as "not in the first place an educational question, but a deep conviction that our children can only be preserved for our People through Afrikaans schools."[110] For the NGK, history was the key to identity, language was the medium, and schools were the vehicle.

There was also the Afrikaner Broederbond (AB), a "brotherhood" founded in 1918 with three political aims: to work for Afrikaner unity; to arouse Afrikaners to national consciousness and love of their way of life, country, and nation; and to further the interests of the Afrikaner nation. Membership of the AB was restricted to "Afrikaans-speaking Protestants who accept South Africa as their fatherland, are of sound moral character and stand firm in the defence of their Afrikaner identity."[111]

"Sisters" were part of the Broederbond's nation as well. According to McClintock, women "were crucial in the construction of a distinctive Afrikaner culture" because it was they who shaped domestic life. The Vrouemonument apparently portrays "the Afrikaner *nation* symbolically as a weeping woman," and after its erection "the cultural power of Afrikaner motherhood was mobilized in the service of white nation building."[112]

McClintock has attributed the exaltation of motherhood to class-based interests, because working-class women drawn into factories in increasing numbers threatened the authority of their own fathers, husbands, and sons. The threat was also understood as racial. Many of the rural women who migrated to urban areas went to work in garment factories. According to Elsabe Brink, garment workers "mostly congregated in the poorest sections of the town or city"—which were not racially segregated. They lived in places like Vrededorp, described by bank inspector M. McLeash in 1921 as "one of the worst slums in existence, harboring as it does in its sea of iron shanties the flotsam and jetsam of low class Colored peoples, Chinese,

Indians and Natives—many of purely criminal class."[113] Although the urban poor received little or no welfare or charity assistance, the NGK insisted that its parishioners should not be "living with and like Kaffirs."[114]

Legislative steps were taken to prevent racial mixing. The Urban Areas Act of 1923 mandated separate living areas for Natives. The "civilized labor policy" introduced in 1924 reserved certain public sector jobs for Whites and Coloreds; it also gave incentives to industry to employ "civilized labor." The 1927 Immorality Act made sexual intercourse across the "color line" illegal. Yet in 1930, a housing inspector complained that poor Whites were still living "cheek by jowl" with Indians, Chinese, Coloreds, and Natives.[115]

National Calling and Racial Purity

The status of different races is a provision of God. National groups like Germans, English etc. came into being because of the wishes of people, because they feel more at home amongst their own with the same language, culture, and value systems.
—*South African businessman, 1988*

After the fall of man, a division of peoples has been authorized and confirmed by God without contradicting the fact that our oneness in Christ is regardless of national groups and peoples. Otherwise, groups' separation would be a sin.
—*Dutch Reformed minister, 1988*

It was not until the turbulent interwar years that the AB (which became a secret organization in 1922) expanded beyond a small group of theology professors at Potchefstroom University. The AB was able to capitalize on the hardships induced by a global economic depression, but its influence was spread through a network of youth and cultural associations. The most prominent were the Federation of Afrikaner Cultural Organizations (known by its Afrikaans acronym, FAK), the Calvinist Bond, the Voortrekkers (an Afrikaner equivalent of the Boy Scout movement), and the Afrikaner National Student Association (the ANS, in Afrikaans). In 1934, the AB organized a Poor White Congress to address the plight of 300,000 White people living in poverty. And in 1935, the Potchefstroom journal *Koers* (mentioned earlier) was founded.

Analyses of Afrikaner nationalism differ on the question of who exactly the AB appealed to, and why. The question generates debate because the AB deployed a diverse array of themes—anti-imperialism, race science, scripture, history, and German national socialism—that taken together constituted a less than unified, coherent doctrine. The very success of AB-promoted Christian-nationalism (a term adapted from "Christian National" education policy in Holland) may be due to the fact that it was all things to all people rather than, as Charles Bloomberg has suggested, a principled alternative to liberal ideology.[116]

Exclusive interpretations of Afrikaner history, culture, and race were propagated primarily by Dutch Reformed ministers and academics. As the 1930s wore on, the meaning of *culture* shifted from an earlier equation with creative expression (Afrikaans poetry, and so on) toward a quasi-religious conception of way of life:

> Culture is the name given to the common spiritual possessions of a People. It is their birthright, left to them by their ancestors, their history and their tradition; a birthright, however, which is carefully preserved against foreign interference and just as carefully supplemented only to the extent that ethnic consciousness increases.[117]

The notion of culture as something inherited from ancestors gave it a racial dimension, without the word *race* ever being used. As Saul Dubow has stated, "The essentialist view of culture which lay at the heart of Christian-nationalism was no less powerful a means of dividing people than an approach based on racial determinism."[118]

Cultural essentialism was apparent among "neo-Fichteans," those exposed to the philosophy of Johann Gottlieb Fichte while studying in Europe.[119] One of the more prominent was Nic Diederichs, an academic and then minister of finance in B. J. Vorster's cabinet. For Diederichs, a nation was constituted through common culture, by which he meant the possession of shared values and principles as well as the struggle to defend them. The diversity of nations was attributed to God (the Tower of Babel story again), as was the possession by each nation of a unique way of life.[120] After criticism from H. G. Stoker and others for failing to pay sufficient attention to race, Diederichs began to insist more on the importance of race in defining the nation.[121]

The intersection of race, nation, and culture had been prevalent before the 1930s in nationalist scriptures that included English speakers. But instead of race being correlated with skin color and European descent, shared race was now premised on descent from Boer stock. In this formulation, even Cape Afrikaners were not true members of the *volk*. In the pages of *Koers,* eugenicists such as G. Eloff described the Boer nation as a distinct "type," the purity of which had to be protected like a "sacred pledge" against "poisonous infiltration." Ironically perhaps, the idea of a "Boer type" was derived from English-language publications in South Africa.[122]

It is also noteworthy that Eloff celebrated racial purity while attributing Boer identity to a process of racial mixing. He argued that Boers had benefited from a unique combination of Nordic (Dutch and German) and Alpine

(French Huguenot) racial traits.[123] Such observations were consistent with the racial theories of Arthur de Gobineau and Karl Vogt, discussed in the previous chapter.

According to Dubow, the person who did most to circulate Eloff's theories was Geoff Cronje. From 1945 onward, recurring themes in Cronje's books were: the need to protect the purity of the Boer nation's blood; God's injunction to respect the diversity of nations; and the Afrikaner's duty to act as a guardian over the nonwhite races.[124]

Before considering the relationship of race and culture to apartheid, it is important to reiterate that the construction of Boers as a racial type with a God-given destiny excluded English-speaking citizens. After refusing amalgamation with Jan Smuts's South African Party (SAP), D. F. Malan and his followers became known as the *Gesuiwerde* (purified) National Party (GNP). English-speaking citizens were the racial "pollution" against which the GNP had to guard.

Boer nationalists sometimes treated Boer and Briton as racially the same but nationally different. In 1931, J. A. Coetzee counterposed the British mind to the Afrikaner soul, arguing that while they belonged to different nations they were members of the same Caucasian race.[125] This argument was echoed by the theologian S. du Toit in 1949, when he said that Afrikaners were from the same racial stock as their English-speaking counterparts even though the latter were not members of the Afrikaner volk. As Dubow has pointed out, these distinctions were less than clear because language and culture—two of the key factors that supposedly constituted the identity of a volk—were often considered expressions of race as well.[126] The racial identities unsettled at Union were still not settled in the 1930s.

Race, Culture, and Apartheid

[It is] not color but culture; not race, but the level of development which forms the basis of discrimination between population groups.   —*G. B. A. Gerdener, 1952*[127]

We don't hate them because they're black. We hate them because they're thieves and murderers.
                    —*South African businessman, 1988*

In Christian-nationalism, racial difference was not reducible to skin color. In the words of A. B. Du Preez in 1959, "Racial differences are always accompanied by differences in culture, civilization, the general mode of living, and religion."[128]

The *Journal of Racial Affairs* defended apartheid in 1971 in the following terms:

> Color is for us important because it is indicative of national and cultural binding. . . . If we say that it turns on cultural and not on color or racial difference, should we not then be prepared to integrate with Westernized non-Whites? . . . But it is not just a matter of the individual. Every individual is a member of a nation and therefore every individual is like the spout of a funnel—the individual we accept is an opening through which a whole nation and a whole culture can flow. . . . Integration with the Coloreds therefore means, ultimately, integration with all others.[129]

The above argument treats color as an indicator of national character, itself synonymous with cultural difference. According to Dubow, this conflation of terms allowed apartheid apologists "to speak about the 'national character' or 'soul' as if these qualities were being transmitted from generation to generation, without the difficulties associated with biological theories of racial inheritance."[130] De Villiers has argued that many Afrikaners speak of language and traditions as "in the blood";[131] culture is treated as a fixed, racial phenomenon and not as a chosen trait amenable to change.

There has always been a contending view of culture in South Africa, one inherent in the colonial idea that blacks might one day learn to be "civilized" like Europeans. Especially after the Soweto riots of 1976, the promotion of an identity based in acquirable middle-class values and interests became more apparent. The former editor of *Die Burger* newspaper remarked in 1977 that the greatest need of Afrikaners "now seems to be to define the common aims of all peoples sharing their land with them. The most obvious of these must surely be defense of a common civilization." In a similar vein, *Die Vaderland* stated a year later that the Afrikaner nation must confront the question of "whether it will continue to exclude, on grounds of color, people who fully accept its language, culture and traditions."[132]

Just how exclusive might be a nation constituted through the above membership requirements is illustrated by the following comment, made to me in 1988 by an executive of the South African Broadcasting Corporation (SABC): "I reject a division which is based exclusively on race and color. An Afrikaans-speaking Colored who is a professional and has an income of, say, 50,000 Rand per annum and who attends an Afrikaans church and who is part of Afrikaner culture must not be excluded merely because he is brown."

A national identity based on professional status, wealth, language, religion, and culture excludes almost all black South Africans from membership, despite the appeal to nondiscriminatory criteria. It is a constitution of identity quite different from the rainbow nationalism of Nelson Mandela, one that makes "attachment to the soil" the only civic sentiment that counts. There is no language movement in contemporary South Africa comparable to the one active in the 1920s, so if a shared culture is to be founded, it will not be through the medium of one official language. The political question is whether a national culture not based in soil, class, or race is being constituted and, if so, how fully inclusive it might be.

Expressions of Common Values: South Africa Multilingua

In South Africa the task of nation-building is formidable because we lack the natural cohesion of a single culture and language. . . . Consequently, we shall have to rely on the other cornerstone—that of common values and ideals.
—*F. W. de Klerk, February 1, 1991*[133]

Lord bless Africa. . . . Listen to our prayers. . . . Come spirit Come Holy Spirit. . . . God bless Our Nation.
—*From "Nkosi Sikelel' iAfrika" (English version)*[134]

Political arithmetic in South Africa has never added up to a unitary nation-state, nationalist mythology notwithstanding. The "thirteen peoples" mentioned by Andries Treurnicht are the "white nation" he claimed to represent; the residents of ten homelands created for Blacks; the "homeless" Coloreds; and the people of Indian descent. If language is the expression of a national "folk spirit," there should have been two homelands for Whites instead of one state with two official languages (English and Afrikaans). Afrikaans-speaking Coloreds would then have been part of the Afrikaner state.

There should also have been four homelands for Blacks, because the 1956 report of the government-appointed Tomlinson Commission divided the African population linguistically into Nguni, Sotho, Venda, and Shangaan-Tsonga.[135] Reflecting the arbitrary nature of colonial boundaries in general, the Sotho group already had its own state in southern Africa, called Lesotho. There was a homeland called Venda, but not one named Nguniland. Besides the four linguistic designations, the Tswana people already had Botswana; they also got BophuthaTswana. The Xhosa were given two separate homelands within the Republic of South Africa—Ciskei and Transkei—and the Zulus one (KwaZulu).

The Natal Mercury expressed the hope that "natural centers of regional authority" will replace the above mélange, as already mentioned. But added to the two official languages of English and Afrikaans in November 1993 were not four but nine African languages: Ndebele, North Sotho, South Sotho, Tsonga, Tswana, Venda, Xhosa, Nguni, and Zulu.

Almost immediately, the endorsement of eleven official languages by the multiparty Negotiating Council generated controversy. To some, eleven was not enough. The Pan Africanist Congress (PAC) proposed to add Tamil, Hindi, and Gujarati, while the Africa Muslim Agency (later Party) of South

Africa wanted Arabic.[136] The council then agreed to the establishment of a language board to promote six more "community languages" in addition to the eleven official ones.[137]

The Pan–South African Language Board, appointed by the new senate, will be responsible for working out the social implications of so many official languages, for example, in public schools. The composition of the board itself is of concern to educators and civil servants, who are divided over whether English and Afrikaans should retain their traditional dominance. In July 1994, a plan by the SABC to relegate Afrikaans on television to the same status as the "family of indigenous languages"[138] was immediately opposed by the Afrikaner cultural organization known as FAK.[139]

The Sowetan put a Gramscian spin on "the internal feuding and seeming chaos at the SABC." It argued that "while the new order has been born, the old not only refuses to die, but has been given a new lease of life. The tension at the SABC arises from this clash of 'cultures.'" One way to create a national culture not based in soil, race, or class is thus to root it in acceptance of change, in new ideas and practices rather than old habits. Reminiscent of a modern/traditional dichotomy, reconfigured boundaries would separate supporters of a new order just born from those "who happily served as their 'master's voice' over decades of apartheid rule."[140]

A different yet complementary way to reconfigure national culture is to found it in "common values and ideals." In a speech to Parliament in 1991, President de Klerk argued that "if we build the new South African nation on the foundation of these values and ideals, a good future awaits us and our children." The values and ideals supposedly shared by "all peace-loving South Africans" were the "four Ps"—peace, prosperity, progress, and participation. They "do not belong exclusively to any single political party" but "are universal," according to de Klerk. If all South Africans accept such values, "a comprehensive South African nation which will include all our people with allegiance and loyalty to our common fatherland" will "be able to unite the rich diversity of our population."[141]

De Klerk's emphasis changed as the election neared, from values supposedly universal to those once placed in the service of anticommunism on the African continent. At a meeting with the Venda rain queen Modjadji, de Klerk apparently "added a new theme of 'Christian values'" to "the NP's [National Party's] support for the maintenance of traditional values." The newspaper *Business Day* went on to report that "his party was in favor of the retention of existing laws on homosexuality which outlawed sodomy. However, he indicated that within the principles of Christian values, it was possible to 'improve' the law governing abortion."[142]

Steve Biko once described Christianity as "the central point of a culture which brought with it new styles of clothing, new customs, new forms of etiquette, new medical approaches, and perhaps new armaments." South

Africa's second official national anthem ("Nkosi Sikelel' iAfrika" has been added to "Die Stem," the "voice" of White South Africa) is a Christian hymn, so there is no question that millions of Africans throughout the continent identify with Christianity. A national culture that includes all South Africans of Christian persuasion is more inclusive than the culture of apartheid. But as Biko went on to say, the spread of Christianity effects a new social division, between "the converted" and "the pagans."[143] De Klerk's Christian-nationalism is no more universal than that of the old Afrikaner Broederbond, recently renamed (in an echo of the past) the Afrikanerbond to reflect its opening to female and black speakers of Afrikaans.[144] Muslims, Jews, and other South Africans not converted to Christianity remain outside the nation. Also excluded is a range of people not opposed, like de Klerk, to homosexuality and abortion.

Commissioning Representation: Affirmative Action and National Symbols

If we want to keep those symbols of Afrikaner history, like the Voortrekker Monument, we'll have to fund it ourselves.
—Jan Pieter de Lange, 1992[145]

The watchword of affirmative action policy in South Africa is not reclassification but balance, as well as the Weberian concept of rationalization. The 1993 constitution guaranteed the jobs of all existing civil servants, even as the racial profile of the public service was a focus of negotiation. Names have been changed: the South African National Defence Force has replaced the old SADF, and the South African Police has been renamed the South African Police Service (SAPS). Quotas have been set: Under its new chief executive, Zwelakhe Sisulu, for example, the SABC aims for a half-black staff by the end of 1997.[146] And guidelines for monitoring "racial representivity" have been established: the public service and administration minister, Zola Skweyiya, announced the promulgation of the Public Service Act in June 1994.[147]

Whether members of racial groups will be able to affirm a different identity than the one created for them by apartheid is yet to be determined.[148] The above measures are intended to give visibility in the higher echelons of the civil service to all races created in the past. The public service is therefore a symbol of national identity as well as a workplace; its reconfiguration complements the activities of those charged with the redesign of national anthems, emblems, and flags.

After three decades, South Africa returned to the Olympic Games in 1992—without the orange, white, and blue national flag, without the national anthem "Die Stem," and without the national sporting symbol, the springbok. The decision of the National Olympic Committee of South Africa (NOCSA) to jettison the old symbols in favor of an interim flag and Beethoven's "Ode to Joy" stirred controversy. Defending the committee's decision, its chairman, Sam Ramsamy, argued that "we had to go for something that will represent national unity."[149] He also proposed a nationwide contest to pick a replacement for the springbok, a proposal that sparked immediate suggestions for a zebra, a hippopotamus, and an ostrich.[150] The logo for the 1996 Games in Atlanta is derived from an ancient rock painting, not from an animal, and the springbok has been replaced by a white protea (the national flower of South Africa).

The new flag suggested in 1993 by the multiparty Commission on National Symbols was greeted with derision. "With its nouveau-ethnic design," The Daily News argued, the flag "will look like a placemat on a pole."[151] Boerstaat Party leader Robert Van Tonder proposed a spotted black-and-white flag "with a Coca-Cola bottle in the middle to symbolize South Africa's new status as an American vassal state."[152] Professional designers were then engaged to work with a TEC Subcommittee on National Symbols.

Just in time for the elections, the TEC approved the second anthem and a different flag. The Y-shaped design was soon likened to a camel: "The unfortunate camel, so the saying goes, was designed by a committee hence it is functional but ugly." The Eastern Province Herald also called it "regrettable, but axiomatic, that the new South African flag could never reflect the tempest of passions that attend the birth of our new nation." If it contained no historic symbols and thus stood for nothing, it didn't matter whether the flag was ugly or pretty.[153] As Die Burgher put it, the flag "has no symbolism, as far as we can see, and it has no historic associations with the past. Some people think it's a hodge-podge of colors and more fitting for a banana republic."[154]

Both newspapers expressed the hope that the "symbol without symbol" would not become an additional source of political conflict. But the inseparability of symbolism from national time was also suggested by Die Burgher.

NATIONAL HISTORIES AND NATIONAL DEVELOPMENT

Suffering, Redemption, and the Time of Apartheid

We will survive just as our pioneer forefathers did. "We will live, we will die for our country" [words from "Die Stem"]. Our morale is high and even if we must suffer, in the end we will get by.   —South African academic, 1988

I'm not a satirist in this at all, I'm on a honeymoon with the
Government. We need to create heroes.
—Satirist and playwright Pieter-Dirk Uys, 1994[155]

In 1938, the Great Trek was reenacted. According to McClintock, the
German-educated members of the AB had learned from the Nazis how to
construct "the illusion of a collective identity through the political staging
of vicarious *spectacle*."[156] The reenactment culminated with the laying of
the foundation stone of the Voortrekker Monument.

One of the most contested of South African "holy days" has been
December 16. Once known as Dingaan's Day, the name of the public holiday was changed to the Day of the Covenant in 1952 and the Day of the Vow
in 1980. This is the anniversary of events that supposedly took place before
the 1838 Battle of Blood River. In the words of Leonard Thompson, the vow
"refers to a pledge made several days before the battle by Afrikaner members of the commando that if God granted them a victory in the coming
struggle they would . . . always celebrate the anniversary of the victory, to
the honor of God."[157] The first political use of the vow was made in 1881,
to commemorate the victory of the Transvaal army over British forces.[158]

Like the frieze of Zulu warriors spearing women and children inside the
circled walls of the Voortrekker Monument, the Day of the Vow celebrates a
God-fearing nation united in suffering against hostile forces. "For how much
longer will official South Africa commemorate the Day of the Vow?" asked
The Eastern Province Herald in 1993. If that day must be celebrated, then
the *Herald* argued that "December 16 should be a day of reconciliation and
understanding, a day of rejoicing in common bonds—not one for accentuat-
ing divisions."[159]

Other anniversaries of historic division are March 21 (Sharpeville Day,
in memory of political protesters shot by police in 1960) and June 16 (which
commemorates the onset of the Soweto uprising of 1976). March 21 has
been renamed Human Rights Day and declared a public holiday. Before
Soweto Day can become official, *The Sowetan* has argued that "any incum-
bent regime must be convinced that 16 June 1976 was a turning point in the
history of South Africa."[160]

The larger question raised by specific days is how a nation newly created should approach a divisive past. The issue has come up in discussions of
political amnesty (a word not unlike amnesia) where a willingness to forget
and bury the past has been counterposed to disclosure for the sake of heal-
ing and catharsis. A parliamentary debate followed Justice Richard
Goldstone's call for a Truth Commission on apartheid atrocities in May
1994. The water affairs and forestry minister, Kader Asmal, said that "the
past controls the present and will shape the future. Amnesty provisions are
therefore based on the fundamental assumption that while we can (legally)

forgive past transgressions, we cannot ever forget them." Democratic Party leader Tony Leon called for legislation "which does not sweep under the carpet the crimes, sins and omissions of the past."[161]

Collective pasts can be forgotten or remembered. *How* they are remembered is driven by the politics of the present, not by searches for an objective truth. This is illustrated by four different recalls of the famed Great Trek. In the teachings of the short-lived OsseweBrandwag (OB), a neo-Nazi organization founded in 1939, the Great Trek was reinterpreted as an act of rebellion instead of suffering.[162] Writing in the mid-1970s, W. A. de Klerk called the Trek a "true response to the challenge of the environment," one taken by people willing to adjust their attitudes, faith, and behavior to altered circumstances.[163] In 1988, two different groups set out to reenact the Trek, during which the Boerstaat Party was launched to demand a volkstaat. Finally, in 1993, F. W. de Klerk compared the country's departure from race-based representation in Parliament to a new Great Trek into the future. On Christmas Eve of that year, *Business Day* called it a "fair analogy" given the "miracle" of change occurring in South Africa.[164]

Instead of remembering distant events, others have sought the origins of a "new" South Africa in the 1955 Freedom Charter. Drafted by a group called the Congress of the People, this document, according to Keyan Tomaselli and Mewa Ramgobin, reflected the wishes of a cross-section of South Africans for national unity and cultural liberation. Despite its absence from museums or "other official cultural spaces," the charter and the mass struggles it represented were "remembered, revived, transformed, and systematized in the 1980s." It was this "popular memory" that supposedly "created the impetus for a national consciousness."[165]

A "rainbow nation" could be constituted through the collective suffering of those who struggled to bring down apartheid. Slated for closure as a penal institution in 1996, Robben Island (the site of a planned new peace institute to be paid for with Scandinavian funds)[166] could become an alternative national monument. And the cell that once housed its most famous political prisoner could be turned into a national shrine.

The transformation of Nelson Mandela from a political leader into a symbol of redemption began during his long incarceration. Rob Nixon has quoted an anonymous Afrikaner as saying in 1990 that "we need a Messiah to lead us out of the wilderness. Maybe Nelson Mandela is that man." This is a sentiment fostered for Nixon by the hold of "metaphors of dawn, birth, revolutionary redemption, or apocalypse and historical closure" on "the nation's black and white cultures."[167] It is one nurtured as well by a continental African vision, one that sees Mandela, according to *The Sowetan,* "as the embodiment of the fight for freedom in the world.[168]

It is debatable whether Mandela the man has done anything to promote his deification. "I stand before you," he declared in his first live speech after the historic walk to freedom, "not as a prophet, but as a humble servant of you, the people."[169] Sovereignty resides in the nation as a whole, not in the person of its cherished figurehead, the affectionately nicknamed "Makela" seemed to suggest. *The Star* cautioned in June 1994 against the false expectations raised for the new president:

> Mr. Mandela is a human leader and a nation's leader, not a messiah and least of all a whole continent's messiah. If he can pull the rabbit of Rwandan mediation out of his hat, that would be confirmation of a new age of miracles; but that is most unlikely. . . . Nor is he Father Christmas to dispense largesse, no matter how badly needed, around the continent. . . . Thus far President Mandela is displaying great levelheadedness on these matters.[170]

Miracle worker or not, Mandela is a "rainbow" nationalist. During his first State of the Nation speech, for example, Mandela read a poem in Afrikaans by Ingrid Jonker, a woman who committed suicide in 1965. He also made a point of insisting that the oppression of women must end.[171] The emotional attachment of so many South Africans to "Makela" may enable support for his policies to outlive the political honeymoon.

Development and Underdevelopment

> What concerns us today is to draw up the necessary measures for the transition period between now and then—to throw up a bridge for the native during the period of transition between the period of semi-barbarism and that of civilization. What will happen after that, how the relationship between native and European will be established then—that we must leave to the future.   —*J. B. M. Hertzog, date unknown*[172]

> Until the level of development is reached where skin color is not the only difference between the population groups, they will have to be kept apart.   —*South African academic, 1988*

In the early years of settlement, the civilized/uncivilized dichotomy did not preclude social interaction. Adam and Giliomee have argued that racial intermarriage was rare but cohabitation was not.[173] Children of all races played together; their parents prayed together.[174] Those further removed from the Cape seemed to be in the habit of providing food, often for several days, to "Kaffers" who came to their farms.[175]

Social mixing did not prevent indigenous peoples from being classified as aliens.[176] Nor did it constrain the colonial practices of land dispossession and slavery. But as antislavery forces gained in influence, the notion of a "civilizing mission" was invoked more and more to justify the treatment of indigenous peoples. An editorial in *De Zuid Afrikaan* in 1832, for example, claimed that the object of government was to bring Hottentots from "their wild and savage state to a civilized communion with each other. . . and at a proper time to become joint Burghers with us of one society."[177]

The suggestion that aliens might at some "proper" (future and unspecified) time expect to become Burghers was meant to realize a twofold objective. On the one hand, it aimed to mitigate external criticism by equating colonial rule with parenting—the principle of guardianship. On the other hand, it sought stability by driving a wedge between "the converted" and "the pagans." As long as "civilization" were not construed too narrowly (so that it could be redefined as circumstances demanded), and the "civilized" themselves did not regress to the level of the rest, then the "proper" time need never arrive.

General Hertzog insisted that Colored people (those whose slave ancestors had cohabited with settlers) differed fundamentally from Africans. For him the "civilized labor policy" adopted after 1924 applied to Coloreds as well. This led in 1925 to the formation of the short-lived African National Bond (ANB), a self-professed "Colored wing or branch of the Nationalist party" that aimed to "cultivate a spirit of national pride" in cooperation with Whites.[178] Despite his insistence that there was "no question of segregation" with regard to Coloreds, Hertzog argued that socially, Coloreds "seek no association with Whites."[179] An argument premised on the idea that difference leads naturally to separation reflected again the influence of racial (typological) thought.

For other black people, Hertzog's policy was that they should "develop on their own lines within their own areas" because they were "children" in all things:

> As against the European the native stands as an eight year old against a man of mature experience—a child in religion, a child in moral conviction; without art and without science; with the most primitive needs and the most elementary knowledge to meet those needs. . . . Differences exist in ethnic nature, ethnic custom, ethnic development and civilization and these differences shall long exist.[180]

Precisely how long it would take to reach maturity, Hertzog was not prepared to say. But he never ruled out the possibility of development:

> When he achieves his majority in development and civilization, and stands on an equal level with the white man, his adulthood will be acknowledged. Then the time will have come to take his claim to political rights into con-

sideration, and further, to establish the relationship which he will have with the European.[181]

Debates about racial adulthood and political rights came in the 1940s. Framing the issue in terms of the principle of guardianship, Prime Minister Jan Smuts addressed Parliament in 1946 as follows:

> That was the policy, it is the policy, and it will remain the policy of the country, viz. the guardianship of the European population in regard to the other portions of the population who are not yet so developed that they can look after their own interests. That is our policy. But the idea and the practice of guardianship also mean that as those portions of the population who are under our guardianship develop, one must to a certain extent gradually grant them political rights. . . . That has been recognized not only by me and my friends, but by nobody less than the late General Hertzog. . . . If we want to save the position of European civilization in South Africa we shall have to keep our eyes open and act justly, and from time to time as these people develop, give them a certain measure of political rights.[182]

Disagreeing fundamentally with Smuts was the National Party, which insisted that national separation was a better guarantor of development than the policy of guardianship and qualified rights. As M. C. De Wet Nel summed up the National Party's attitude in 1959:

> First is that God has given a divine task and calling to every People in the world, which dared not be destroyed or denied by anyone. Second is that every People in the world, of whatever race or color, just like every individual, has an inherent right to live and to develop. . . . In the third place, it is our deep conviction that the personal and national ideals of every individual and of every ethnic group can best be developed within its own national community. Only then will the other groups feel that they are not being endangered. . . . This is the philosophic basis of the policy of apartheid.[183]

By the early 1990s, the National Party had abandoned its commitment to separate development and appeared ready to acknowledge that the appropriate time for national inclusion had arrived. In recognition of political change, South Africa has been returned to international sport; to international forums such as the United Nations and Organization for African Unity; and to relations with former investors and trading partners. Countries such as China and Malaysia have sought economic ties with South Africa, while the World Bank, the International Monetary Fund, and the Group of Seven industrial countries have promised to aid the new Reconstruction and Development Program (RDP). With all of these changes has come a debate about reclassification, not of South Africa's multiple races but of the identity of the country itself.

Development and Reclassification

In the classificatory order of things, South Africa has moved up in the world by being removed from the ranks of global pariahs. But the country has simultaneously moved down, or gone backward, through efforts to reclassify it as developing instead of developed.

The shift was initiated by the National Party in 1993. Its attempts to have South Africa reclassified from a developed nation to a developing one within the GATT system were supported by economists working for the African National Congress. The de Klerk regime was responsible too for the spatial reorientation of South Africa from a bastion of anticommunism on the African continent to what de Klerk called "the vanguard of the developing countries of the world."[184] Once Mandela became president, South Africa "firmly placed itself among developing countries," according to *Die Burgher,* by becoming the 130th member of the Group of 77 in the United Nations.[185]

Postapartheid development in South Africa is conditioned by the global capitalist economy within which the country is now—as an ex-pariah—more fully situated. At the same time, the category of "developing" is not race-neutral. *The Pretoria News* did not mention race when it said in June 1994 that "this is a developed country, but only in parts. In other parts we are woefully undeveloped, never mind developing."[186] But a report quoted a couple of weeks earlier in *Business Day* linked race explicitly to development. It said that "if white South Africa were a separate country it would rank 24th in the world (just after Spain). Black South Africa would rank 123 in the world (just above the Congo). South Africa was placed 93rd on the Human Development Index."[187]

By pushing black South Africans literally and conceptually beyond the boundaries of the Republic, the policy of separate development facilitated the construction of South Africa as a developed country. The more it was scrubbed clean of "black spots," the more developed must it be. The political transformation of "resident aliens" into citizens has complicated that vision, and the RDP has replaced apartheid as the means to national development. If reconstruction is not forthcoming, it will matter little to the majority that development is no longer separate. Political struggle, in a variety of forms, will continue.

NOTES

1. Quoted in *The New York Times,* May 11, 1994, 8.
2. Holiday, "White Nationalism in South Africa as Movement and System," 80.

3. The racial identity "white" is referred to as White to reflect its official status in the South African constitution and the Population Registration Act of 1950.

4. When *black* is used as an inclusive term to encompass those classified as Colored, Asian, and African, it appears without a capital B. In South Africa, *Black* is used as a synonym for African only.

5. Van Schaik, *Groot Woordeboek: Afrikaans/Engels,* 523.

6. All translations of Afrikaans words have been checked against those in Van Schaik, *Groot Woordeboek.*

7. The phrase is Steve Biko's. Quoted in Woods, *Biko,* 127.

8. Manzo, "The Limits of Liberalism," 117.

9. Sparks, *The Mind of South Africa,* 42.

10. McClintock, "'No Longer in a Future Heaven,'" 106.

11. De Villiers, "Afrikaner Nationalism," 367.

12. On this see Manzo, *Domination, Resistance, and Social Change in South Africa,* 168–185.

13. Quoted in Moodie, *The Rise of Afrikanerdom: Power, Apartheid, and the Afrikaner Civil Religion,* 73.

14. This chapter draws in part on research conducted in South Africa in 1988. A total of 438 questionnaires—which asked a diverse array of questions relating to national identity and South African politics—were received from Afrikaans-speaking academics, politicians, bureaucrats, journalists, media executives, and businesspeople. What has been reproduced here in quotations but without notes is a small portion of open-ended commentary received from respondents (the actual sources of which must remain anonymous). For more information about the conduct and findings of the survey, see Manzo and McGowan, "Afrikaner Fears and the Politics of Despair: Understanding Change in South Africa."

15. De Villiers, *White Tribe Dreaming: Apartheid's Bitter Roots as Witnessed by Eight Generations of an Afrikaner Family,* 8.

16. Patterson, *The Last Trek: A Study of the Boer People and the Afrikaner Nation,* 3.

17. De Villiers, *White Tribe Dreaming,* 8.

18. Quoted in De Villiers, *White Tribe Dreaming,* 31.

19. Quoted in Adam and Giliomee, *Ethnic Power Mobilized: Can South Africa Change?* 91.

20. "Ex-Koevoets May Return," *The Star,* June 9, 1994.

21. See Du Toit and Giliomee, *Afrikaner Political Thought, Volume I: 1780–1850,* 211–213.

22. Adam and Giliomee, *Ethnic Power Mobilized,* 97–98.

23. Adam and Giliomee, *Ethnic Power Mobilized,* 99.

24. Quoted in Adam and Giliomee, *Ethnic Power Mobilized,* 99.

25. Patterson, *The Last Trek,* 25.

26. Quoted in Du Toit and Giliomee, *Afrikaner Political Thought,* 213–223.

27. Quoted in Du Toit and Giliomee, *Afrikaner Political Thought,* 217–218.

28. Quoted in Du Toit and Giliomee, *Afrikaner Political Thought,* 216–219.

29. Quoted in Du Toit and Giliomee, *Afrikaner Political Thought,* 223.

30. Moodie, *The Rise of Afrikanerdom,* 32. The exclusion of Cape Afrikaners may have reflected the influence of Schalk Burger (chairman of the *Volkraad,* or "parliament") rather than Kruger himself. According to Adam and Giliomee, Kruger believed that anyone who spoke Dutch or Afrikaans was an Afrikaner, whereas for

Burger the term *Afrikaner* was synonymous with Transvaler (see Adam and Giliomee, *Ethnic Power Mobilized,* 102). Kruger made language the hallmark of identity; for Burger it was loyalty to (and residence in) the Transvaal.

31. Quoted in Patterson, *The Last Trek,* 26.

32. Quoted in Adam and Giliomee, *Ethnic Power Mobilized,* 101.

33. Adam and Giliomee, *Ethnic Power Mobilized,* 101.

34. Quoted in Vatcher, *White Laager,* 24.

35. Quoted in Thompson, "Great Britain and the Afrikaner Republics, 1870–1899," 303.

36. Quoted in Harrison, *The White Tribe of Africa,* 27.

37. Lord Selbourne, quoted in Lewis, *Between the Wire and the Wall: A History of South African 'Coloured' Politics,* 47.

38. Quoted in de Klerk, *The Puritans in Africa: A Story of Afrikanerdom,* 78.

39. Quoted in Moodie, *The Rise of Afrikanerdom,* 74.

40. Quoted in Moodie, *The Rise of Afrikanerdom,* 77.

41. Quoted in Moodie, *The Rise of Afrikanerdom,* 78.

42. On this see O'Meara, *Volkskapitalisme: Class, Capital and Ideology in the Development of Afrikaner Nationalism, 1934–1948.*

43. Moodie, *The Rise of Afrikanerdom,* 15.

44. Moodie, *The Rise of Afrikanerdom,* 130–131.

45. Quoted in Botha, *Verwoerd Is Dead,* 55.

46. Quoted in Hepple, *Verwoerd,* 177–178.

47. Of the 1,800,748 whites entitled to vote, 1,663,872 did so. Those in favor of a republic totaled 850,458, and those against 775,878. See Hepple, *Verwoerd,* 178.

48. Quoted in Moodie, *The Rise of Afrikanerdom,* 248.

49. Quoted in Moodie, *The Rise of Afrikanerdom,* 265.

50. Quoted in Vatcher, *White Laager,* 136.

51. Quoted in O'Meara, *Volkskapitalisme,* 169–170.

52. De Villiers, "Afrikaner Nationalism," 407.

53. Quoted in Dubow, "Afrikaner Nationalism, Apartheid, and the Conceptualization of 'Race,'" 9.

54. Quoted in Dubow, "Afrikaner Nationalism," 18.

55. Quoted in Dubow, "Afrikaner Nationalism," 22.

56. Quoted in Moodie, *The Rise of Afrikanerdom,* 246.

57. Quoted in Geyser, *B. J. Vorster: Select Speeches,* 74.

58. On this point see Manzo, *Domination, Resistance, and Social Change in South Africa,* 94–99.

59. The quote is from the 1948 report of the government-appointed Sauer Commission. See De Villiers, "Afrikaner Nationalism," 406.

60. Both quotes are from McClintock, "'No Longer in a Future Heaven,'" 111.

61. "Reincorporation," *Business Day,* April 29, 1993.

62. The date depends on whether "birth" is signaled by the adoption of an interim constitution by the multiparty Negotiating Council, or by the approval of the new constitution by the South African Parliament. See "Birth of the New South Africa," *The Star,* November 18, 1993; and "Parliament Approves New Constitution," *This Week in South Africa,* December 21–27, 1993, 1.

63. See Manzo and McGowan, "Afrikaner Fears and the Politics of Despair," 20.

64. Quoted in David Beresford, "De Klerk Says White Homeland Could Be Up for Discussion," *The Guardian Weekly,* February 2, 1992, 9.

65. Andries P. Treurnicht, "South Africa Will Never Be One Nation," *The Los Angeles Times*, May 20, 1991, B5.

66. Quoted in Scott Kraft, "Rallying Rightists," *The Los Angeles Times*, July 2, 1991, 5.

67. See Liz Sly, "Homeland Dream Dims for White South Africans," *The Chicago Tribune*, March 12, 1992, 13.

68. "Verwoerd Grandson a 'New Generation Symbol,'" *Die Burgher*, May 14, 1993.

69. "Party Wants the Cape to Secede," *Business Day*, December 24, 1993.

70. See Christopher Wren, "A Homeland? White Volk Fence Themselves In," *The New York Times*, May 8, 1991, A4.

71. "AVF Volkstaat to Include Most Boer Republics," *Die Burgher*, July 5, 1993.

72. Quoted in Bill Keller, "Circle the Wagons? Or Just Start a New Country?" *The New York Times*, October 15, 1993, A4.

73. "Unitary State Threat Binds Front: Viljoen," *Die Burgher*, May 11, 1993.

74. "General Viljoen Addresses Huge Conservative Rally," *The Weekly Mail*, May 14, 1993.

75. "Right Has Two Choices, Oblivion Or . . . ," *The Sunday Times*, March 6, 1994.

76. "Front Split Looms as Viljoen Quits," *The Sunday Times*, March 13, 1994.

77. "Mangope Warns TEC," *Business Day*, January 20, 1994.

78. "Right Has Two Choices."

79. Pik Botha as South African minister of foreign affairs on March 12, 1994. Quoted in *This Week in South Africa*, March 8–14, 1994, 2.

80. See "ANC Scorns Plan for Independent Natal," *The Guardian Weekly*, December 13, 1992, 9.

81. "Hands Off KwaZulu, Says King," *The Star*, July 26, 1993.

82. "Perilous Gambit," *The Star*, February 16, 1994.

83. "Progress on Regions," *The Natal Mercury*, July 9, 1993.

84. David Beresford, "Mandela Supports Whites' Land Bid," *The Sydney Morning Herald*, June 3, 1995.

85. "Buthelezi in TV Studio Scuffle," *The Canberra Times*, September 27, 1994, 7.

86. See, for example, "The Houses That Tokyo Will Build," *The Weekly Mail*, July 15, 1994.

87. "Land Rights," *Business Day*, November 10, 1994.

88. "U.N. Refugee Agency, South Africa Sign Accord," *Business Day*, September 8, 1993.

89. "Deal on Mozambican Refugees," *Die Burgher*, October 15, 1993.

90. "Right Place, Right Time," *The Star*, July 22, 1994.

91. See "South Africa and Mozambique Agree on Arms, Crime Clamp," *The Star*, June 15, 1993; and "Mozambique Pact," *Business Day*, July 18, 1994.

92. "Over 1-M Illegal Aliens on Reef," *The Star*, October 15, 1993.

93. "Minister Botha's Plan to Ease Trauma of Mine Closures," *Business Day*, July 15, 1994.

94. "Government Acts to Stem Floods of Immigrants," *Business Day*, October 22, 1993.

95. "New Immigration Policy Is Unveiled," *Business Day*, August 9, 1994.

96. "Final Round," *Business Day*, February 18, 1994.

97. "President Mandela Hints at Clamps on Right," *Business Day,* November 8, 1994.

98. Quoted in Du Toit and Giliomee, *Afrikaner Political Thought,* 212.

99. Adam and Giliomee, *Ethnic Power Mobilized,* 85.

100. Quoted in Giliomee, "The Development of the Afrikaner's Self-Concept," 10.

101. Adam and Giliomee, *Ethnic Power Mobilized,* 85.

102. Loubser, *The Apartheid Bible: A Critical Review of Racial Theology in South Africa,* 15.

103. Du Toit and Giliomee, *Afrikaner Political Thought,* 87.

104. Coetzee, *White Writing: On the Culture of Letters in South Africa,* 25.

105. Quoted in Adam and Giliomee, *Ethnic Power Mobilized,* 91.

106. Quoted in Du Toit and Giliomee, *Afrikaner Political Thought,* 73.

107. McClintock, "'No Longer in a Future Heaven,'" 107.

108. Moodie, *The Rise of Afrikanerdom,* 81.

109. Moodie, *The Rise of Afrikanerdom,* 86–88.

110. Quoted in Moodie, *The Rise of Afrikanerdom,* 70–72.

111. Quoted in Moodie, *The Rise of Afrikanerdom,* 50.

112. McClintock, "'No Longer in a Future Heaven,'" 109–110.

113. Quoted in Brink, "'Maar 'n Klomp "Factory" Meide': Afrikaner Family and Community on the Witwatersrand During the 1920s," 190.

114. Quoted in Harrison, *The White Tribe of Africa,* 71.

115. Quoted in Brink, "'Maar 'n Klomp "Factory" Meide,'" 190.

116. Bloomberg, *Christian-Nationalism and the Rise of the Afrikaner Broederbond in South Africa, 1918–1948,* 101.

117. From *Die Republikein,* 1935, quoted in Bloomberg, *Christian-Nationalism,* 107.

118. Dubow, "Afrikaner Nationalism," 12.

119. Moodie, *The Rise of Afrikanerdom,* 153–155.

120. Moodie, *The Rise of Afrikanerdom,* 157.

121. Moodie, *The Rise of Afrikanerdom,* 160–162.

122. Dubow, "Afrikaner Nationalism," 20–21.

123. Dubow, "Afrikaner Nationalism," 20.

124. Dubow, "Afrikaner Nationalism," 22.

125. Dubow, "Afrikaner Nationalism," 27.

126. Dubow, "Afrikaner Nationalism," 28.

127. Quoted in Dubow, "Afrikaner Nationalism," 24.

128. Quoted in Dubow, "Afrikaner Nationalism," 14.

129. Quoted in de Klerk, *The Puritans in Africa,* 249.

130. Dubow, "Afrikaner Nationalism," 30.

131. De Villiers, "Afrikaner Nationalism," 403.

132. Both quotes are from Adam and Giliomee, *Ethnic Power Mobilized,* 124.

133. F. W. de Klerk, "Address to Parliament," February 1, 1991, 1–2. Transcript supplied by the South African Consulate, Beverly Hills, California.

134. From a translation on an African National Congress T-shirt.

135. See Ashforth, *The Politics of Official Discourse in Twentieth Century South Africa,* 159.

136. "More South African Languages," *Business Day,* November 16, 1993.

137. "Board to Develop Languages," *Die Burgher,* November 17, 1993.

138. "Afrikaans on T.V. Row Deepens," *Die Burgher,* July 25, 1994.

139. "Afrikaans," *The Natal Witness,* July 25, 1994.

140. "Comment," *The Sowetan,* July 25, 1994.

141. F. W. de Klerk, "Address to Parliament."

142. "President de Klerk and Rain Queen Ignore the Weather," *Business Day,* March 11, 1994.

143. Biko, *I Write What I Like,* 56.

144. "Afrikaner Will Be Minority," *Die Burgher,* November 29, 1993.

145. De Lange was the chairman, at the time of writing, of the Afrikaner Broederbond. Quoted in Bill Keller, "Will Apartheid's Inner Circle Open Up to Blacks?" *The New York Times,* December 1, 1992, 3. The chairman of the Afrikanerbond is Tom De Beer.

146. "Board Sets Affirmative Action Target for 1997," *Business Day,* August 8, 1994.

147. "Changes in Civil Service," *Die Burgher,* June 9, 1994.

148. On affirmative action and race classification see Manzo, *Domination, Resistance, and Social Change in South Africa,* 264–271.

149. Quoted in Christopher Wren, "An Era Ends, Another Begins: South Africa to Go to Olympics," *The New York Times,* November 7, 1991, B25.

150. The Reverend Allan Hendrickse, leader of the Colored house in Parliament, proposed the zebra, but its black and white stripes suggested racial segregation rather than harmony to some. The left-of-center Afrikaans-language weekly *Vrye Weekblad* reasoned that the hippo "is the only animal upon which the divided country could possibly agree." As for the ostrich, it was said by Botswana resident Norman Lock to be a bird that "best portrays your national character over the last four decades and more." See Scott Kraft, "Usual Symbols of South Africa Won't Be at the Olympics," *The Los Angeles Times,* November 19, 1991, H2.

151. "No Time for Clashing Symbols," *The Daily News,* October 21, 1993.

152. Quoted in Michael Hill, "South Africa Unfurls New Flag, But Not Everyone Salutes," *The Baltimore Sun,* October 22, 1993, 8A.

153. "The Flag: Like the Camel . . . ," *The Eastern Province Herald,* March 17, 1994.

154. "New Flag," *Die Burgher,* March 17, 1994.

155. Quoted in Bill Keller, "South Africa's Rulers Discover Priscilla Politics," *The Sydney Morning Herald,* December 23, 1994, 11.

156. McClintock, "'No Longer in a Future Heaven,'" 108.

157. Thompson, *The Political Mythology of Apartheid,* 144.

158. Thompson, *The Political Mythology of Apartheid,* 169.

159. "Day of Unity?" *The Eastern Province Herald,* December 17, 1993.

160. "Comment," *The Sowetan,* June 17, 1994.

161. Both quotes are from "Disclosure Vital for Amnesty," *The Star,* May 26, 1994.

162. Moodie, *The Rise of Afrikanerdom,* 223.

163. de Klerk, *The Puritans in Africa,* 321–325.

164. "The New Trek," *Business Day,* December 24, 1993.

165. Tomaselli and Ramgobin, "South Africa and the Freedom Charter: Culture and Violence."

166. See "Peace Institute Plan for Robben Island," *Business Day,* July 7, 1994.

167. Nixon, "Mandela, Messianism, and the Media," 47.

168. "Comment," *The Sowetan,* June 3, 1994.

169. Quoted in Nixon, "Mandela, Messianism, and the Media," 51.

170. "St. Nelson's Temptations," *The Star,* June 16, 1994.

171. "Comment," *The Sowetan,* May 26, 1994.

172. Quoted in Moodie, *The Rise of Afrikanerdom,* 261.

173. Adam and Giliomee, *Ethnic Power Mobilized,* 89.

174. de Klerk, *The Puritans in Africa,* 51–52.

175. Du Toit and Giliomee, *Afrikaner Political Thought,* 157.

176. Adam and Giliomee have argued that Khoikhoi and San were classified as aliens at the Cape. See *Ethnic Power Mobilized,* 86. In the Transvaal, President Kruger apparently assumed that no black man, heathen or Christian, could ever be a member of the Transvaal people. See Moodie, *The Rise of Afrikanerdom,* 29.

177. Quoted in Du Toit and Giliomee, *Afrikaner Political Thought,* 107.

178. Lewis, *Between the Wire and the Wall,* 128–147.

179. Quoted in Moodie, *The Rise of Afrikanerdom,* 262.

180. Quoted in Moodie, *The Rise of Afrikanerdom,* 261.

181. Quoted in Moodie, *The Rise of Afrikanerdom,* 261.

182. Quoted in Lewsen, *Voices of Protest: From Segregation to Apartheid, 1938–1948,* 210–211.

183. Quoted in Moodie, *The Rise of Afrikanerdom,* 265.

184. de Klerk, "Speech to Parliament," *The South African Press Association,* April 19, 1993.

185. "South Africa Joins 'Group of 77' World Body," *Die Burgher,* June 25, 1994.

186. "Cold Advice from One Who Should Know," *The Pretoria News,* June 13, 1994.

187. "Gulf Divides South Africa's People," *Business Day,* June 1, 1994.

4

Turnip Seeds in the Parsnip Fields: British Empire and Island Nation

As Others See Us

There were the Scots
Who kept the sabbath
And everything else they could lay their hands on

Then there were the Welsh
Who prayed on their knees and their neighbors

Thirdly there were the Irish
Who never knew what they wanted
But were willing to fight for it anyway

Lastly there were the English
Who considered themselves a self-made nation
Thus relieving the Almighty of a dreadful responsibility.
—*Anonymous, date unknown*[1]

Like Afrikaner nationalism, *British nationalism* is an umbrella term for an array of different scriptures. The British nation has been gendered—usually but not always—as female. Its best-known symbol is the warrior-woman Britannia, but the nation has also been personified as a female monarch (in the Elizabethan age), as an evil old man (by George Orwell), as an old white[2] woman (by Enoch Powell), and as a brave young man (by Margaret Thatcher). Race and religion have been bound up at different times and in different ways with sovereign space, culture, and time. And debates about identity have been most evident during periods of globally induced change—transformations occasioned in this case by wars against France and later Germany; by the administration of the British Empire and its subsequent transformation into a commonwealth; and by the formation of the

113

European Economic Community, which evolved into the European Community (EC).

As with the inclusive Afrikaner nationalism that suppressed a Boer/Briton distinction, the British nation has been welded from the competing nationalisms of the English, the Irish, the Scots, and the Welsh. As Linda Colley has pointed out, "We can plausibly regard Great Britain as an invented nation . . . superimposed over an array of internal differences in response to contact with the Other, and above all in response to conflict with the Other."[3] Internal and external enemies have served to paper over an array of regional, class, and national divisions within Britain itself. But as in South Africa, an inclusive nationalism has been enabled only by the suppression of racial differences among so-called white people. Irish Catholics have been among the most enduring of Britain's four "races," but they are not the only white Britons to have been historically racialized. National identity has moved in tandem with racial identity, so that Britishness has been enabled by the idea of whiteness, and vice versa.

Britain has long been constructed in opposition to Europe, even as the peoples of the British nation have been taught to identify with other "civilized" peoples. National identity has been forged (as in South Africa) out of a sense of geographic isolation from the European continent and from the threat of superior powers and aggressive intentions. To Cape Afrikaners, "Europeans" were represented by the employees of the Dutch East India Company. To the first Britons they were personified by the French army. But in both cases, a notion of European tyranny has been a powerful impetus to national identity.

Physical and conceptual separation from Europe has coexisted with a sense of shared achievement and superiority vis-à-vis colonized peoples. Precisely because of the historic association of Europe with force and power, British nationalists have looked to Europeans for assistance in offsetting perceived national decline. Britain's entry into the EC cannot be separated from the effects of decolonization and nostalgia for global influence. But the reaching out to those scripted in the past as hostile races has not been automatic or without ongoing tensions. Debates about whether it is possible to be simultaneously British and European have accompanied the movement into Europe.

British and South African nationalisms have treated colonized peoples as aliens and as threats to the nation. The obvious fact that black[4] people have formed the overwhelming majority of South Africa's population and only a small percentage of Britain's (even with postcolonial reverse settlement) has not precluded a common predisposition toward them. Along with Jewish workers and refugees, so-called colored people (a term that in Britain has applied to people of Asian, African, and Caribbean descent) have been considered innately different. Even when race has not been mentioned, aliens have been associated with unwanted competition for jobs, houses, and women; with dirt, disease, and lawlessness; with social intolerance and political disloyalty; and with national decline and contamination.

Vaughan Bevan has pointed out that the principal metaphor for racial immigration into Britain has been aquatic: "References abound to floods, torrents, rivers, streams, pools, flows, trickles, dams, barriers and flood-gates."[5] Nationalists such as Enoch Powell have inveighed against "swamp-ing," even though black people constitute only about five percent of the British population. Specific factors, such as high birthrates and citizenship rights, have been mentioned as indicators of danger. But underpinning con-structions of black people as sources of trouble have been wide-ranging assumptions reflective of racial thought and a Protestant heritage. All these assumptions have reduced, in scriptures like Powell's, to one powerfully exclusionary sentiment: the sentiment that considers all black people in Britain—whether born in the country or not—to be in the wrong place at the wrong time.

And yet, the British Nationality Act of 1948 gave citizenship to the res-idents of Commonwealth countries. The rights of black people to settle in Britain have been rolled back at routine intervals since then, but it remains the case that the British government gave citizenship to nonresidents of the British Isles in the same year that the National Party came to power in South Africa on a platform of apartheid.

Britain is legally a "nonracial" society, meaning that all races have the same rights and duties under the law. Antidiscrimination legislation has been placed in the statute books, so that those who can prove discrimination on the basis of race, creed, or gender are entitled to compensation. Reconstruc-tions of British culture as tolerant, democratic, nonracist, and superior to the national cultures of countries like apartheid South Africa depend to some extent on a race-blind legal system.

The remainder of this chapter is organized as follows. Part one exam-ines a tension between island defense and "ruling the waves." Britons, metaphorically speaking, have sometimes been rallied to build seawalls to keep back the foreign floods and at other times exhorted to construct solid ships (now a Channel tunnel) to enable departure. In examining British nationalism within the context of Europe and empire, this section shows how racial thought (the notion that each race is best suited to its own terri-torial space) has conditioned attitudes toward movement.

Part two considers the relationship of supposedly shared ways of life and their symbols—Protestantism, monarchy, Parliament, tolerance, law and order, and forms of entertainment—to constructions of racial difference. In each case, people of different races who do not share these cultural com-mitments are rendered as non-British, whether they reside in Britain or not. But what is also evident is that national character is sometimes considered instinctive, as something that cannot be learned or chosen. Nationals are born with it; those who must be taught are always inferior derivatives.

Finally, part three looks at time as a shared possession and as a journey to perfection. Selective recall of British history, especially the history of the empire and war, is highlighted here and throughout the chapter.

DEFENDING THE ISLAND AND RULING THE WAVES

French and British Races

> It is quite true that the so-called races of Britain feel themselves to be very different from one another. A Scotsman, for instance, does not thank you if you call him an Englishman. . . . But somehow these differences fade away the moment that any two Britons are confronted by a European.
> —*George Orwell, 1944*[6]

> Let us be frank. In their social contacts, the British and French are not always each other's favorite people. . . . Each gets on more easily with other races.   —*The Times, 1976*[7]

As with most nationalisms, efforts to pinpoint the exact date of origin of British nationalism have generated scholarly debate and little consensus. At the earliest end of the scale is Colley, whose analysis suggests that British national identity emerged out of earlier, separate nationalisms in the course of repeated warfare with eighteenth-century France. At the latest end is Hugh Kearney, who has argued that it was only during two world wars in the twentieth century that a concept of Britishness appeared and nation-building began.[8] The difference seems to hinge on whether national identity comes at the moment of its invention (Colley's position) or from its universalization among a mass population. Either way, both authors highlight the debt that British identity owes to warfare in Europe and to the fear of island invasion.

Colley's thesis is persuasive. She has argued that during the age of warfare with France (from the Act of Union joining Scotland to England and Wales in 1707 to the start of the Victorian era in 1837), Great Britain never experienced a major invasion. Yet the sense of persistent danger and fear of its imminence enabled the invention of a single British nation. The fact that these wars were perceived by both sides as religious in nature[9] means that defense was always of culture as well as of territory. In addition, the willingness of France to support the dynastic claims of the Catholic Stuarts against those of Protestants blurred the boundaries between inside and outside and heightened fears of internal subversion by an enemy presence.

Colley has shown that British nationalism was superimposed onto older alignments and loyalties. Yet she resists the notion that England, Scotland, and Wales were united in themselves and were understood as distinct. Scotland and England had separate political institutions (despite drawing closer since the Protestant Reformation) and the Welsh their own language. England, as mentioned in Chapter 1, had a national identity in the sixteenth century, one forged in opposition to imperial Rome. But the three countries were not separate and distinct nations because they were rift, among other things, by perceptions of racial difference. Lowland Scots "regarded their highland countrymen as members of a different and inferior race, violent, treacherous, poverty-stricken and backward. They called them savages or aborigines, labels that some Lowlanders continued to use well into the 1830s."[10]

If Colley is correct, British nationalism emerged before rather than after that of Scottish and Welsh (if not English) nationalisms. Still, it was the actual or potential threat of war with France over a long period that enabled Britons to suppress racial differences and to think of themselves as one.

Alien Acts: Immigration and Racial Statecraft

Although the intersection of war and Protestantism forged the British nation, an official sense that foreign difference existed beyond France was already well established. As early as the fifteenth century, according to Bevan, restrictions were imposed on the economic activities of mainly Jewish "foreigners." Protectionist measures were taken, and in some cases those deemed alien were physically attacked and driven out of the country.

The sixteenth century began a tradition of official compassion for religious refugees, as well as a tighter identification of citizenship with territory and religion. Aliens were those not born within the Crown's dominions. Those who moved there could apply either for naturalization (which required an Act of Parliament) or for the more limited status of denizen (which afforded some legal and trading rights). Under an act of 1609, however, the "grace and favor" of naturalization were open only to "such as are of the religion now established in this Realm," a move that rendered all non-Protestants—not just Catholics but also European Jews—as permanently alien.[11]

Restrictions and exclusions thus predated eighteenth-century warfare. But it was only at the end of that century, pending yet more conflict with France, that efforts to police "resident aliens" became more routine. Bevan has argued that the novelty of the 1793 Aliens Act (one strengthened in 1798) "lay in the fact that so many of the features of modern control appeared within it, for example entry via designated ports, licenses to enter, a central system of record keeping including reports of hoteliers, control on internal movement by passports and an unfettered and expeditious power of removal."[12] Surveillance of the racially different has thus been central to modern statecraft in Britain.

When hostilities with France ended in 1802, the earlier acts were replaced. But when warfare erupted again only a year later, the terms of the 1798 law were revived.[13] Exclusion of "enemy aliens" has thus been practiced at moments of perceived threat. Selective exclusion is not an aberration from an otherwise inclusionary norm. As practiced in Britain, exclusion does more than limit access to a given territory. The alien is one who cannot and must not enter, so the national is anyone already there—the native. Breach of physical borders by those constructed as alien complicates the conceptual distinction (leading to demands for expulsion or internment at one extreme and assimilation at the other). But this does not obviate the dependence of nationalism on excludability.

Immigration controls slackened again after hostilities ended with France, and the idea of Britain as a tolerant and open society began to take effect in the nineteenth century. There were few official attempts until 1906 to restrict the entry of Irish people (who came in large numbers in the mid-1800s to escape famine) or of the mainly Jewish refugees from Russia and Poland. Yet as Colin Holmes has pointed out, Irish immigrants were widely perceived as constituting an economic and social problem. Portrayed as a savage race, they suffered distrust and discrimination in consequence.[14]

As for Jewish settlers, unease about their desire to live "according to their traditions, usages and customs" translated into recurring doubts about their loyalty to the country.[15] Efforts to legislate against entry came in 1894 and 1898, the proponents of control frequently connecting the presence of alien "types" to moral and social decline. Lord Hardwicke, for example, argued in 1898 as follows:

> It would be a very serious matter if the type of population which is now to be found in many districts of the East End, where there is a strong alien element, were to become at all a common type in the poorer districts of our large cities. It would mean, my Lords, that these classes would become to a great extent non-English in character, and that, both in physique and in moral and social customs, they had fallen below our present by no means elevated standard.[16]

Such efforts failed, but they gave rise to attempts by groups such as the British Brothers' League (founded in 1901) to channel anti-Semitism. Bevan has shown that the league added to the usual anti-alien sentiments (questions about lifestyles and loyalty) the charge of racial inferiority based on Darwin's theory of transmutation. Vigilance was demanded to offset "the dilution of the strength of native Anglo-Saxon stock by breeding with inferior races."[17]

In 1903, a Tory Member of Parliament (MP), Major William Evans
Gordon, likened Jewish immigration to the entry of diseased cattle from
Canada. He was delighted, according to Paul Foot, "to receive some support
from the Liberal benches."[18] That same year the allegations of crime, disease, and moral profligacy circulating about Jews were not borne out by the
findings of a Royal Commission established in 1901. Yet having undermined the case for immigration control, the commission then recommended
prohibitions on the entry of "undesirable aliens." These were defined as
"criminals, prostitutes, idiots, lunatics, persons of notoriously bad character
or likely to become a charge upon public funds."[19]

With the 1905 Aliens Act, the unrestricted entry of immigrants from
Europe was ended. That act mandated the berthing of "immigrant ships" at
designated ports and empowered immigration officials to deny entry to their
passengers. It also provided for the expulsion from the country of certain
categories of undesirables, particularly criminals and spies. The few hun-
dred German gypsies then residing in Britain were among the first to go.[20]

Internment and Deportation

By the time Britain entered war against Germany in 1914, attempts to contain and sometimes expel certain Europeans had become routine. As
Kearney and others have suggested, mass warfare served to heighten the
sense that Europeans in general were different from a distinct and unified
British people. But some Europeans were still considered more threatening
and alien than others.

The Aliens Restriction Act passed through Parliament in 1914. The legislation—which had German-born residents of Britain in mind, according to
Holmes—empowered the home secretary to control the registration, movement, and deportation of anyone deemed alien. Those who could demonstrate probable persecution were to have political asylum, a concession that
worked to reinscribe the image of Britain as just and tolerant even as the act
moved it in the opposite direction. The act also provided for internment, the
immediate effect of which was the establishment of internment camps
across the country. More than 32,000 men (the majority for the duration of
the war) were interned and almost 29,000 repatriated. Of those "enemy
aliens" deported, most were of German origin.[21]

No sooner was the spotlight shone on resident Germans than its shadow
fell over others. Especially after the introduction of military conscription in
1916, official and popular ire was directed at those Russian (primarily
Jewish) Poles who declined to serve in the British army. The outcome was
the Military Service (Allied Conventions) Act of 1917, which enforced
enlistment in either the British or the Russian army.[22] Essentially a loyalty
test to Britain, this legislation established another marker of difference

between nationals and aliens. The former were not only those ineligible for deportation and incarceration; they were also those who would willingly die for the country.

Warfare with Germany thus heightened a sense of Britishness, one defined to contrast British people with those of German and Jewish as well as French origin. According to George Orwell, the "sole result" of contact between Britons and foreigners during the Great War was that the former "brought back a hatred of all Europeans, except the Germans, whose courage they admired. In four years on French soil they did not even acquire a liking for wine."[23] But even if the treatment of those thought threatening could be justified by wartime fears and their own behavior (itself a dubious proposition), the continued deportation of Jewish aliens *after* the war could not.

Outbreaks of collective violence against Jews and so-called coloreds occurred throughout Britain in 1919, the same year that a new aliens act extended the provisions of the 1914 legislation to peacetime. The proximate cause of the violence, according to Holmes, was economic: "Competition for employment, particularly in an overstocked labor market in the shipping industry and a general white resentment at the gains achieved during the war by the 'colored' population . . . helped to generate the violence."[24] Yet it seems pertinent to mention the mortal influenza epidemic that came with the end of war, because the established equation of racial difference with disease may have been partially responsible for the attacks that took place.

Whatever the reasons for the trouble, the government attempted to suppress it by activating the machinery of the Aliens Act, in particular the clause allowing for the expulsion of those attempting to foment sedition or disaffection.[25] The underlying premise was that each race should stay in its own place and that those who moved were responsible for the resentments their presence generated. Once set, the precedent of punishing the victim proved tenacious.

Foot has argued that as the Tory Party adopted the anti-Semitism of its extreme right, the language of Tory MPs became increasingly racist. In a speech that constituted the British nation as both a single race and four separate races, for example, Charles Crook, MP, argued that "these four limbs of the race—Saxon, Norman, Dane, and Celt—have given the nation the power that it is today by the mingling of their strength. I am content to maintain our stock as nearly as possible from these four races."

W. P. C. Greene, MP, provided a somewhat different rationale for immigration control in 1925. He asserted that the British must avoid the sort of racial degeneration that had apparently befallen the United States:

The Americans have noticed . . . that the whole type of race in the U.S. has tremendously altered in the last 50 to 100 years. The old Nordic type is absolutely changing, and becoming what may be called the Alpine or Mediterranean type—a type far inferior to the fine old original English and Scottish colonist type. It is absolutely essential to preserve the purity of our race and to prevent contamination with the riff-raff of Eastern Europe, the stiffs of the Mediterranean and the dead beats of the world.[26]

Given this background, and the circulation of Jewish conspiracy theories in the 1920s, it is not surprising that official compassion for religious refugees was severely tested by the flight of Jews from Nazi Germany. Fascist groups such as the Imperial Fascist League and the British Union of Fascists were in their heyday in the 1930s, and anti-Semitic sentiment was diffused in popular novels. Holmes has argued that despite the arrival of some 56,000 Jews from Central Europe in that decade, the right to enter Britain until 1938 was granted mainly to those with plans to move on.[27]

The effect on British national identity of renewed warfare with Germany needs to be understood in a threefold sense—in terms of German militarism, Jewish flight, and civic sentiment. First, there was the stimulus to unity occasioned by the renewed fear of military defeat and invasion. In the wartime words of Orwell, "Economically, England is certainly two nations, if not three or four. But at the same time the vast majority of the people *feel* themselves to be a single nation." To what could this national feeling be attributed? Orwell continued with a combination of biblical references and sociobiological imagery:

> There can be moments when the whole nation suddenly swings together and does the same thing, like a herd of cattle facing a wolf. There was such a moment, unmistakably, at the time of the disaster in France. After eight months of vaguely wondering what the war was about, the people suddenly knew what they had got to do: first to get the army away from Dunkirk, and secondly to prevent invasion. It was like the awakening of a giant. Quick! Danger! The Philistines be upon thee, Samson![28]

What the "herd" did *not* do, according to Orwell, was "drive hundreds of thousands of its nationals into exile or the concentration camp."[29] And yet when Germany defeated France in early 1940, the British government *did* institute a policy of interning all "enemy aliens." The internment of 30,000 people within a matter of weeks (on the Isle of Man and overseas) reflected established practices of expulsion. It was a practice, it should be noted, that reasserted itself during the 1991 Gulf War with Iraq. The Tory government ordered the internment of Iraqis, Palestinians, and other Arabs suspected of sympathy with Saddam Hussein or "terrorism."[30]

The imprisonment during World War II of Italian restaurateurs, anti-Nazi activists, and an array of sundry other long-term residents of Britain was certainly "tragic and absurd," in the words of James Walvin. But this was not only the effect of a "hysterical climate."[31]

Walvin has quoted one MP as saying that "you cannot trust any Boche at any time," and described the man's defense of internment on those grounds as "extreme."[32] Yet Bill Williamson has argued that editorials in such newspapers as *The Times* were rife during the war with the imagery of organic community.[33] The nation was constructed as a single body with its own spirit, one rooted by Orwell in individual liberty and Christian feeling rather than German Romantic nationalism. Orwell precluded for Britain the "kind of regimentation" that allowed elsewhere for party rallies, youth movements, colored shirts, Jew-baiting, "spontaneous" demonstrations, and the Gestapo.[34] If all members of a warfaring nation were fundamentally the same, all would be equally threatening, regardless of where they lived or for how long. This nationalist logic, and not merely the climate of mass hysteria, produced the Churchill government's internment program.

As with other nationalisms, Orwell's construction of the essential nature of the British people downplayed or overlooked any commonalities between nationals and aliens. His notion that Britons were not capable of "Jew-baiting," for example, required the active forgetting of both recent history and wartime behavior. Only 10,000 Jews were admitted to Britain from Europe between 1939 and 1945. While the government considered the feasibility of diverting Jewish refugees to far-flung corners of the empire, it treated German Jews who had escaped to Britain before 1939 as eligible for internment.[35] More subtle evidence of anti-Semitism was debates about presumed Jewish involvement in black market activity, and tolerance of openly Fascist organizations.[36]

British nationalism during World War II thus fed on historic fears of invasion as well as hostility toward European Jews. And regardless of how tenacious existing social divisions may have been, the idea of shared sacrifice within a community united in opposition to tyranny enjoyed broad appeal. As Williamson has pointed out, the notion of a British nation joined in war and ready to act in times of danger has been continually revived. The Victory Parade at the end of the war, the Festival of Britain in 1951, and the annual Remembrance Day celebrations have shaped popular memories of the war as well as reinvented the character and spirit of Britain.[37]

If revival must be practiced, it is because the same conditions and forces that give sustenance to national identity can work simultaneously to undermine it. This is so for World War II, because the arrival in Britain of European refugees, Allied troops, and recruited workers turned the supposed home of one nation into "a fascinating mix of nationalities and races."[38] Many of these, such as the large contingent of U.S. soldiers stationed in Britain, departed once the war was over. But many did not, and the exigencies of postwar economic reconstruction only served to swell their numbers.

That so many of these new arrivals were people from the British colonies gave nationalism a different twist in the postwar era. Instead of being defined in opposition to assorted Europeans, Britons became those who were not "colored." The ways in which British has meant white will be discussed again. But first it is necessary to show how spacial inscriptions of race have been conditioned by Britain's imperial heritage.

Britannia Rules the Waves

But, Lord, how surprised when they heard of the News,
That we were to be servants to circumcis'd Jews,
To be Negroes and Slaves instead of the Blues,
which nobody can deny.   —*Eighteenth-century ballad*[39]

Rule Britannia, Britannia rule the waves,
Britons never, never, never will be slaves.
                                        —*British national hymn*

The British Empire expanded after the Seven Years War with France and Spain ended in 1763. Before then, Britain's imperial links were predominantly with the transplanted fellow nationals in North America. Connections to future colonies were through print and commerce. Literates were joined to the rest of the world via travelers' tales and sailors' diaries, the equivalent of latter-day UFO stories. There was also direct contact with West Africans, in particular, through the slave trade centered in Liverpool. Until outlawed in 1807, the trade was highly profitable to those who operated it. But the settlement of Africans within Britain was not without its opponents, for reasons that were not all humanitarian.

By the mid–eighteenth century, a minority black population was resident in Britain. Most were poor and employed as domestics, but a few became famous as boxers, musicians, and entertainers.[40] Whatever their occupation, most black settlers in Britain were male, and some of these men formed relationships with white women. The capacity of black men and white women to parent a "little race of mulattoes" (as one commentator put it in 1710)[41] became linked to national decline. In the following plea for controls on black immigration by historian Edward Long, for example, bestiality is a contagious disease located in "lower-class" women:

> We must agree with those who declare, that the public good of this Kingdom requires that some restraint should be laid on the unnatural increase of blacks imported into it. . . . The lower class of women in England, are remarkably fond of the blacks, for reasons too brutal to mention; they would connect themselves with horses and asses if the laws permitted them. . . . Thus, in the course of a few generations more, the English blood will become so contaminated with this mixture . . . as even to reach the middle, and then the higher orders of the people. . . . This is a venomous and dangerous ulcer, that threatens to disperse its malignancy far and wide, until every family catches infection from it.[42]

When postcolonial immigration became more systematic, the association of a black presence with contamination and national decline was thus well established. As the ballad that opened this section also suggests, spacial coexistence with those deemed racially inferior has signified the enslavement of the nation. Subjugation and containment of aliens, within the framework of such logic, is then necessary for national strength and renewal. Racial proximity excites fears of how the mighty fall.

With the loss of the slave trade the main impetus to black settlement in Britain disappeared, and the focus of nationalist concern was redirected. Instead of the West African within, the expanded empire without brought with it nagging questions about possible national destruction.

According to Colley, the acquisition of an empire sustained by force and military control—one that included the Catholic inhabitants of French Quebec as well as large portions of Asia—produced a crisis of identity. Established images of Britons as a nation defined by Protestantism, commerce, and liberty were unsettled by imperial expansion. With the fall of the Roman Empire as a historical referent, nationalists worried that the British Empire could not be sustained, that it would decay and destroy the nation in the process. Apparently, "the British were in the grip of collective agoraphobia, captivated by, but also adrift and at odds in a vast empire abroad and a new political world at home."[43]

In the wake of these anxieties, two different and contradictory nationalisms emerged from London, the administrative center of British nation and empire. One took the form of a reasserted Englishness, a celebration of English identity that depended for its effect on constructions of Scottish difference. Traced by Colley to the figure of John Wilkes, "Wilkite" nationalism stressed the inherently alien character of the Scots. Scottish people were portrayed as an authoritarian nation, in contrast to the liberty-loving English.[44]

Those who wanted to construct one British nation had already had difficulty including certain Scots within its boundaries. As already mentioned, Highlanders were deemed an inferior and savage race by Lowlanders, a construction reinforced by the Jacobite (Highland) rebellion against Parliament in 1745. John Free told the Laudable Association of Anti-Gallicans in 1756 that Englishmen, Lowland Scots, and the Hanoverian kings were all descended from the same Saxon race. They should therefore work together and with the Welsh, who were Ancient Britons.[45]

Wilkite nationalism differed from this earlier racism in a double sense. First, it cast all Scots as alien and not just those from the Highland areas. Scots were invariably portrayed in tartan kilts—a Highlander garment banned by Parliament after the 1745 uprising.[46] Historic boundaries between different Scottish people were deliberately fudged, and the kilt-wearing traitor was made to stand for all.

The second and less obvious racism in Wilkite nationalism was its use of a racial analogy. Colley has reproduced a playbill from a London satire of 1792. Entitled *Sawney Scot and John Bull,* the photo is of two men standing face-to-face and staring fiercely and malevolently at one another. Since one is wearing a thistle in his hat and the other a rose on his lapel, it is not difficult to tell Scot from Bull, the personifications of Scotland and England, respectively. But what is also noticeable, aside from the mutual hostility, is that Sawney Scot is portrayed in the stereotypical image of a Jew. In contrast to the short bulbous nose of the Englishman, that of the Scot is long and hooked. Intentional or not, such images worked to racialize Scottish people and make them appear more threatening.

Historically, it was the very success of Jewish artisans and traders—their supposed capacity to "take our jobs" and turn "us" into "servants" (as the ballad went)—that made them a threat. In the context of imperial anxiety, the Semitization of the Scot may have been motivated by similar concerns. For as Colley has argued, Wilkite nationalism was a reaction to Scottish power and influence.

The British army as a path to social advancement increased with the military and administrative requirements of empire. English insecurity in the face of a greater Scottish political presence was displayed in an obsession with Scottish sexuality, one that symbolized anxiety over the "penetration" of England by Scottish men.[47]

As in the past it was renewed warfare—this time with the American colonies—that worked to suppress national and racial differences within Britain. Particularly after France began aiding American rebels in 1778, the notion of the country being persecuted by an alliance of traditional enemies and rebellious nationals fostered unity. In addition, many Scots used the war as an opportunity to demonstrate loyalty to Britain.[48]

Colley has argued that imperial anxieties largely disappeared by 1783 (one year after Irish independence).[49] No obvious signs of decay helped bury the fears of national destruction. But imperial advancement and attitudes toward it remained linked to the racial assumptions that both informed and conditioned it. Concerns circulated about whether Britons could go and plant roots overseas, about whether the race could flourish in other climes, and about how it was possible to avoid "contamination."

Prior to imperial expansion, Britannia literally ruled the waves through commercial shipping. But this was rule of a deterritorialized, unpopulated space and so did not raise concerns about the effects of national transplantation. With the acquisition of new territories, "ruling the waves" took on a different meaning. The sea was no longer simply a natural boundary separating the island from the continent, but a metaphor for alien lands and their indigenous races.

The ways in which British colonial administration operated are well known. After sending lone men, the government transported families so as to create national enclaves and preclude the possibility of "going native." Colonial isolation reinforced the view that "niggers" (a term used for Indians as well as West Africans) were inferior, that Britons were destined by God to rule over others, and that the British were the only race not to degenerate when transplanted. As one MP succinctly put it, "I believe in this race, the greatest governing race that the world has ever seen; in this Anglo-Saxon race, so proud reaching, self-confident and determined, this race, which neither climate nor change can degenerate, which will infallibly be the predominant force of future history and universal civilization."[50]

As Britain continued to colonize, belief in a "great chain of being" was lent respectability by racial science. But until then it seems that imperial attitudes were fed by implicit comparisons between white settlers overseas and black settlers within Britain. Unlike the latter, the former were presumed to thrive rather than degenerate in foreign climes; they were masters rather than slaves; and they did not partner lower-class women. Informed by this logic, the British Empire meant national greatness and immigration meant national decline, even though both involved the movement of races from their home territory.

Seawalls and Settlers: Immigration and Reverse Settlement

> Taking Negroes is a certain sign that the house is going down. Look at the place next door. Milk bottles left outside, the sheets never changed: a dirty house—no wonder they take blacks.
> —*London landlady, date unknown*[51]

> Numbers are of the essence. . . . We must be mad, literally mad as a nation to be permitting the annual inflow of some 50,000 dependents, who are for the most part the material of the future growth of the immigrant-descended population. It is like watching a nation busily engaged in heaping up its own funeral pyre.   —*Enoch Powell, 1968*[52]

Although the immigration of Africans was largely halted by the abolition of slavery, a small number of students and workers (many of them seamen) continued to live in Britain. In his autobiography, the Ghanaian leader Kwame Nkrumah recalled feeling quite at home in the London of 1945. "There was nothing to stop you getting on your feet and denouncing the whole of the British Empire," according to Nkrumah, even as "many landladies objected to taking in colored lodgers" and "occasionally someone would end in trouble with a girl."[53]

The living conditions available to black people were investigated by

Nkrumah through his work for the Colored Workers' Association of Great Britain and found to be appalling.[54] West Indian factory workers, seamen, and forestry workers recruited during the war had to be lodged in hostels because of the difficulties they experienced in the private housing market.[55]

Yet black workers continued to be recruited to meet postwar labor demands. Walvin has noted that "London Transport, a number of British hotels and restaurants, regional hospital boards and the British Transport Commission all made prominent recruiting drives in the Caribbean to satisfy their own particular labor shortages."[56] West Indians were joined by hundreds of thousands of Poles (and other Eastern European workers) and by people from Ireland, all of whom were portrayed in racial terms. Polish men, for example, were cast as "a race of Casanovas," while hostile and racialized images of Irish people persisted. The most easily tolerated Irish people, according to Holmes, were those who renounced their Irishness.[57]

Jewish immigration into postwar Britain was minute; only 1,000 settled there between 1946 and 1951.[58] And the emerging story of the Holocaust did not put an end to anti-Semitism. If anything, it was given sustenance by events in Palestine. After the Irgun group hanged two British sergeants in 1946, Jewish shops in England were attacked; Jewish meetings were disrupted; and "Death to All Jews" was daubed in the dockland area of Liverpool.[59]

The British Nationality Act of 1948 challenged established traditions in British immigration policy. The act guaranteed unrestricted entry into the United Kingdom of citizens of Commonwealth countries—whether independent or not—and so constituted Commonwealth peoples as British. What Bevan has called the "source of all subsequent debate and controversy in immigration and race relations"[60] was "madness" in the sense that it deviated from normal practice. The act was a global constitution of national identity, one rooted in the shared space of the Commonwealth and not in the soil of the British Isles. Through residence in the "household" of the collapsing empire, "coloreds" were to be considered legally British.

Challenges were launched from the Labour cabinet and the Civil Service almost as soon as the act was passed.[61] As John Rex has pointed out, the situation of the new immigrants as colonial, "colored," and poor was much noted. Given the differential distribution of housing opportunities—which tended to push new arrivals into multiple-occupancy lodging houses—perceptions of racial inferiority were fed by reinvigorated fears of urban deterioration, disease, prostitution, and violence.[62]

Unease over "colored" immigration, particularly as the proportion of women and children increased in the 1950s, *did* lead to an outbreak of collective violence in 1958. More will be said in part two about these and other "race riots," since they have figured prominently in constructions of national character. But here it should be noted that the official response to them signaled the writing on the wall for the British Nationality Act. It was the same logic that underpinned the deportation of foreigners for inciting "sedition and disaffection."

No sooner were the Nottingham riots (which began as an attack on West Indians) under way than local MPs called for restricted immigration. According to J. K. Cordeaux (the Conservative MP for Nottingham Central), the problem "attaches to our Government for allowing unrestricted immigration."[63] At the height of the rioting, *The Daily Mail* ran an article by a Labour MP with the headline: "Should We Let Them Keep Coming In?" The next day the same newspaper praised the two MPs, arguing that "Britain is already an overcrowded island, haunted always by thoughts of unemployment. If immigration is allowed to go on unchecked the evil will not diminish but will grow. Now it must be tackled." Edward Pilkington has pointed out that this coupling of denunciations of violence with calls for immigration control was not restricted to the tabloid press. *The Daily Telegraph* suggested that "even if West Indians or Pakistanis had white skins, it would be necessary to consider whether this small island could absorb a limitless number."[64]

There were voices of opposition to this sentiment. *The Observer* argued that restriction "would be a shameful admission that the problem is too difficult for us to solve and that a multi-racial society is impossible."[65] Months of debate followed in Parliament, with objections to unrestricted immigration voiced, as Bevan has pointed out, in the same terms used against Jewish refugees at the turn of the century.[66] For example, Cyril Osborne told Parliament that unless immigration were stopped, "Britain would become so cramped with black people carrying tuberculosis and leprosy, living off the dole and turning whole areas into slums, that there would hardly be standing room." To mitigate threat from black people already present, George Rogers suggested scattering them across the country, increasing the powers of the police, and deporting convicted criminals.[67]

If immigration controls were not immediate, Pilkington has suggested it was because of smirking coverage of the riots in places like South Africa and the U.S. South, as well as diplomatic pressure from the colonies.[68] Pressure was placed in turn on the governments of India and Pakistan to exercise tighter control over passport allocation. According to Walvin, this effectively "ensured that the uneducated and unskilled were no longer able to travel to Britain, unless they were dependents of settlers already there."[69]

Whatever the reasons for hesitation, the Conservative government exercised controls via the Commonwealth Immigrants Act of 1962. This was one year after Britain applied for full membership in the EC. It was against a backdrop of activities by organizations such as the Birmingham Immigration Control Association (BICA).[70] And it was the same year that a safe Labour seat in Birmingham was lost to a Conservative candidate with a campaign similar to that of the BICA.

The 1962 legislation initiated an entry system based on work vouchers issued by the Ministry of Labour. It set a legal precedent of allowing for the deportation of Commonwealth citizens. But the act did not prevent the entry of dependents of those already admitted, an omission that was to become the focus of many of Enoch Powell's later speeches.

The 1962 act was not supported by the opposition Labour Party. Yet once in power, the party issued its own White Paper on immigration. The focus of the 1965 paper was numbers, and the intention was to limit black immigration to skilled workers or those with guaranteed employment. The paper was accompanied by the first Race Relations Act, one that lacked powers of enforcement and did not cover two areas of routine discrimination, namely housing and employment.

Both the White Paper and the Race Relations Act codified established scriptures of race and nation. The former "played the numbers game" (as Robert Moore has put it[71]), while the latter invented a British national character distinctively different from that of South Africa and the U.S. South. Difference, once officially constructed, was to be socially tolerated.

It was within this context that "Powellite" nationalism emerged. Critics such as Bill Smithies and Peter Fiddick have been at pains to show how the Birmingham MP played fast and loose with statistics and arithmetic.[72] That is important. But nationalism is always more myth than reality. What made Powell a popular hero was less the veracity of his statements and more their metaphorical power.

Through martial metaphors and a willingness to "play the numbers game," Powell connected the presence of "coloreds" in Britain to military defeat and invasion. At times Powell placed danger in the future and made it avertable in the present. In April 1968, for example, he stated that "in fifteen or twenty years, on present trends . . . whole areas, towns, and parts of towns across England will be occupied by different sections of the immigrant and immigrant-descended population."[73] At other times Powell suggested that through official folly (he routinely described Britain as "crazy" or "bonkers"), danger was already present.

There was said to be a "huge reservoir" of immigrants in need of "assisted repatriation." In November 1968, Powell claimed that "whole areas which lie at the heart" of Britain had been "transformed . . . into alien territory." He railed against "that unparalleled invasion of our body politic" and described it as "nearer the truth to think in terms of detachments from communities in the West Indies or India or Pakistan encamped in certain areas of England."[74] Whether in the future or the present, continued immigration and high birthrates were said to be turning "the existing population" into "strangers in their own country."[75]

A recurring theme in Powell's speeches was that "numbers are of the essence." He sought to distinguish between those Commonwealth citizens (like Nkrumah) who came to study from those who came to settle. Any number of students seemed acceptable because they would not stay. Settlers were a problem because their presence was permanent. Those in the "wrong place" should be repatriated. The question is why Commonwealth citizens—those constituted as British by the 1948 Nationality Act—should be considered so wrong for Britain.

Here Powell separated national character from alien cultures. Describing immigrants' "customs and their social habits and expectations" as "widely different" from those of the native population, Powell insisted he was not assuming immigrants to be "more predisposed to vicious or spiteful behavior." The issue was not that immigrants were more criminal than "our own people" but that they were "strangers."[76] Faulting the legal system for allowing "an Englishman born in Birmingham and a tribesman from the North-West Frontier" to be "indistinguishable in the law of the United Kingdom," Powell insisted that the possession of British citizenship did not turn an alien into a Briton.[77]

Like other nationalisms, this one defined the national by default. As Smithies and Fiddick asked, "Who are the Englishmen? Mr Powell himself does not answer the question, but contents himself with enumerating some examples of non-Englishmen."[78] Powell's favorite examples were Sikhs, because of their supposed "campaign to maintain customs inappropriate to Britain." Through a metaphor of disease, Powell described "communalism" as a "canker" that "has been the curse of India" and was contaminating Britain.[79]

A historic association of communalism with barbarism should be noted,[80] for the invocation of communalism within Britain was destined to incite fears of national decline and decay. But Powell did not resort to crude racism. He appeared as a guest of talk show host David Frost in January 1969, and in response to continual charges of "racialism," Powell rightly insisted that he never described one race as inherently superior to another. When Frost asked for comment on "the fundamental differences between white and black people, right? . . . the unchanging, unchangeable differences," he was more in tune with Powell than he seemed to realize.[81]

What made both men "racialist" was the shared assumption that differences in customs and character are fixed and permanent. This is perhaps most apparent in the conclusion to a speech delivered by Powell in Eastbourne:

> The West Indian or Asian does not, by being born in England become an Englishman. In law he becomes a U.K. citizen by birth; in fact, he is a West Indian or an Asian still. Unless he be one of the small minority . . . he will

by the very nature of things have lost one country without gaining anoth-er, lost one nationality without acquiring a new one.[82]

Powell did not call Commonwealth peoples "riff-raff," "stiffs," or "dead beats." But he did revive the equation of immigration and national decline, via a political metaphor and gendered imagery.

Commentators on British nationalism have argued that in the postwar era, immigration into Britain symbolized loss of national standing as well as foreign invasion. Walvin, for example, has said that "the rapid growth of black and Asian communities provided the very evidence and proof of Britain's demise."[83] Foot, also, has suggested that "[coloreds] are symbols to the British not only of strangeness but also of failure."[84] To understand that symbolism, it is necessary only to return to the quote from the London landlady that opened this section of the chapter.

Due to the historic association of the racially different with dirt, disease, and urban decay, only a place that is "going down" would "take blacks." Better establishments that would follow suit (thinking, perhaps, to make a quick profit) would be sowing the seeds of their own demise. The landlady was speaking literally about her neighbor's house and not metaphorically about a nation. But as earlier chapters showed, the concept of the household became a metaphor for the imperial nation-state in the eighteenth century, and nations have been conceived as neighborhoods and social clubs as well as extended families. Powell played to great effect on the symbolism of houses and neighborhoods.

In February 1968, Powell predicted an "invasion" of "entire areas" and their attendant transformation. He warned that "the previous native inhabi-tants . . . might be driven from their homes and their property deprived of value." The years from 1954 to 1966, according to Powell, were "the years when a 'For Sale' notice going up in a street struck terror into all its inhab-itants." Lest the listener doubt his veracity, Powell added: "I know; for I live within the proverbial stone's throw of streets which 'went black.'"[85]

By weaving together two troubling images—a native people fleeing in terror from an invading force and a familiar street "gone black"—Powell rendered national decline in a form understandable to Britons like the London landlady. Thanks to official refusal to "distinguish between one British subject and another,"[86] Powell suggested the national home was up for sale, the foreigners were moving in, and the "house" itself was on the way down.

Powell later foresaw "the River Tiber foaming with much blood" from "our own neglect," a classical image of Britain reminiscent of God's first plague upon the biblical Egyptians. He also told the apparently true story of an old-age pensioner, a white woman who refused to rent rooms in her boarding house to "negroes" and was now the only white person left in a once "respectable street." The woman's life was linked to fear, isolation, and torment:

> She is becoming afraid to go out. Windows are broken. She finds excreta pushed through her letterbox. When she goes to the shops, she is followed by children, charming, wide-grinning piccaninnies. They cannot speak English, but one word they know. 'Racialist,' they chant. When the new Race Relations Bill is passed, this woman is convinced she will go to prison. And is she so wrong? I begin to wonder.[87]

Smithies and Fiddick cast doubt on whether the "lone old lady" whose story was retold many times ever existed.[88] But real or not, the old lady wielded enormous representational power. As Paul Gilroy has argued, Powell's old white woman was less flesh and blood than an allegory for the national body.[89] Surrounded by "grinning picaninnies," she represented the once great and homogeneous imperium seeing national decline reflected in the shiny skin of its former colonials. Here is the once mighty Britannia: frail, alone, and living in terror.

Powell's speeches were sufficiently embarrassing to the Conservative Party that he was dismissed from the shadow cabinet. As for the ruling Labour Party, it simultaneously extended the provisions of the Race Relations Act to cover housing and employment and introduced the 1968 Commonwealth Immigrants Act. The latter restricted the right of entry to those with a close ancestral link to the United Kingdom and subjected all other potential immigrants to a quota system.

Thanks to diplomatic pressure, the British government accepted Asians forced out of Uganda by Idi Amin in 1972.[90] But such compassion came only after passage of the 1971 Immigration Act. That legislation tied settlement rights for Commonwealth citizens born outside the British Isles to "patriality"; that is, it asked for proof that at least one *paternal* grandparent or parent of the applicant had been born in the United Kingdom. [91] In overturning the constitution of identity in the 1948 Nationality Act, the 1971 act retied the nation more tightly to the geographical space of the British Isles. The only dispersed "relatives" eligible for return were to be the descendants of male emigrants.

The Immigration Act of 1971 was promulgated in the same year that British membership in the EC was finally granted. The decision to apply for full membership was first taken, as already mentioned, by a Conservative Party government in 1961. It was renewed in 1967 by a Labour government. Expressed most forcefully by France's General de Gaulle in 1963, exclusion had been premised on Britain's supposed insularity from Europe in conjunction with its colonial networks. Britain was said to be "linked through her exchanges, her markets, her supply lines to the most diverse and often the most distant countries."[92]

Although important, questions such as why British membership was accepted when it was, whether entry should have been preceded by a national referendum, and who if anyone benefited will not be addressed here. Two aspects of Britain's rapprochement with Europe are more pertinent to this book. The first is that movement did not come about—despite efforts by Winston Churchill after World War II[93]—until after the British Empire began to collapse and the immigration of colonial peoples excited fears of national decline. Amid debates on a range of issues, British entry into the EC was celebrated as a way to reverse decline and revive lost influence. The fact that Britain moved into Europe while immigration tightened was no coincidence.

The second key point is that Britain's relationship to Europe had to be ambivalent, given the dependence of national identity on constructions of European threat. Were the British now supposed to surrender their national character for the sake of survival and a place in Europe? Or was the nation strong enough to retain its identity and export its achievements? In the discussions surrounding acceptance of British membership in 1971, and then again after Britain joined the EC in 1973, it was these sorts of questions that informed nationalist debate.

Fanfare for Europe? British and European Nations

Why should we go in? . . . We must go in, if we want to remain Great Britain, and have the chance of becoming a Greater Britain. . . . Today we don't occupy the place in the world we once did. . . . For 25 years we've been looking for something to get us going again. Now here it is.
—*Edward Heath, 1971*[94]

One can hardly hold it against Frenchmen that they feel no inclination to shed crocodile tears over the alleged passing of a certain way of life; or share the average Englishman's instinctive distaste for having to "muck in" with all those "niggers south of the Channel," in some sort of continental hotch-potch.
—*The Times, 1973*[95]

As *The Times* pointed out in July 1971, the Labour Party had earlier "fully understood the strength of the case for entering the European Community." It was an understanding supposedly fostered by recognition that Commonwealth power could not rival that of the United States, the Soviet Union, the EC, China, and Japan. Instead of opposing the government's White Paper on membership, the Labour Party was asked to welcome a means to "end this atmosphere of staleness and pettiness of purpose."

Acceptance was said to mean that the young "can now look forward to leading life with the whole of Western Europe as a home land," whereas rejec-
tion "would be a sort of suicide, a turning away from the challenge of life
and a withdrawal into the supposed security of rigor mortis." Movement,
according to *The Times*, was a British trait:

> Britain has always moved out in the world; has chosen to be an island from
> which development comes and not merely an island into which its citizens
> retreat. The White Paper marks the completion of the Government's poli-
> cy. It also marks the start of a new and much more promising phase in
> British history, a phase in which the British revive their own strength and
> prosperity in contributing to the collective strength and prosperity of
> Europe.[96]

The White Paper generated much debate in European media. It was
described by the German newspaper *Die Zeit* as a document that "had at last
lifted the discussion from the level of butter and mutton to . . . the political
fate of the nation."[97] Yet the White Paper was more a pastiche of the mun-
dane and the lofty than an elevation of politics above agriculture.

Having warned in messianic fashion against the dangers of isolation—
"in a single generation we should have renounced an imperial past and
rejected a European future"[98]—the paper estimated the effect of membership on such things as European institutions, industrial tariffs, New Zealand
cheese, and Commonwealth sugar. Under the heading "Free Movement of
Labor," the paper also offered reassurance that "community regulations
would not affect controls over immigration from countries outside the
EEC."[99] This excited fears that "kith and kin" in Australia, New Zealand,
and Canada would be unable to enter Britain, that the 1971 Immigration Act
was somehow in peril. It led to unsuccessful demands in Parliament that
immigrants from the "old Commonwealth" should have the same status as
citizens of EC countries.[100]

Lord Walston pointed out in *The Times* that "too many people talk of the
old Commonwealth as if it were synonymous with the white Commonwealth," and argued that the value of the Commonwealth lay in "the
fact that it is multiracial." Still, he linked "the need to combat racial
prejudice" to "the need to control immigration into this country."[101] The
assumption that only those in the Commonwealth with British male ancestors were members of the national "family" was scarcely contested at
all.[102]

Although Parliament did vote to accept the terms of British membership, proponents had to work hard to sell the notion (in the words of opposition leader Harold Wilson) that "Britain is finished if we do not go in."[103]
At the time the White Paper was published, opponents were numerous and
diverse. They ranged from the majority of the British population (57 percent

of whom were apparently against EC membership),[104] to the Parliamentary opposition, to MPs like Enoch Powell (who left the Tory Party over the issue). While the average "woman in the street" seemed concerned about rising prices and the alien nature of French cheeses (said by one to be "so unlike Cheddar types in consistency that a major swing to them by the majority of the British people is likely to be extremely slow"[105]), her fears were not unlike those expressed in loftier terms.

Enoch Powell and other Conservative dissidents opposed a surrender of British sovereignty to European institutions. In response to the warlike imagery that was Powell's forte, supporters of Europe offered two contradictory arguments that continue to inform British attitudes toward Europe. On the one hand, they argued that Europe was not a threat because "real power remains firmly in the hands of member nations."[106] In the words of the foreign and Commonwealth secretary, Sir Alec Douglas-Home, "Influence that is not backed by strength declines. That is the first and clearest sense in which our political future—that is our ability in the future to safeguard British national interests—depends on Europe."[107]

On the other hand, proponents argued that "a 'surrender' of sovereignty is not necessarily a bad thing" because "to enlarge the area subject to a single sovereignty, albeit federal, is to enlarge the area of (usually) assured peace." Enlargement was said to depend on the existence of "a sufficient community of sentiment on the part of the people or peoples concerned." Supposed growth of such a community since 1945 meant that loss of sovereignty was to be rejoiced, not lamented.[108]

These debates over sovereignty were less about the nature of political power—whether it resided in the British Parliament or in the institutions of the EC—and more about what it meant to be British in a world without empire. In the racial terms of the newspaper correspondent cited earlier (who was playing on the British saying that "niggers begin at Calais," the first port of entry into France), the issue was how much Britons could associate with "niggers south of the Channel" without becoming contaminated with their traits.

Reassurances were given that "no one wishes to override the member countries' national, constitutional and cultural characteristics."[109] Unique national characters were simultaneously constructed and highlighted. Readers of *The Times* were told, for example, of German orderliness, conformism, love of nature and music, and traditional romanticism and idealism. Despite the "many wrongs in West German society," Britons were told to admire German strength, even if the German people were not relaxed enough to enjoy it.[110]

Just as a British identity was made possible by the suppression of internal differences, a European "nation" was imagined for the member countries of the EC. Exemplified by *The Times,* this took the form of a Euronationalism, one expressed in the conviction that "the people of Europe should be able to see themselves as a European nation with a particular character and aims." As in the past, national culture was defined in opposition to alien difference. "The European ideal," intoned the editorial, "is one of civilization, that is the free development of individual character in a free society." More than market relations or common institutions, Europe was an idea: "The idea of community with individuality is the theme of the political future of the European nations. It is also the theme of the development of the society of the European peoples."[111] European culture was civilization not barbarism, individualism not communalism, and (implicitly) white not black.

Although not inconsistent with the emphasis on a shared European civilization, the idea that Britain could contribute to the development of a "single [European] political personality while still respecting national differences" appeared in tandem with Euronationalism.[112] Not only Britain's future but its past as well was now remembered as less imperial than European. This attitude was summed up by Edward Heath, who said that "the truth is that Britain has always been part of Europe." Instead of the necessity for national defense, Heath took from the two world wars the lesson that "we are inevitably involved in the fate of Europe."[113]

Not only through renewed interpretations of warfare was a novel past created. As its contribution to a ten-day, countrywide extravaganza named Fanfare for Europe, *The Times* published a two-part series entitled "Forward into Europe." The first edition went backward in time. In its polyvocal reflections on "Britain's influence, past and present, on the evolution of European ideas and culture,"[114] the report constructed a European past for Britain in academia, literature, finance, science, design, and sport.[115]

Such constructions were accompanied during the first weeks of 1973 by teachings on European institutions.[116] But these did not silence concerns expressed in metaphors of warfare. Farmers worried about "fewer defenses" against European agricultural imports;[117] workers feared a "wholesale invasion of Britain by workers from across the Channel";[118] and university principals such as Lord Bowden asserted that EC bureaucracy would "wreck the English education system" by assuming administrative control.[119] Proponents were vigilant at refuting every charge, but the British public remained split on the eve of entry.[120]

Fanfarers for Europe then changed tactics, turning surrender into a military conquest and the invasion of Britain by Europe into its opposite. This strategy was aided by fears of British invasion expressed in France,[121] but its most complete articulation appeared in the second edition of "Forward into Europe." Accompanied by a series of friezes mimicking the Bayeux tapestry, the report depicted twelve years of epic struggle to conquer Europe, under such headlines as: "The First Assault"; "Edward the Bold Sets Forth";

"Skirmishes on the Home Front"; "Diplomatic Blitzkrieg"; "Death of a French Warrior"; "Triumph of the Faithful Geoffrey"; and "At Westminster a Bloody Victory." The style was humorous, but the comic relief did not mask the seriousness of the representation.[122]

Britons were not all certain that conquering Europe was a better option than strategic withdrawal. Conservative MP Richard Crossman said at the end of 1972 that "if we are to withdraw from the EEC and live happily as an offshore island, we must become a nation of little Englanders. I should like to see this happen."[123] But proponents of Europe could count on *The Times*. A "reluctance" to join Europe, readers were told on the day of entry, was "entirely understandable":

> It was always so when the British faced another frontier: when brave but uncertain men and women followed Captain John Smith to settle in the New World, when the first merchant adventurers established their factories in India, and when Britons of all conditions set sail for Australia, New Zealand, and other unknown territories beneath the horizon. Men were ever reluctant to change the known for the unknown, and this time reluctance is the greater because the entire nation rather than a few adventurers is confronted with a new frontier.[124]

In implicit contrast to colonial experiences, readers of *The Times* were reassured that Britain was welcomed in Europe, that national culture was admired, and that the country could aid European development and progress. Although somewhat tongue-in-cheek, the metaphor of disease used by President Pompidou of France captured neatly the neocolonial theme:

> Tell them that the natives are more civilized than they think and that they will be warmly welcomed into the Community. . . . Britain's entry will have positive aspects. She will bring to the Community her outward looking attitude towards the world, her sense of space. . . . Finally, it is a stable democracy that is entering the Community. I hope we shall not infect it with this old virus of instability that has resisted Gaullist antibiotics.[125]

The Times did not invent presumptions of British superiority. But it did play an active part in disseminating them. Again reminiscent of colonialism, Britons were asked to make contributions to European defenses[126] and to the continent's "Christian tradition."[127] The country's armed forces, churches, scientific achievements, education, business acumen, and arts were all lauded in "Forward into Europe" and other articles. More than any other aspect of Britons' "own and very special character,"[128] articles and editorials emphasized the country's Parliament as a symbol of democracy.[129] Even an engineering firm got in on the act, by placing next to a photo of the leaning tower of Pisa the slogan "If they'd let us into Europe sooner. . ."[130]

There *was* doubt about the ability of "the British race" (as Lord Goodman of the Fanfare for Europe Committee called the nation in 1973)[131] to bring "civilization" to Europe. The issue was whether "anything of such implied consistency as a national character" really existed. According to *The Times* correspondent T. J. O. Hickey, consistency was missing because differences in Britain's "racial stock" produced conflicting and contrasting attitudes toward Europe.[132] These were not racial differences between white and "colored."[133] Hickey's races were the Normans, the Anglo-Saxons, and the Celts. This type of thinking may have been atypical in the Britain of 1973, but that it coexisted with references to a British race and appeared in a "respectable" newspaper illustrates the strength of historical memories.

Ambivalence over the EC was formally resolved in 1973 via a mechanism known as the Luxembourg Compromise. According to Anthony Barnett, "This was understood to be a crucial safeguard which meant that no member state could have its vital interests over-ruled by a majority vote of the others." As Barnett has also pointed out, this tacit promise was broken in 1982, when member states of the EC "voted through agricultural price increases against Britain's protests."[134]

Outrage might have been more vocal were it not for war with Argentina over the Malvinas. Reminiscent of her predecessor eleven years earlier, Prime Minister Margaret Thatcher claimed that the Falklands War "has put the Great back into Britain." As for why such a domestically popular war was necessary, Thatcher defended it in different ways. She claimed that "British sovereign territory has been invaded"; that "the people of the Falkland Islands, like the people of the United Kingdom, are an island race"; and that "the principles that we are defending are fundamental to everything that this Parliament and this country stand for. They are the principles of democracy and the rule of law."[135]

Thatcher was too preoccupied to do battle with Europe in 1982. "Iron Britannia's"[136] subsequent skirmishes with the EC are legendary. Conservative revolt against her belligerent attitude toward Europe cost her the leadership of the party in 1991. Refusal by some Tories to endorse Prime Minister John Major's support for enlargement of EC powers via the 1992 Maastricht Treaty may be due in part to Thatcher's continued influence.[137]

Yet Thatcher's nationalism—despite her insistence that Britain could stand alone if necessary—was not a "little Englandism" of the Richard Crossman variety. During and after the Falklands War, Thatcher's speeches made clear that hers was an imperial nationalism, a desire for a homogeneous Britain with global reach. Like Powell a decade earlier, Thatcher opposed immigration in 1978 by invoking cultural difference and numbers:

> People are really rather afraid that this country might be rather swamped by people with a different culture and you know, the British character has done so much for democracy, for law and done so much throughout the

world that if there is any fear that it might be swamped people are going to react and be rather hostile to them coming in. So, if you want good race relations, you have got to allay people's fears on numbers.[138]

Nostalgia for empire was manifest also in a desire—a "bounden duty" in Thatcher's terms—to export the rule of law and free enterprise to new sites, such as Eastern Europe. For Thatcher in 1992, the problem with a (Western) European identity for Britain was that "it's not big enough minded." To confine the cultural influence of a country that once ruled a quarter of the globe to one-half of a continent was to deny it the chance to "show our paces."[139]

SOLID BREAKFASTS AND GLOOMY SUNDAYS

There *is* something distinctive and recognizable in English civilization. It is a culture as individual as that of Spain. It is somehow bound up with solid breakfasts and gloomy Sundays, smoky towns and winding roads, green fields and red pillar boxes. It has a flavor of its own. Moreover it is continuous, it stretches into the future and the past, there is something in it that persists, as in a living creature.

—*George Orwell, 1944*[140]

Academic analysts have noted connections in British nationalism since the 1970s between immigration and racial harmony. Some have argued that the former is policed with greater vigilance than the latter—that is, that immigration control is implemented with greater gusto than the Race Relations Acts.[141] Others have shown how race is linked to culture in discussions of familial and social values. Culture has been treated as a gene (a "living creature" in Orwell's words) passed along from one generation to another, so denying the possibility that black people can become British.[142] Even when not mentioned, race has been found in discussion of such social issues as the growth of unemployment, policing of inner-city areas, and urban "riots."[143]

This section will set those nationalist practices in historical context to demonstrate continuities over time. The inscriptions written onto settlers from the "new Commonwealth" since the 1970s may be novel, but they are analogous in many ways to those used before—hence the comparisons found between political protest in urban Britain and on the streets of Northern Ireland.

Protestant Individuals

Protestantism was central to first English and then British nationalism. Greenfeld has described religion as "perhaps the most significant among the

factors that furthered the development of the English national consciousness." The authorization of a King James Bible stimulated literacy and
instilled in the common people who read it "a novel sense of human—individual—dignity, which was instantly to become one of their dearest posses-
sions."[144]

The persecution of Protestants by Queen Mary aided a correspondence
between Protestant revolt and national identity. Transformed into national
heroes and saints, religious martyrs were offered up as examples of a distinctively English Christian character in John Foxe's 1563 *Book of Martyrs*.
The Reformation was a nationalist struggle against the Church of Rome.[145]

Colley has argued that Foxe linked religious tyranny to Roman
Catholicism everywhere. Catholics were traitors, especially during social
unrest and war. The Anglican Church and newspapers reinforced that view,
as did different historic events. Among the most significant were the attempt
in 1605 by a Catholic, Guido Fawkes, to blow up the Houses of Parliament;
the Counter-Reformation movement in Europe in the early 1700s; and continental support for Stuart claimants to the throne.[146]

Fear of Catholics fed what Colley has labeled "intolerant Protestantism," a Christian-nationalism that treated Catholicism as un-British and
excluded those who practiced it from political office. The so-called
Toleration Act of 1689 was for Protestant nonconformists, not for Roman
Catholics. Religious intolerance furthered British nationalism, according to
Colley, by serving "as a powerful cement between the English, the Welsh
and the Scots, particularly lower down the social scale."[147]

It is not only against Catholic France that Britain has been defined.
Compared at different times to dogs and Africans, Irish people in England
"were described by many Victorians in racial terms."[148] Without much fac-
tual evidence, Irish immigrants to England were said to be diseased, crimi-
nally inclined, and lazy.[149] After World War I, "No Irish" signs appeared in
the Midlands of England, and hostility toward Irish Catholics was evident in
areas of heavy settlement such as Liverpool. In Scotland, militant Protestant
organizations opposed Irish immigration. A report, "The Menace of the Irish
Race to Our Scottish Nationality," for example, was given to the 1923 synod
of the Church of Scotland.[150]

As Holmes has pointed out, images of Irish people as apes were reinforced but not solely dependent on the activities of the Irish Republican
Army (IRA), for they came from an established tradition of racial stereo-
typing. Such images "smacked of the same hostility that identified Jews as
responsible for all social problems of the inter-war East End of London."[151]

Irish people are still associated in Britain with lawless savagery and
mental stupidity. The former image is reinforced by coverage of the IRA and
events in Northern Ireland, while the latter finds continual expression in
popular comedy. "Have you heard the one about the Irishman" is a standard

opening to a British joke. But Catholicism is less a marker of difference than it once was. This may be because, as George Orwell claimed in 1944, "the common [British] people are without definite religious belief, and have been so for centuries."[152] It may also be because the rational individualism traceable by Marx and Weber (among others) to the Protestant Reformation has been redirected as a weapon of exclusion.

As previous discussion demonstrated, the idea of Sikhs as communal was tied by Enoch Powell to repatriation and immigration control. Margaret Thatcher also constructed an image of "the basic drives and instincts of the overwhelming majority of free men and women" in Britain from Protestant individualism. British "instincts" were turned against an assortment of "collectivist" enemies in the Mineworkers' Union, the IRA, the Greater London Council, and the Labour Party.[153]

In 1993, Winston Churchill's grandson (of the same name) called for a halt to a "relentless flow of immigrants" into Britain to avert the prospect of "the muezzin . . . calling Allah's faithful to the high street mosque" for Friday prayers. Many of those to distance themselves from Churchill's remarks heard echoes (not surprisingly) of Enoch Powell. Yet some critics were not as far from either man as they seemed. Prime Minister John Major, for example, tied British national identity to traditional religion and the safety of old white women when he expressed confidence that in fifty years' time, "spinsters will still be cycling to Communion on Sunday morning."[154]

Royal Families

The French are no less French, the Dutch no less Dutch for being members of the [European] community for 20 years. . . . Nor shall we be any less British. The other countries have their own royal families. So shall we. Indeed, when the four new members join, six out of 10 members of the community will be monarchies.　　*—Edward Heath, 1971*[155]

If the Protestant Church is less a national symbol than it once was, the situation of the British monarchy is less clear-cut. The separation of church, monarchy, and nation is also historically novel. In the sixteenth century (thanks again to the influence of Foxe's *Book of Martyrs*), nationalism and Protestantism converged in the body of Queen Elizabeth I. The successor to Mary and head of the Anglican Church, "Elizabeth was a sign of God's recognition of the nation's goodness, of England's being a chosen people."[156] It was via the embodiment of England in Elizabeth that the nation was gendered for almost fifty years as a woman.

The reigns of two Stuarts, James and Charles, broke the association of nation and monarchy. Their policies were interpreted as assaults on freedom, and the religious confrontation one of Crown against nation. A reconciliation was effected briefly in the Restoration, only to be torn asunder by the 1688 revolution. For Oliver Cromwell and others, "Nationalism was about the right of participation in the government of the polity—it was about liberty, and not monarchy or religion."[157]

The monarchy became a *British* symbol (as opposed to a symbol of England or a resurgence of royal political power) during the reign of George III. In an era of military defeat and political change, George seemed reassuringly stable and normal (despite his famed insanity). As one after another European monarchy fell, the king's personal and royal longevity was contrasted favorably to events in revolutionary France. According to Colley, British culture was "an essentially 'masculine' culture . . . caught up in an eternal rivalry with an essentially 'effeminate' France."[158] Through the Royal Jubilee of 1809 and subsequent ritual, "British patriotic and public display was rendered distinctive by focusing it on the monarch."[159]

If Elizabeth I symbolized liberty, the monarchy after George III became a sign of domestic stability and order. That is why Margaret Thatcher recalled the spirit of Sir Walter Raleigh and Elizabeth I when celebrating individualism,[160] and Edward Heath found European community in the institution of the royal family.

Houses of Parliament

British democracy is less of a fraud than it sometimes appears. . . . At any time the ruling class will rob, mismanage, sabotage, lead us into the muck; but let popular opinion really make itself heard . . . and it is difficult for them not to respond.
—*George Orwell, 1944*[161]

It was the British people who took the lead in asserting liberty as a fundamental human right and who devised political institutions to protect and to promote it. We have planted that doctrine and those institutions in every quarter of the globe.
—*Margaret Thatcher, 1975*[162]

The symbolic significance of Parliament is displayed in a uniquely British ritual. Eschewing Halloween on October 31, Britons instead fete Guy Fawkes Day. This begins in the last week of October when children construct straw men known as Guys. The Guys are paraded for several days— with the expectation of pecuniary reward—to admiring neighbors ("a penny for the Guy" is the standard refrain). Large communal or private bonfires are meanwhile constructed in preparation for a night of festival. On November

5, the Guys are placed atop the bonfires and set alight, while observers eat treacle toffee, roast chestnuts, and explode fireworks.

The Guy represents not an ordinary man but the Catholic plotter Guido Fawkes. To the populace, Guy Fawkes Day probably means nothing more than a party and pocket money. But in a nationalist sense the event symbolizes the longevity of British institutions and their capacity to withstand enemy assault.

The Houses of Parliament are the home and guarantor of individual liberty and popular democracy. This inscription dates from the time of John Locke, when liberty and democracy were tied to popular representation in government. Whatever its origins or worth, the idea that a democratic polity guarantees the right of private individuals to do as they please—as Orwell said, "to have a home of your own, to do what you like in your spare time, to choose your own amusements instead of having them chosen for you from above"[163]—has been used to justify racial discrimination.

As mentioned earlier, discrimination has been practiced routinely in housing and employment. The Race Relations Acts were written to give legal redress to its victims. To Enoch Powell, the legislation and not the behaviors it was designed to forestall was inconsistent with British culture. Equality before the law, he argued, "does not mean that the immigrant and his descendants should be elevated into a privileged or special class, or that the citizen should be denied his right to discriminate in the management of his own affairs between one fellow citizen and another." Britons should not support laws "enacted to give the stranger, the disgruntled and the *agent provocateur* the power to pillory them for their private actions."[164]

The mere presence and continuity of the parliamentary household has been taken as a sign that the national culture is democratic, regardless of how its members act. The corollary is that peoples without parliaments are strangers to democracy and thus to British culture. This produces a tendency for Commonwealth countries to be dismissed, in Holmes's words, as "assorted mango dictatorships and for the Commonwealth itself to be written off as a dud institution."[165]

Hospitable Tolerance

Two myths, basic to the philosophy of propagandists against immigrants, have sustained prejudice against them. . . . One of them is that Britain has always had a tradition of hospitable tolerance towards previous waves of immigrants. The other is that present settlers are so inferior to them that they are, and will remain, more of a liability to modern, civilized Britain than an asset.   —*The Times, 1976*[166]

We have proved to be over the generations an extremely tolerant society. I am sure everyone hopes that we shall continue to
be so. Our position as a nation depends on being a tolerant
and generous society.   —*William Whitelaw, 1981*[167]

Examples of intolerance mentioned by *The Times* in 1976 were: the expulsion of 16,000 Jews in 1290, "after many of them were victims of violence
and others of murder"; the eighteenth-century fear that "negroes" would
swamp the country; the 1905 Aliens Act; the riots against "coloreds" in
1919; and the 1962 Commonwealth Immigrants Act.[168] This list was by no
means exhaustive. Yet the nineteenth-century inscription of Britain as a tolerant and open society has proved remarkably tenacious. It is an inscription
tied to race in a twofold sense.

First, as Holmes has argued, white people have been constructed as tolerant of black immigrants, despite all evidence to the contrary. The national
myth is that "these groups have been positively and voluntarily endured and
that a pronounced degree of self-restraint has been evident in the responses
they have encountered."[169]

Second, acts of violence and murder by nationals have been blamed on
aliens for being in the country. Victims of racial attack have then been scripted as intolerant for resisting. In 1976, for example, youth leaders in the
Southall area of London organized a demonstration against repeated attacks
on Asian settlers. Following the murder of Gurdip Chaggar (for which five
white teenagers were subsequently charged), more than 2,000 Asian and
West Indian Britons "threatened to take the law into their own hands and to
search for the killer." The demonstration "suddenly got out of hand" and
Southall—described by a local MP as "a model as far as toleration is concerned in view of the number of immigrants"—remained tense for several
days.[170]

Sydney Bidwell, MP, blamed poor race relations on recent statements
by Powell.[171] Spokespersons for Asians faulted the newly formed British
National Party (BNP) for inflaming "relatively harmless antagonism
between Asians and the host community."[172] Labour MP Andrew Faulds
cited discrimination and "the inherited assumptions of our imperial past,"[173]
while Margaret Thatcher (then leader of the Conservative Party) pointed to
"endless numbers in a country which was more densely populated than
Pakistan or India."[174]

As in the past, violence was accompanied by demands for a total ban on
"the tide of immigrants" supposedly flowing into the country.[175] Even those
who resisted demands for repatriation made similar assumptions about the
effects of settlement. An article in *The Times,* for example, described how
"within memory Southall has changed from a small, neat and clean village
in the country into a foreign town,"[176] the assumption being that the town

was purely foreign and not a hybrid. Another article described research that "shows that one immigrant in every seven born in Bradford is part-colored,"[177] thus applying the word *immigrant* even to British-born children with one native parent.

Perhaps the most telling response came from the Labour Party government. Deploring the demonstrations that followed it and not the murder itself, Prime Minister James Callaghan "urged people not to allow passion to destroy Britain's reputation as a tolerant, cohesive and unified society." The Race Relations Bill before Parliament was simultaneously offered as evidence that racialized minorities "are free to live here as free and equal citizens with everybody else."[178]

As for the BNP, it won a local election in the East End of London in 1993, in an area where "marriage of Asian and English customs is unabashed and potent." Derek Beackon, the candidate who won by seven votes, did so with a combination of demands for repatriation and reforms to housing policy.[179] According to Tory MP Winston Churchill, "The very large scale of immigration . . . adds to the pressure in these communities and provokes reactions."[180]

Law and Order

> Everyone believes in his heart that the law can be, ought to be, and on the whole, will be impartially administered. . . . The hanging judge, that evil old man . . . who will at any rate interpret the law according to the books and will in no circumstances take a money bribe, is one of the symbolic figures of England.
> —*George Orwell, 1944*[181]

> Riot in the streets is a catching disease, and an epidemic in Britain is raging now. . . . Plenty of high-unemployment British cities still confine mob violence to its natural home in and around the football grounds. . . . There is a pan-European spread of street-mobs of the young, not just in Britain so vulnerable to televised contagion from Ulster.
> —*The Economist, 1981*[182]

The association of race with criminality, savagery, and disease has a long history in British nationalism. This association has taken one of two (not unrelated) forms. Either diseased aliens provoke national lawlessness and undermine stability or lawless aliens infect the nation with their savage criminality. The law itself is assumed to be "impartially administered" and racially blind.

The nineteenth-century serial killer Jack the Ripper was imagined to be

Jewish. After one particularly gruesome murder, a pogrom almost occurred in the East End of London. *The East London Observer* wrote in 1888 that "it was repeatedly asserted that no Englishman could have perpetrated such a horrible crime . . . and that it must have been done by a JEW—and forthwith the crowds began to threaten and abuse such of the unfortunate Hebrews as they found in the streets."[183]

Sander Gilman has shown that once the murderer was rumored to be infected with syphilis, he became more quickly Jewish. Jews were associated with sexual corruption (the frequenting of prostitutes) and with the incidence and spread of disease. Absence of material evidence to support the "Jewish Jack" thesis did not negate its force. Statistical evidence that Jews had a lower incidence of syphilis than the general population was read as proof of immunity through centuries of exposure. According to Gilman, "Studies assumed that biological difference as well as the social difference of the Jews was at the root of their seeming 'immunity.'"[184]

Syphilis, in turn, was thought to turn skin black. Jews were described by some race scientists as a "mongrel race," the product of racial mixing between Israelites and ancient Egyptians. Thus, "Jews are black because they are different, because their sexuality is different, because their sexual pathology is written on their skin."[185] From this combination of ideas sprang the assumption that Jack the Ripper was no Englishman.

These same inscriptions of law and order were at work again almost a century later, in nationalist assessments of the so-called race riots of the 1980s. The government-appointed Scarman Inquiry of 1981 has generated almost as much scholarly analysis as the events themselves.[186] Some reporters at the time resisted any easy analogy to the United States in the 1960s and argued that British cities (with the exception, perhaps, of battles between Asian Britons and skinheads in Southall) were not in the grip of racial violence between white and black.[187] Yet evidence that these were multiracial affairs did not prevent the attribution of blame to a "colored" presence in the country.

The events of 1981 were read as a predictable effect of liberal immigration policies. As Walvin has noted, "For many, the riots were the fulfilment of Enoch Powell's infamous prophecy, couched in classical imagery in 1968, which predicted future violence in British cities."[188] Powell himself asked William Whitelaw (the home secretary) and his government to "bear in mind in view of the prospective increase of the relevant population, that they have seen nothing yet."[189]

In many respects the "riots" were anything *but* a triumph for Powell, who had suggested in contradictory fashion in 1968 that Britons would flee before the enemy hordes and at the same time rout the invaders. The centers of unrest (Brixton and Southall in London, Toxteth in Liverpool, and Moss Side in Manchester) were in areas of racial mixing and so defied prediction of whole towns "gone black." Also, it was only in Southall that white Britons sided with the police against local blacks. The following description by *The Economist* of what happened in Brixton paints a different portrait:

> Those who consider the Brixton drama a "racial confrontation" should ponder the scene last Sunday morning, in the brief interlude between violent clashes. Outside about half of the neat, ugly little houses in the side-streets off Railton Road stood their owners—elderly white Cockneys, mostly women, all wretched. Beside them, protective, stood bunches of their younger black neighbors, watching to keep the trouble off.[190]

Absent from this and other scenes (such as those where whites and blacks queued outside stores to loot them of their contents and collectively hurled missiles at police from behind street barricades) was Powell's image of the "wide-grinning piccaninnies" who terrified old ladies. The complex effect of economic reconstruction, housing deterioration, racial discrimination, and police campaigns against "mugging" (a crime attributed to a black youth subculture since the 1970s),[191] the urban Britain of 1981 was not one predicted by Powell. *The Times* described the riots as "a severe blow to British self-esteem" and a contributor to feelings of "national anguish," not as the fulfilment of a racial prophecy.[192]

Those who refused to follow Powell's lead still assumed that the law—personified not by hanging judges but by British "bobbies"—was impartial. Amid questions about police practices when stopping, searching, and detaining anyone suspected of a crime (the so-called sus laws),[193] Conservative MP Eldon Griffiths insisted that "there is no justice in suggesting that the Metropolitan Police are in any sense racially motivated."[194] Suggestions that the police were not only impartial but also the innocent victims of well-planned attacks were used to justify the first-ever use of CS gas outside of Northern Ireland (against rioters in Liverpool)[195] and government plans to "snatch people from the streets" and detain them in army camps.[196]

Publications such as *The Times* and *The Economist* did not follow the Tories in absolving the police of responsibility for the unrest. Media willingness to uncover racist attitudes among policemen challenged their reputation for impartial administration of race-blind laws. Denying an upsurge in racially motivated attacks in Southall, for example, a local policeman claimed that "these people [Asians] generalize from the particular."[197] The chief constable of Merseyside police, Kenneth Oxford, said his force was attacked in Toxteth because "we are the readily identifiable symbols of authority and discipline which is anathema to these people.[198] Three months earlier in Brixton, a bus full of policemen chanted "good old Enoch, send the bastards home."[199]

Despite such probing and seemingly objective reporting, those sources just cited managed simultaneously to draw a portrait of an innocent polity (as represented by the police) under attack from an enemy presence. Photographs of "blood spattered and weary" policemen[200] were accompanied by detailed tallies and descriptions of their injuries (which clearly outnumbered those inflicted upon the rioters);[201] by the classification of events as "battles";[202] and by the prominence given to police interpretations of the unrest. These shifted attention from the "sus" laws to such factors as "an almost inbred tendency for the colored people to believe they ought to be able to do their own thing";[203] a misdirected disaffection with social deprivation;[204] and an irresponsibility on the part of parents who allowed their children to go on an "uncivilized rampage."[205]

What remains to be demonstrated is how the 1980s riots—when they were not attributed to "contagion from Ulster" and thus blamed on Irish people—could be made the responsibility of "colored" people alone. For there was no shortage of white people willing to stray from their "natural home" at the soccer clubs and take violence into the streets.

Were it not for the presence of "coloreds" among them, white Britons would not have vented their frustrations on public property and the forces of law and order. This message was conveyed via reports suggesting no white person initiated any of the 1981 riots (the notion that whites only joined in later, when the looting started) and in stories that downplayed the presence of white Britons by describing the rioters as "mostly black."[206] It was conveyed, more subtly, by headlines that singled out blacks for blame. The "black youths" who attacked police in one incident, for example, were marked by color,[207] whereas the "rioters" in Liverpool with irresponsible parents were revealed to be exclusively white only in the accompanying text.[208]

Perhaps nowhere was the above message more manifest than in one particular prediction of future "civic breakdown." Accompanying an analysis of "the deprived areas that spell danger" was a map of "where the colored population is concentrated." It was the "flammable" mix of "unemployment, substandard housing and racial concentration" that apparently rendered these areas susceptible to trouble, not the mere presence of "colored" people. Nonetheless, only "colored" areas were identified as dangerous and only in them was a "firewatch" deemed necessary.[209] Unemployment and poor housing were symbols of deprivation; but people with African, West Indian, or Asian backgrounds were the actual danger.

If the 1981 "riots" were molded to the theme of national contamination, those that occurred four years later tapped into a somewhat different (though not unrelated) set of assumptions. This time the trouble began in the Handsworth area of Birmingham following an altercation between a policeman and a local youth. During the subsequent "trail of violence," two brothers of Asian origin were beaten and burned to death by "black rioters" who set fire to their property.[210] Weeks later an "orgy of violence" occurred (once again) in Brixton after police accidentally shot and paralyzed an innocent woman.[211] In October, the arrest of four men sparked violence in Toxteth, Liverpool.[212] Finally, policeman Keith Blakelock died from knife and machete wounds in the Tottenham area of London.[213]

Murder and mayhem in areas of predicted danger reinforced expectations of lawless savagery and mindless cruelty. Despite some attribution of blame to "powerlessness, poverty and racism,"[214] emphasis on "malice and criminal inspiration" seemed more widespread than four years earlier. In contrast to its demands for a public inquiry into the 1981 Brixton riots, for example,[215] *The Times* now demanded "unequivocal" support for the police on the grounds that "democratic politics itself is threatened."[216] Describing as "appropriate" an emphasis on "the criminality of the outburst," the newspaper then favored an "internal Whitehall review" rather than a "wide-ranging inquiry into the origin of the night's events in Birmingham."[217]

Traditional stereotypes were not undermined by the apparent presence of heroin and cocaine dealers in Handsworth. The lord mayor of Birmingham, Frank Carter, was probably not alone in blaming "absolute thuggery gone mad on drugs" for the troubles.[218] But more than a preoccupation with criminality and drugs was at work in analyses of the violence. From the statements of new Home Secretary Douglas Hurd[219] to the reports of newspaper correspondents,[220] it was stressed repeatedly that trouble broke out in precisely those areas that had been the major beneficiaries of government funding, private enterprise schemes, and community policing. Something other than social deprivation must therefore account for what had happened.[221]

Critical questions could have been asked about the presumed efficacy of government "aid" or the assumption that progressive change had indeed occurred. Instead, *The Times* offered descriptive, demographic profiles of the Handsworth area of Birmingham and the Broadwater Farm Estate in Tottenham (the scene of the initial violence). Both were identified as predominantly black (in the latter case, because of white flight from "the trouble") and as disproportionately young.[222]

Was there something not understood about the combination of being young (therefore born British?), black, and poor? Was it possible that when expectations of equal opportunity met the reality of racial discrimination, feelings of despair, hopelessness, and social alienation were the predictable outcome? Found in U.S. newspaper coverage of events in Britain,[223] these sorts of questions were missing from British sources such as *The Times*. In their absence, stories that highlighted only numbers and the "higher density of young people"[224] played to historic fears (so forcefully articulated by Powell) of swamping by an enemy presence. They also reworked the idea inherent in the "mugging" scares of the 1970s that black youth are prone for no particular reason to criminality and violence. As Lawrence has pointed out, this is a notion that feeds in turn on constructions of the black family as pathological and its home life as culturally inferior.[225]

Finally, accounts of brutal murder and suggestions of money wasted were reminiscent of colonial scriptures. These can be traced back to the period following the abolition of slavery in 1838 and the Indian Mutiny of 1857. At those times, according to Walvin, "many became disillusioned with the altruism which had been invested in the black cause." Earlier faith in the capacity of Christian peoples to "civilize the natives" gave way to essentialist arguments about the "original nature" of the "damned nigger" (who was not only African but Indian as well). The "nigger" was deemed unworthy of the effort invested in his development because he would not or could not retain civilization in the absence of white control and guardianship.[226]

The conviction that "coloreds" will throw off the trappings of civilization once the white man's back is turned is consistent with an aspect of what Banton has called the "English world-view," namely the assumption that culture cannot be taught. "The Englishman," according to Banton, "is irritated rather than flattered by imitation." If culture is unique to a particular nation or group, those who imitate do not necessarily become fellow nationals: "Like 'half-castes,' they are neither the one nor the other."[227]

Sports and Entertainment

> All the culture that is most truly native centres round things which even when they are communal are not official—the pub, the football match, the back garden, the fireside and the 'nice cup of tea.'   —*George Orwell, 1944*[228]

> Most of us feel no sense of identity with Ulstermen, Falkland Islanders or Gibraltarians but will cheer unequivocally for John Barnes or Nigel Benn.   —*The Guardian, 1990*[229]

The presence of black people in sports and entertainment in Britain stands in some contrast to their near total absence from those other symbols of the nation's culture discussed above. As Lawrence has pointed out, sports and entertainment have long been considered appropriate venues for those with "natural" rhythm and athletic ability.[230] Even in eighteenth-century Britain there were black boxers and successful musicians, such as Billy Waters, the one-legged fiddler.[231] It is not only Irish people who are the butt of popular jokes: "The stand-up comic has only to effect an Asian or 'West Indian' accent to raise a laugh, and of course language in particular and 'race' in general have become popular themes in situation comedies."[232]

Yet in "truly native" culture is found support for Gilroy's argument that "blacks are British even as their presence redefines the meaning of the term."[233] That staple of the British pub lunch, the pork pie, has been joined by such exotic fare as French-bread sandwiches filled with tandoori chicken and mayonnaise. John Barnes of Liverpool ("Niggerpool" is one of its local nicknames) is only one of a number of black men (not to mention Europeans) who play for top British soccer teams. Curry is as likely to be eaten in the late hours of the day as fish and chips. A genre of popular music known as "two-tone" (because the bands were multiracial) sprang up in the 1970s. As for popular entertainment, the satirical comedy "Spitting Images" once ran a sketch where the queen gave her crown to the black boxer Frank Bruno instead of to her son Prince Charles.

It is because British culture is *not* fixed and impervious to change that sports and entertainment (as in South Africa) are important sites of nationalist activity. Just as evidence of white Britons throwing petrol bombs at police undermines constructions of a law-abiding nation, the presence of curried meat in a French baguette shows the hybridity of postcolonial British culture. So if it is to reinvent a static national character, nationalism must stand vigilant against any and all such practices. The seemingly harmless amusements of black and Asian Britons (those certainly considered a private affair if engaged in by whites) have thus been subject to nationalist scrutiny.

Two examples will suffice. The first is perhaps the most creative in the way it linked annual holidays to plans for of a ministry for repatriation. Here again stands the figure of Enoch Powell. In 1968 Powell suggested that because people from the West Indies, India, or Pakistan went "back home" for every holiday, they were not really loyal to their adoptive Britain. In recognition of this, an "organized, financed and subsidized repatriation and re-emigration" effort would be "as profoundly humane as it is far-sighted."[234] Needless to say, the logic of the argument that those who spend two weeks a year in the same place should remain there for the other fifty has not been applied to white Britons.

The second example concerns reggae music, a genre associated by some with drugs, noise, overcrowding, unemployment, and prostitution.[235] In response to an "eleven day non-stop party" that allegedly took place in Birmingham at the end of 1980, Tory MP Jill Knight proposed to ban all West Indian house parties. Having outraged the local black community with this suggestion, she later blamed urban unrest on bad parents who failed to "teach discipline and restraint."[236]

Curry, reggae music, house parties, and visits to Asia—such seemingly harmless amusements have been treated as alien imports and a threat to British culture. None of them is the exclusive preserve of "immigrant" people and households. But evidence of their dissemination to the "natives" (the ones that welcome difference and not merely tolerate it) gives cold comfort to those who consider it evidence of contamination and national decline.

TALES OF NATION AND EMPIRE

[Britain] resembles a family, a rather stuffy Victorian family, with not many black sheep in it but with all its cupboards bursting with skeletons. . . . It is a family in which the young are generally thwarted and most of the power is in the hands of irresponsible uncles and bedridden aunts. Still, it is a family. It has its private language and its common memories, and at the approach of an enemy it closes its ranks.

—*George Orwell, 1944*[237]

As Orwell's words suggest, the idea of Britons as a family—however dysfunctional—depends in part on a stock of common memories. As with any national history, this one has been raided selectively for significance and meaning. The same events have been reinterpreted at various times to produce different lessons, as when Edward Heath found a European identity for Britain in its history of warfare. But certain memories endure through continuous revival. The most stable in the British context are those that recur to the Protestant past and World War II; another is the memory and practice of empire, where the twin notions of time—as a possession and a journey—come together to create the British nation as a progenitor of global development.

Common Memories: A Puritan Family at War

As one surveys the passing crowd, one remembers George Orwell's description of the British as a people with knobbly faces and decent instincts.

—*The Daily Telegraph, D-Day Anniversary, 1994*[238]

Kraut-bashing is a disease that is rotting Britain from the head down. . . . It is an outlook that is prejudiced against anything new, different or foreign. . . . Nostalgia for the Second World War and hostility to everything German are among its most powerful ingredients.   —*The Independent, 1994*[239]

If there is anything akin in British nationalism to the Afrikaner mythology of the Great Trek, it is the Protestant story of the Puritan Rebellion. Described by Greenfeld as a "momentous move whose significance was not to be appreciated until two centuries later,"[240] this was the emigration of some 60,000 people from England in the mid–seventeenth century in the name of religious freedom. Retained for posterity in John Bunyan's

Pilgrim's Progress, the story of this enforced exile has been retold in ways that reinforce two different (but not incompatible) inscriptions of the British nation.

The first is the notion of Britain as analogous to the biblical people of Israel. Britons have been imagined as a chosen people, a nation that finds God's grace through suffering and death in His name.[241] Amid the battles of World War II (an event that reinforced this particular image), Orwell suggested that the historical memories of the "common people" are devoid of victory. Popular battle poems such as "The Charge of the Light Brigade" are always tales "of disasters and defeats."[242] It is not a celebration of incompetence that is at work here, but an expectation of redemption after a period of sacrificial suffering.

Related to this is the idea of the Puritans as bearers of truth, liberty, and courage. Being true to the spirit of "our fathers and grandfathers" might mean a willingness to strike out for territories unknown (and plant therein the old British virtues), or simply a willingness to stand up (at home or abroad) to the forces of tyranny and oppression.

Perhaps no one in recent times has used the legacy of the Puritans— their spirit of Protestant individualism—to greater effect than Margaret Thatcher. According to the magazine *The New Statesman and Society,* Thatcher "plundered" history "at will" while casting herself as "the solitary pilgrim of Protestant England's first tale, *Pilgrim's Progress.*"[243] She found an essentially masculine spirit of Britain (one personified in her speeches in the figure of Sir Walter Raleigh) in mercantile England, in the Victorian age, and in (not surprisingly) her own Conservative government. The "iron lady" unleashed the ghosts of the ancestors in support of the Falklands War and against various domestic adversaries. Britain must remember, she said in 1980, "that a nation is an extended family."[244] Her stories cast the Labour Party and assorted like minds as Britain's "irresponsible uncles and bedridden aunts," while her own party defended the interests of its brave young men.[245]

As much as it has recurred to the Puritan past, British nationalism has kept alive the memory of World War II. As mentioned in part one of this chapter, memory of war has been ritualized in annual Remembrance Day celebrations; it has also been retained through such fictional productions as the 1970s television series *A Family at War.* What is remembered is an instinctive national character, not the social divisions, low morale, and popular radicalism identified by some historians[246] but an organic community coming together (in Orwell's words) "like a herd of cattle."

Also recalled is opposition to Nazi tyranny, a celebration of democracy that can shade into "Kraut-bashing." As Williamson has noted, active forgetting has accompanied memory, because even in wartime "there were

many signs that the values for which Nazi Germany had been opposed—
racism, anti-semitism and authoritarianism—were themselves part of
British society."[247]

Williamson went on to suggest that "no account of racism in British
society could be complete if it neglected the question of change in the
British Empire and the post-war patterns of colonial politics."[248] The British
Nationality Act and subsequent immigration into Britain are obviously a
cornerstone of any such account. But so too is the way in which that empire
has been remembered.

Global Development

The Afro-Asians are feckless peoples with cultures different
from our own. By our standards they are barbarous. No one
really bothers about the Irish. They don't peddle dope and they
don't kill chickens in the kitchen. This civilization of the North
Sea and of Kipling's five nations is in danger of destruction
through this flood coming in. It must be stopped.
                                            —*John Sanders, 1961*[249]

We can look back at the history of our empire in the confidence that it was not a scourge to other people, but contributed to the well-being of mankind.
                                      —*Margaret Thatcher, 1979*[250]

The British people are not noted for knowledge of imperial history.
According to Orwell, the "sheer hypocrisy" of the working class "takes the
form of not knowing that the Empire exists."[251] Banton made a similar point
in the 1950s. In response to a survey showing that most Britons could not
distinguish a colony from a dominion, Banton suggested that "the colored
man would appear less of a stranger were British people better informed
about the background and aspirations of colored immigrants."[252]

There is a difference between knowing where to find a colony on a map
and knowing how to justify British rule there. Having described the
hypocrisy of "the English," Orwell went on to tell them that "life within the
British Empire was in many ways better than life outside it," even if "the
Empire was underdeveloped" and "India slept in the Middle Ages."[253] What
nationalism has taught is not the situation of colonialism but the idea of
empire as a gift, an idea predicated in turn upon a construction of the
colonies as "backward."

In a study of British racial thought from the late 1890s to the early
1960s, Paul Rich has documented the survival into the twentieth century of
Victorian notions about race. Distinguishing between the "middle opinion"

of the liberal mainstream and the hereditarian doctrines of the conservative right, Rich identified a number of shared assumptions that "left an indelible mark on British attitudes toward race and color."[254]

The general ethos of "middle opinion" was one of faith in the progressive evolution of scientific rationality, an ethos that contrasted with social Darwinist predictions of the extinction of certain races. At least until the Indian Mutiny—after which the idea of India as a static Eastern culture separated permanently from the Western Enlightenment gained greater currency[255]—the former supported a "civilizing mission" while the latter considered it a waste of time. But both differentiated the British nation from more "backward" peoples without scientific reason.

The idea of Britain as a preeminently scientific (rather than literary or religious) nation predates the Victorian age. According to Greenfeld, it was circulating in England as early as the sixteenth century. The contrast then was between the scientific genius of England and the more artistic characters of Italy, France, and Spain.[256] The empiricist science of the nineteenth century used cranial and facial measurements, observations, comparisons, experiments, and classification to rank order races. Scientific reasoning showed that the capacity to reason scientifically was racially given. This tautological logic was resisted by "middle opinion" with the claim that races were not permanently retarded, any more than normal children.

Many centrists believed in the transformatory powers of Christian proselytization and direct rule. Others followed ethnologists like Mary Kingsley (who distinguished between convertible African societies and a permanently Eastern India) in advocating indirect rule. Kingsley believed dissemination of scientific knowledge would "assist these West Africans in their thirteenth century to rise into the nineteenth century state."[257] But in both cases, science was a hallmark of national achievement and racial superiority.

Rich has argued that with the increasing influence of sociology in the early 1900s, the language of "advanced" and "backward" races was replaced with "higher" and "lower" levels of "civilization."[258] Some joined William Arthur in thinking that Indians were not a black race but "sunburnt whitemen." Arthur drew a distinction between the "low development" of black Africans and an Indian civilization that had "fallen."[259] Around the turn of the century also, a multiracial commonwealth of nations with different religions and "degrees of civilization" became a political objective. First suggested by the Labour Party in 1918, the notion of harnessing scientific expertise to imperial development produced the Colonial Development and Welfare Act of 1940.

Rich has pointed out the irony of a British government embracing colonial development—which meant in 1940 "everything which ministers to the physical, mental or moral development of the colonial peoples of whom we are trustees"—just when its guardianship was ending.[260] But if an openness to autonomy and self-rule for the colonies was novel, there were continued linkages to the past. One was the assumption of British cultural superiority. As Lawrence has put it, "The 'end of Empire' was suffused with [a] general attitude of paternal superiority; the talk was all of 'trusteeship,' 'standards,' 'conditions,' 'building up,' 'guidance,' 'responsibility' and 'granting.'"[261]

A second linkage was to geographic (as opposed to cultural) theories of difference, namely the presumption that racial difference requires physical separation. The question of whether colonized peoples share the same cultural traits and thus a single racial identity (they are all "colored" or "heathen") has been answered in different ways. Nationalism still homogenizes (danger is "colored" regardless of who the "rioters" are) and differentiates (older Asians have been scripted as the most law-abiding yet alien residents of Britain).[262]

How the above question is answered would seem to have implications for the drawing of colonial and postcolonial boundaries. A division between Kenya and Tanzania, for example, might be racial as well as territorial. But the only boundary that has really mattered is the one that separates the "highest" level of "civilization" from all the rest. A commonwealth of nations inside the British Isles was not imagined in the 1940s or earlier. Even when black workers were recruited into Britain during World War II, the Colonial Office considered them not as immigrants but as trainee developers for their own countries.[263]

The idea of development erects the same memorial to imperial history that a "civilizing mission" once did. British rule of the colonies is to be remembered in its totality as a gift to humankind, regardless of what its naysayers might claim about specific instances. As a 1946 government pamphlet for schools, entitled *Britain and the Colonies,* expressed it:

> Even the critics of empire now begin to appreciate that the maintenance and strengthening of the British Commonwealth is no sinister imperialism in the worst sense, and that all of us who have a common loyalty to the Throne are honestly trying to create a better world not only for ourselves but for mankind generally.[264]

Given its intended audience, that quote is a reminder of the role schools have as disseminators of nationalist thought. Schools have figured in nationalism in Britain in three different ways. First, the story of the "invasion" of Britain's schools by aliens—like that of the neighborhood that has "gone black"—has been allegorical. The school symbolizes the nation in decline rather than the parlous state of its children's education. One of Enoch Powell's favorite stories, for example (one he often defended against charges of untruth), was of "a constituent whose little daughter was the only white child in her class at school."[265] Young or old, in school or at home, the lone white female was Powell's preferred symbol of a nation under threat. (That Britannia was portrayed as surrounded by black *children* is also significant, for here Powell played upon traditional images of black people as members of childlike races.)

Other nationalist scriptures have focused more literally on children and education. Sometimes, as Rex has pointed out, concern over the impact of immigration on neighborhood schools seems to proceed from the premise that contact with black children as such is retarding.[266] Demands for racially exclusive schools—expressed as a need to maintain standards of excellence and discipline—presuppose that black children have lower standards than whites or are more prone to misbehavior. Despite the officially nonracial nature of the state, such demands have been received sympathetically by the Conservative Party in office. In 1990, for example, the secretary of state for education moved to allow parents to select schools according to racial criteria on the grounds that family preferences supersede the requirements of race relations legislation.[267]

At other times, the concern has been less with the existence in British schools of "immigrant" children per se than with changes to the traditional school curriculum that their presence might suggest. Although not to the same extent as in the United States, there *has* been public debate in Britain—stimulated in some measure by poor exam results and high dropout rates among minority children—about the adequacy of existing curriculums.[268] Government policy in 1987 was for a nationwide core curriculum and standardized tests, an agenda interpreted by detractors and supporters alike as "a struggle for the entrepreneurial heart of the next generation."[269]

Overall, British nationalism continues to remember a benign, nonviolent, and progressive empire. Faith in the gradual evolution of scientific rationality would seem to live on in the "middle opinion" of development thinking and practice, not only in Britain but on a global scale. What is not entirely clear is whether, in Rich's words, the "legacy of a patrician imperial benevolence" has proven adaptable to race relations within Britain itself.[270] The sense that the nation's mission is to develop other races wherever they might be seemed to inform the various domestic welfare agencies that sprang up in the 1950s to help new immigrants assimilate. That sense may also inform government investment in minority communities and other racially based schemas of various sorts.

What is evident is that these projects have coexisted with redoubled efforts at social control and physical expulsion, justifications for which are routinely sought in inscriptions of permanent cultural difference and the unsuitability of Commonwealth peoples for life in Britain.

The idea of a nation closing ranks to defend its territory from invasion is not new—nor is the attempt to cast a mantle of respectability over racial exclusion by treating it as instinctive. But as Martin Barker's study of the "new racism" has shown, what is noteworthy in contemporary Britain is how racial thought has been cloaked in the language of sociobiology. As Barker put it, when racism is "rooted in the genes," demands for racial exclusion and control cannot be condemned. They are forgiven instead as "simply the extension of loving one's family."[271]

In this context, it is not surprising that arson attacks and other incidents of racist violence (which have been written off as "neighborhood disputes") have proliferated since the late 1970s.[272]

At least some of the conditions that made possible the invention of Britain—particularly warfare with Europe and the possession of an empire—have now disappeared. These changes may have enabled the country's "ethnic" nationalisms to gain renewed authority. For example, a novel brand of "little Englandism"—one more easily contained in the past than Scottish or Welsh nationalism—has reappeared since the mid-1980s.[273]

It remains to be seen whether racism against "immigrants" is a glue strong enough to hold Britain together in a changed global context. The construction of black people as a threat and a problem gives continued meaning to the idea of Britain—and Europe. It is not a construction that has gone unchallenged. But unless and until alternative understandings of the nation are more widely embraced, Britishness will remain associated with whiteness.

NOTES

The title of this chapter is drawn from a work of nonfiction by George Orwell. While "highly civilized human beings" were flying overhead during the aerial bombings of World War II, Orwell reflected on the national character of the British/English nation (the two terms were used interchangeably). Acknowledging that national character may change, Orwell yet wrote that "certain alternatives are possible and others not. A seed may grow or not grow, but at any rate a turnip seed never grows into a parsnip." The weeding out of "turnips" is an established practice in Britain. See Orwell, *England Your England,* 37.

1. These words appear on a linen tea towel sold in a tourist shop in the north of England.

2. The racial term *white* as conventionally understood (to refer to "pink" people) is not written *White,* because it is not an official classification in Britain.

3. Colley, *Britons: Forging the Nation, 1707–1837,* 5–6.

4. Here *black* is used instead of *colored,* as an inclusive term for people of Asian, Caribbean, and African descent.

5. Bevan, *The Development of British Immigration Law,* 28.

6. Orwell, *England Your England,* 47–48.

7. John Ardagh, "Barriers to Break Down Before We Can Become Vrai Amis," *The Times,* June 22, 1976, VI.

8. Kearney, "Four Nations or One?" 2.

9. Colley, *Britons,* 3–6.

10. Colley, *Britons*, 15.

11. Bevan, *The Development of British Immigration Law*, 52–57.

12. Bevan, *The Development of British Immigration Law*, 60.

13. Bevan, *The Development of British Immigration Law*, 61–62.

14. Holmes, *A Tolerant Country? Immigrants, Refugees, and Minorities in Britain*, 16–17.

15. Holmes, *A Tolerant Country?* 21.

16. Quoted in Foot, *Immigration and Race in British Politics*, 87.

17. Quoted in Bevan, *The Development of British Immigration Law*, 63–68.

18. Foot, *Immigration and Race in British Politics*, 89.

19. Quoted in Bevan, *The Development of British Immigration Law*, 69.

20. Bevan, *The Development of British Immigration Law*, 30; Holmes, *A Tolerant Country?* 19–23.

21. Holmes, *A Tolerant Country?* 24.

22. Holmes, *A Tolerant Country?* 25–26.

23. Orwell, *England Your England*, 49.

24. Holmes, *A Tolerant Country?* 28.

25. Holmes, *A Tolerant Country?* 27–28.

26. Both quotes are from Foot, *Immigration and Race in British Politics*, 110.

27. Holmes, *A Tolerant Country?* 31–33.

28. Orwell, *England Your England*, 48 and 50.

29. Orwell, *England Your England*, 52.

30. On this and other internments in Britain see Ceserani and Kushner, *The Internment of Aliens in Twentieth Century Britain*.

31. Walvin, *Passage to Britain: Immigration in British History and Politics*, 92.

32. Walvin, *Passage to Britain*, 92.

33. Williamson, "Memories, Vision and Hope: Themes in an Historical Sociology of Britain Since the Second World War."

34. Orwell, *England Your England*, 40.

35. Walvin, *Passage to Britain*, 91–92.

36. Holmes, *A Tolerant Country?* 37.

37. Williamson, "Memories, Vision and Hope," 168.

38. Walvin, *Passage to Britain*, 90.

39. Cited in Bevan, *The Development of British Immigration Law*, 58.

40. Walvin, *Passage to Britain*, 33–35.

41. Walvin, *Passage to Britain*, 34.

42. Quoted in Lawrence, "Just Plain Common Sense: The 'Roots' of Racism," 57.

43. Colley, *Britons*, 102–105.

44. Colley, *Britons*, 111–113.

45. Colley, *Britons*, 90.

46. Colley, *Britons*, 114.

47. Colley, *Britons*, 121–128.

48. Colley, *Britons*, 140–144.

49. Colley, *Britons*, 145.

50. Quoted in Walvin, *Passage to Britain*, 44–45.

51. Quoted in Banton, *White and Colored: The Behavior of British People Towards Colored Immigrants*, 102.

52. Quoted in Smithies and Fiddick, *Enoch Powell on Immigration*, 37.

53. Nkrumah, *Ghana: The Autobiography of Kwame Nkrumah*, 48–52.

54. Nkrumah, *Ghana*, 58.

55. Walvin, *Passage to Britain*, 42–43.

56. Walvin, *Passage to Britain*, 108.

57. Holmes, *A Tolerant Country?* 48–51.

58. Walvin, *Passage to Britain*, 104.

59. Williamson, "Memories, Vision and Hope," 173.

60. Bevan, *The Development of British Immigration Law*, 76.

61. Holmes, *A Tolerant Country?* 53.

62. See in general Rex, *Race, Colonialism and the City*.

63. Quoted in Pilkington, *Beyond the Mother Country: West Indians and the Notting Hill White Riots*, 111.

64. All quotes from Pilkington, *Beyond the Mother Country*, 129–131.

65. Quoted in Pilkington, *Beyond the Mother Country*, 131–132.

66. Bevan, *The Development of British Immigration Law*, 77.

67. Pilkington, *Beyond the Mother Country*, 133–134.

68. Pilkington, *Beyond the Mother Country*, 125–135.

69. Walvin, *Passage to Britain*, 109.

70. Foot, *Immigration and Race in British Politics*, 134.

71. Moore, *Racism and Black Resistance in Britain*, 27.

72. See in general Smithies and Fiddick, *Enoch Powell on Immigration*.

73. Quoted in Smithies and Fiddick, *Enoch Powell on Immigration*, 36.

74. Quoted in Smithies and Fiddick, *Enoch Powell on Immigration*, 74–75.

75. Quoted in Smithies and Fiddick, *Enoch Powell on Immigration*, 40.

76. Quoted in Smithies and Fiddick, *Enoch Powell on Immigration*, 68.

77. Quoted in Smithies and Fiddick, *Enoch Powell on Immigration*, 63.

78. Smithies and Fiddick, *Enoch Powell on Immigration*, 94.

79. Quoted in Smithies and Fiddick, *Enoch Powell on Immigration*, 42.

80. See Manzo, *Domination, Resistance, and Social Change in South Africa*, chapter 1.

81. Quoted in Smithies and Fiddick, *Enoch Powell on Immigration*, 119–122.

82. Quoted in Smithies and Fiddick, *Enoch Powell on Immigration*, 77.

83. Walvin, *Passage to Britain*, 15.

84. Foot, *Immigration and Race in British Politics*, 232.

85. Quoted in Smithies and Fiddick, *Enoch Powell on Immigration*, 20.

86. Quoted in Smithies and Fiddick, *Enoch Powell on Immigration*, 20.

87. Quoted in Smithies and Fiddick, *Enoch Powell on Immigration*, 41–43.

88. Smithies and Fiddick, *Enoch Powell on Immigration*, 59.

89. Gilroy, *There Ain't No Black in the Union Jack: The Cultural Politics of Race and Nation*, 46.

90. Bevan, *The Development of British Immigration Law*, 82.

91. Bevan, *The Development of British Immigration Law*, 83.

92. Quoted in Smith, "Britain in the New Europe," 164.

93. See Smith, "Britain in the New Europe," 158.

94. Quoted in *The Times*, July 9, 1971, 5.

95. Charles Hargrove, "At Last, an Amicable Settlement to That Torrid 'English Affair,'" *The Times*, January 1, 1973, 14.

96. See the editorial "Towards a European Britain," *The Times*, July 8, 1971.

97. Quoted in Roger Berthoud, "British White Paper Praised for Its Style and Expression of the Ideals of the Case for Entry," *The Times*, July 9, 1971.

98. Quoted in Denis Taylor, "White Paper Says Terms Are Fair and Reasonable," *The Times*, July 8, 1971, 1.

99. Taylor, "White Paper Says Terms Are Fair," 5.

100. The government argued that citizens of the "old Commonwealth" were already provided for. Hence there was no need to write special provisions into EC regulations. See John Groser, "Only Minor Changes in Immigrants Policy," *The Times,* January 2, 1973, 1.

101. See Lord Walston, "Definition of British Nationality," *The Times,* December 2, 1972.

102. For one such contestation see Jerome Caminada, "Kith and Kin: A Myth Wearing Thin?" *The Times,* December 2, 1972.

103. See "Text of Mr. Wilson's Broadcast on the Common Market," *The Times,* July 10, 1971, 4.

104. A Harris poll published by *The Daily Express* showed that 20 percent of respondents were in favor of joining the EC, 57 percent were against, and 23 percent were undecided. The number against was lower than the 62 percent reported in a similar poll conducted two months earlier, leading *The Times* to headline that "Public Support for Entry Is Growing." See the article published July 8, 1971, 1.

105. See the letter by Mrs. C. K. Allington, Letters to the Editor, *The Times,* July 8, 1971.

106. See Mr. Charles Longbottom, "Sovereignty in the EEC" (in Letters to the Editor), *The Times,* July 5, 1971.

107. See "Sir Alec Sees Greater Political Influence for Britain Inside the Common Market," *The Times,* July 10, 1971.

108. See Mr. A. E. Holdsworth, QC, in Letters to the Editor, *The Times,* July 3, 1971.

109. This reassurance was given by Jean Rey, president of the European Commission in 1970. See "Confidence on EEC Entry," *The Times,* July 5, 1971.

110. See Roger Berthoud, "Conformity at Home and Ease at Work," *The Times,* July 6, 1971.

111. See "A Great Day for Europe," *The Times,* January 1, 1973.

112. The quote is from Walter Behrendt of West Germany while he was president of the European Parliament. See "Chance to Develop Unified and Democratic Europe," *The Times,* January 17, 1973. See also Ralf Dahrendorf's discussion of the EC's "search for a European personality," in Roger Berthoud, "Dr. Dahrendorf's Appeal for a Liberal and Outward-Looking European Foreign Policy," *The Times,* January 11, 1973, 6.

113. See Edward Heath, "Opening of an Era Offers Britons the Chance of Guiding Events," *The Times,* January 2, 1973.

114. Louis Heren, "The Times: Meeting Challenge of New Frontier," *The Times,* January 1, 1973, 1.

115. See "Forward into Europe: 1," *The Times,* January 2, 1973, VIII–XII.

116. See, for example, "The European Community, 1973," *The Times,* January 3, 1973, xii; and "Twenty Years of the European Court," *The Times,* January 10, 1973.

117. See Leonard Amey, "Fewer Defences and More Competition in Bacon Market," *The Times,* January 3, 1973.

118. See Ian Murray, "No Fear of a Two-Way Wholesale Invasion Across the Channel," *The Times,* January 3, 1973, v.

119. See Stephen Jessel, "Lord Bowden Says EEC Civil Servants Are Trying to Wreck English Education," *The Times,* January 6, 1973.

120. See *The Times,* January 1, 1973, 1.

121. See, for example, Charles Hargrove, "France Hears of Britain's Invasion

of Europe," *The Times,* January 6, 1973; and Peter Gaskel, "A Rash of Union Jacks on the Map of France," *The Times,* January 26, 1973.

122. See "Forward into Europe: 2," *The Times,* January 3, 1973, I–V.

123. Richard Crossman, "Let's All Be Little Englanders," *The Times,* December 6, 1972.

124. Heren, "The Times: Meeting Challenge," *The Times,* January 1, 1973.

125. See Charles Hargrove, "President Pompidou Assures Any Doubting Britons that Natives of Europe Are Friendly," *The Times,* January 3, 1973, 4.

126. Henry Stanhope, "Chance of Influencing the French," *The Times,* January 3, 1973.

127. Michael Cantuar, "Prospect of a More Christian Community," *The Times,* January 2, 1973.

128. The phrase is that of musician Yehudi Menuhin, in "English Music—Uncertain and Temperate Like the English Climate," *The Times,* January 2, 1973, x.

129. See, for example, David Wood, "Strasbourg Seeks Democratic Lead from UK," *The Times,* January 3, 1973, III; "Democracy for Europe," *The Times,* January 4, 1973; "Chance to Develop Unified and Democratic Europe," *The Times,* January 17, 1973; and "Power to the Parliament," *The Times,* January 17, 1973.

130. See the full-page advertisement that appeared in *The Times,* January 2, 1973.

131. See Lord Goodman, "Fair Wind for a Fanfare," *The Times,* January 2, 1973, IX.

132. See T. J. O. Hickey, "Three Contrasting Attitudes Discernible Beneath the Surface," *The Times,* January 2, 1973.

133. The only article in *The Times* in 1973 to mention the attitudes of black Britons toward Europe occurred in a report about ravings in "the heartland of British democracy and free speech—Speakers' Corner in Hyde Park." According to the reporter, "One of the black speakers, who draw the biggest Corner audiences these days, mentioned Europe in passing as a 'massive neo-colonialist conspiracy to castrate black men everywhere.'" It did not occur to the reporter to solicit black opinion on Europe, or to ask why black speakers were drawing such large crowds. See "The Times Diary: Keeping Up with the Euroclichés," *The Times,* January 1, 1973, 15.

134. Barnett, "Iron Britannia," 51.

135. All quotes from Barnett, "Iron Britannia," 51, 62, 16, 18, 89.

136. The title of Barnett's monograph (just cited) evidently plays on the idea of Thatcher as an "iron lady."

137. See William E. Schmidt, "British Leader Hit by Tory Rebellion," *The New York Times,* March 11, 1993; and Schmidt, "A Setback for European Unity," *The New York Times,* May 6, 1993.

138. Quoted in Bevan, *The Development of British Immigration Law,* 85.

139. See Robert Lenzner's interview with Margaret Thatcher, "It Just Won't Do. It's Not Big Enough Minded," *Forbes,* October 26, 1992, 42–45.

140. Orwell, *England Your England,* 37.

141. This point is made by Bevan in *The Development of British Immigration Law,* 27.

142. See Gilroy, *There Ain't No Black in the Union Jack,* especially chapters 1 and 2.

143. The Center for Contemporary Cultural Studies, *The Empire Strikes Back: Race and Racism in 1970s Britain,* 29.

144. Greenfeld, *Nationalism,* 51–54.

145. Greenfeld, *Nationalism,* 60–61.

146. Colley, *Britons,* 23.

147. Colley, *Britons,* 23.

148. Walvin, *Passage to Britain,* 42.

149. Foot, *Immigration and Race in British Politics,* 81.

150. Cited in Holmes, *A Tolerant Country?* 29.

151. Holmes, *A Tolerant Country?* 29–30.

152. Orwell, *England Your England,* 40.

153. Quoted in "Tales of Thatcher," *The New Statesman and Society,* April 28, 1989, 8–11.

154. See William Schmidt, "A Churchill Draws Fire with Remarks on Race," *The New York Times,* June 1, 1993.

155. See "Text of Mr. Heath's Broadcast on EEC Entry," *The Times,* July 9, 1971, 5.

156. Greenfeld, *Nationalism,* 65.

157. Greenfeld, *Nationalism,* 74.

158. Colley, *Britons,* 252.

159. Colley, *Britons,* 216.

160. See "Tales of Thatcher," 10.

161. Orwell, *England Your England,* 51–53.

162. Quoted in "Tales of Thatcher," 10.

163. Orwell, *England Your England,* 40.

164. Quoted in Smithies and Fiddick, *Enoch Powell on Immigration,* 38–40.

165. Holmes, *A Tolerant Country?* 13.

166. Peter Evans, "Optimism and Pessimism About Race Relations," *The Times,* July 30, 1976.

167. Whitelaw was home secretary in 1981. The comment was made during a parliamentary inquiry into "race riots" in London. See "Brixton Riot Inquiry: We Cannot Buy Our Way Out of These Problems," *The Times,* April 14, 1981, 10.

168. The article was part of a six-part series by correspondent Peter Evans entitled "The New Britons." This one was subtitled "Myths That Spell Trouble" and appeared at a time when Asian communities in London began to organize protection against ongoing racist violence.

169. Holmes, *A Tolerant Country?* 2.

170. See Diana Geddes, "Asians Clash with Police in Protest Over Killing," *The Times,* June 7, 1976, 1; and Robert Parker, "Five Charged with Murder of Southall Asian Youth," *The Times,* June 8, 1976, 1.

171. Geddes, "Asians Clash with Police."

172. See Robert Parker, "Race Tension Blamed on National Party," *The Times,* June 7, 1976, 1.

173. Andrew Faulds, "Laws Alone Do Not Bring Racial Harmony," *The Times,* August 23, 1976, 10.

174. "Mrs. Thatcher Explains British Race Problems," *The Times,* September 7, 1976, 6.

175. See Ronald Bell and Roger Alford's letters to the editor under the heading "Racial Tensions and the Fears of Native Britons," *The Times,* June 17, 1976.

176. See Philip Howard, "Immigrants in Southall Form a Tightly Knit Community," *The Times,* June 9, 1976.

177. Robert Parker, "Asians Criticize Anti-Racialist Demonstration in Bradford," *The Times,* June 21, 1976, 2.

178. Quoted in Neville Hodgkinson, "Prime Minister and Mr. Jenkins Try to Ease Race Tension," *The Times,* June 9, 1976, 1.

179. Edward Pikington, "Bark of the Dogs Revives Old Fears," *The Guardian Weekly*, September 26, 1993.

180. Vivek Chaudhary, "Clashes Follow Racists' Poll Win," *The Guardian Weekly*, September 26, 1993.

181. Orwell, *England Your England*, 45–46.

182. See "Fire Over England," *The Economist*, July 11, 1981, 12.

183. Quoted in Gilman, "'I'm Down on Whores': Race and Gender in Victorian London," 159.

184. Gilman, "'I'm Down on Whores,'" 165.

185. Gilman, "'I'm Down on Whores,'" 166–167.

186. On Scarman see Benyon, "Going Through the Motions: The Political Agenda, the 1981 Riots and the Scarman Inquiry"; Norman Gelb, "The Scarman Report: Reading Britain's Riots," *The New Leader*, January 11, 1982, 8–9; and Glazer, "The Scarman Report: An American View." On the 1981 riots in general see Phillips, "Black Britain Explodes"; Rex, "The 1981 Urban Riots in Britain"; Solomon, "Problems, But Whose Problems: The Social Construction of Black Youth Unemployment and State Policies"; and Taylor, "A Summer of Discontent."

187. See, for example, Louis Heren, "Echoes of America's Long Hot Summers," *The Times*, April 13, 1981, 12; "Britain's Riots: Lessons from Abroad," *The Economist*, May 15, 1982; Godfrey Hodgson, "Beware the Easy Explanations," *The Times*, July 8, 1981, 10; and Henry Fairlie, "How America Found the Answer to Its Long Hot Summers," *The Times*, July 15, 1981, 12.

188. Walvin, *Passage to Britain*, 169–170.

189. Quoted in *The Times*, April 14, 1981, 10.

190. See *The Economist*, April 18, 1981, 55.

191. Much has been written on how "mugging" was attributed to black culture in the 1970s. For the most detailed overview see Hall, *Policing the Crisis: Mugging, the State, and Law and Order.*

192. See "Where Are We Going?" *The Times*, July 13, 1981, 11.

193. See, for example, "Police Off Brixton's Map," *The Economist*, April 18, 1981, 54.

194. Quoted in *The Times*, April 14, 1981, 10.

195. See "Police Use CS Gas After Admitting Riot Is Out of Control," *The Times*, July 6, 1981, 1.

196. See George Clark, "Army Camps in Readiness for Riot Offenders," *The Times*, July 14, 1981, 1.

197. Quoted in John Witherow, "Southall: The Pride and the Apprehension," *The Times*, July 6, 1981.

198. See "Chief Constable Puts Blame on Parents," *The Times*, July 6, 1981, 1.

199. Quoted in "Police Off Brixton's Map."

200. See, for example, the photo of the "blood spattered and weary" Liverpool policeman in *The Times*, July 6, 1981, 1; and that of a policeman with "blood streaming from a head wound" in *The Times*, April 13, 1981, 4.

201. Describing the Brixton riots, for example, *The Times* noted that "of the 192 injuries in Saturday's rioting 165 were police officers, of whom 18 were still in hospital today. Constable Danis Ozols . . . had an emergency operation late on Saturday night after receiving a fractured skull." See the article that appeared under the subheading "Running Battles in Streets for Second Night," *The Times*, April 13, 1981, 1.

202. "Running Battles." See also the photo captioned "Battle of Toxteth," *The Economist*, July 11, 1981, 28.

203. This was from a "middle-aged officer" in Brixton. Quoted in Stewart Tendler, "Why We Stop Black Youngsters," *The Times,* April 14, 1981, 4.

204. This explanation was given by Wilford Gibson, assistant commissioner at Scotland Yard. See "The Police View: Force on Streets 'Was No Provocation,'" *The Times,* April 13, 1981, 4.

205. The quote is from Kenneth Oxford, chief constable of Merseyside, in a condemnation of the parents of *white* rioters. See Ronald Kershaw, "Police Chief Condemns Parents of Rioters," *The Times,* July 8, 1981, 2.

206. As an example of both types of representation see Martin Huckerby, "Looters Moved in as the Flames Spread," *The Times,* April 13, 1981, 4.

207. "15 Police Are Injured in Attacks by Black Youths," *The Times,* April 21, 1981, 1.

208. According to a previously cited article, "Mr [Kenneth] Oxford said that in the Park Road disturbances on Monday night there were young white people but no black people." The fact that his condemnation was directed toward the parents of whites only was not apparent from the headline: "Police Chief Condemns Parents of Rioters."

209. See David Walker, "The Deprived Areas That Spell Danger," *The Times,* July 8, 1981, 10.

210. For coverage of the events see *The Times,* September 10 and 11, 1985.

211. See *The Times,* September 30, 1985.

212. See *The Times,* October 3, 1985.

213. See *The Times,* October 8, 1985.

214. These factors were cited by Clare Short, the Labour MP for Birmingham, Ladywood, in connection with the Handsworth riots. See "Handsworth: Thatcher's Legacy," *The Times,* September 12, 1985, 14.

215. See "There Must Be an Inquiry," *The Times,* April 13, 1981, 13.

216. See "To Stop a Riot," *The Times,* October 8, 1985, 15.

217. See "Focus on the Facts," *The Times,* September 13, 1985, 11.

218. Quoted in Craig Seton and Colin Hughes, "Drugs and Poor Policing Blamed for Violence in Birmingham," *The Times,* September 11, 1985.

219. Hurd described as "ironic" the outbreaks of violence in the two places— Brixton and Handsworth—that had received the most public and private investment. See Richard Evans and Philip Webster, "Hurd Rejects Calls for Public Inquiry into Latest Violence," *The Times,* September 30, 1985, 1.

220. See, for example, Pat Healy, "Black Jobs Gloom Worsening," *The Times,* September 11, 1985, 2.

221. See, for example, Robin Young, "Blame May Lie Beyond Poverty," *The Times,* October 2, 1985, 2.

222. On Handsworth see "Blame May Lie Beyond Poverty." On the Broadwater Farm Estate in Tottenham see Colin Hughes, "Whites Leave Riot Estate and Blame Outsiders for Trouble," *The Times,* October 9, 1985, 2.

223. *The Los Angeles Times* tied national identity to racial discrimination when it argued that "the current generation of young blacks is the first to view itself as 100% British, to believe it has the right to equal opportunity, yet is faced with shrinking prospects of getting it." See Tyler Marshall, "Britain: The Turmoil of Adjustment," *The Los Angeles Times,* October 22, 1985, 10.

224. Young, "Blame May Lie Beyond Poverty."

225. Lawrence, "Just Plain Common Sense," 75.

226. Walvin, *Passage to Britain,* 40–44.

227. Banton, *White and Colored,* 77–78.

228. Orwell, *England Your England,* 39.

229. Quoted in Crick, *National Identities,* 168.

230. Lawrence, "Just Plain Common Sense," 74.

231. Walvin, *Passage to Britain,* 34.

232. Lawrence, "Just Plain Common Sense," 73.

233. Gilroy, *There Ain't No Black in the Union Jack,* 155.

234. Quoted in Smithies and Fiddick, *Enoch Powell on Immigration,* 312.

235. See, for example, the account of life in Brixton given by a "young, white, 'professionalish' woman" at the height of unrest there in 1981. Robin Young, "How the Reggae Music Soured for Mrs. X," *The Times,* April 13, 1981, 4.

236. Quoted in Lawrence, "Just Plain Common Sense," 53.

237. Orwell, *England Your England,* 53–54.

238. See "Vanished Britain," *The Daily Telegraph,* June 7, 1994, 4.

239. Kenan Malik, "A Britain Still at War with Germany," *The Independent,* June 6, 1994, 15.

240. Greenfeld, *Nationalism,* 71.

241. See Colley, *Britons,* 28–31.

242. Orwell, *England Your England,* 42.

243. See "Tales of Thatcher."

244. Quoted in "Tales of Thatcher," 9.

245. See also Malcolm Bradbury, "Mrs. Thatcher's Children," *The New York Times,* December 11, 1988, 44–51.

246. See Williamson, "Memories, Vision and Hope," 168.

247. Williamson, "Memories, Vision and Hope," 171.

248. Williamson, "Memories, Vision and Hope," 172.

249. Sanders was a supporter of Albert Mucklow, founder of the Birmingham Immigration Control Association. Quoted in Foot, *Immigration and Race in British Politics,* 196.

250. Quoted in "Tales of Thatcher," 10.

251. Orwell, *England Your England,* 42–43.

252. Banton, *White and Colored,* 88.

253. Orwell, *England Your England,* 56.

254. Rich, *Race and Empire in British Politics,* 201.

255. Rich, *Race and Empire,* 27.

256. Greenfeld, *Nationalism,* 78–79.

257. Quoted in Rich, *Race and Empire,* 31.

258. Rich, *Race and Empire,* 97.

259. Rich, *Race and Empire,* 66.

260. The quote is from Malcolm Macdonald, minister of health, in introducing the Colonial Development and Welfare Bill. See Rich, *Race and Empire,* 145–146.

261. Lawrence, "Just Plain Common Sense," 66.

262. Lawrence, "Just Plain Common Sense," 72–73.

263. Rich, *Race and Empire,* 162.

264. Quoted in Rich, *Race and Empire,* 65–66.

265. Quoted in Smithies and Fiddick, *Enoch Powell on Immigration,* 19.

266. Rex, *Race, Colonialism and the City,* 119.

267. Holmes, *A Tolerant Country?* 7.

268. See, for example, John Slater, "History and Controversy in the Classroom," *History Today,* January 1987, 6–7.

269. Jim Bencivenga, "School Reform in Britain," *The Christian Science Monitor,* November 9, 1987.

270. Rich, *Race and Empire,* 11.

271. See Barker, "Biology and the New Racism," 35.

272. See Peter Martin, "The Color of Blood," *The Independent Magazine,* June 12, 1993, 20–28.

273. See Raphael Samuel, "Little Englandism Today," *The New Statesman and Society,* October 21, 1988, 27–30.

5

Wattles in the Bush: White Australia and the Multicultural Family

In Australia, everyone is welcome to join our multicultural family and contribute to our future, no matter where they come from. It's one of the things which makes our Australian family unique, and of which we are justly proud.

—*Australian Citizenship Information, 1994*[1]

If South Africa is known globally for apartheid and Great Britain for its empire, Australia probably owes whatever reputation it possesses to the *White*[2] *Australia* policy. That term encapsulates a range of official practices, from the Immigration Restriction Act of 1901 to the abandonment of immigration quotas in 1973. In the words of Richard White, White Australia was "invented within a framework of modern Western ideas about science, nature, race, society, and nationality."[3] White Australia has also been *re*invented and refashioned, particularly during the course of colonial relations with Great Britain and then after the two world wars of the twentieth century.

The Australian nation has been created within a larger context of relations involving Great Britain, the countries of Asia, and the United States. Humphrey McQueen has argued that periods of rapprochement between Britain and Japan or China have fed nationalist fears that the "noble bonds of race" tying Britain to her colonies would break, leaving Australia vulnerable to invasion.[4]

Marie de Lepervanche has argued that White Australia was "simultaneously structured by, and in opposition to, power relations with Britain."[5] The idea of conquering settlers[6] as a British race suppressed racial and other differences among them, uniting them against Aborigines (who were exterminated and expected to become extinct, like a species of animal) and so-called Asiatics. As the British "type" extended its grip over the antipodes (including Pacific islands such as Fiji), the image of the landscape changed. From

169

an inhospitable, foreign territory the bush became a welcoming site of sunlight, wattle, and the real Australia. The "type" itself transmuted into a
"coming man" and became racially ambiguous.

McQueen has noted that Australian nationalism is rife with the imagery
of Britain as a mother country and Australia as a child, one that reaches
maturity by flexing its independent muscles.[7] The nation has been gendered
as a boy, one initiated into manhood via the camaraderie and sacrifices of
war. Australian national character and spirit have been found in the religious
order of warfare. In battle the Australian has supposedly proven his physical
mettle while displaying personality traits shared with his mates. Yet the battles fought for Britain only throw into sharp relief the historic tensions in
Australian identity. As White has suggested, independence and adulthood
have been achieved only within the context of a continuing relationship with
Britannia.[8]

Australia entered a strategic alliance with the United States during
World War II. Said by W. F. Mandle to have been "born out of fear and con-
venience,"[9] that relationship owed as much to a constructed sense of racial
kinship and solidarity as it did to the Japanese army; Australia used the
racial experiences of its Anglo-Saxon "cousins" to justify the White
Australia policy in the first place.

Coexistent with a program of postwar immigration from Europe to bol-
ster the population, Australia's refocused strategic gaze signified a loss of
faith in British defense. It combined with a certain mimicry of U.S. culture
to undermine nationalist identification with Britain. This meant that the
White Australia under the nuclear umbrella of the United States was quite
different from the entity once protected by the British Empire.

The postwar White Australia policy reversed the previous practice of
excluding from the country "certain European peoples very dissimilar to
Australians."[10] It welcomed instead those "who have been described pejora-
tively as Dago, Wog, Wop and Balt."[11] Instead of a synonym for British, the
White in Australia was to refer henceforth to people of European descent.

Although not without its tensions, the racial assimilation of "certain
European peoples" has been effected with relative ease, because Australia
has not been defined against Europe (or religious difference) to the same
extent as South Africa or Great Britain. Yet all three nationalisms share two
main commonalities. First, each has been willing to suppress racial differences among Europeans for the sake of national survival from "colored"
people. Second, aliens have been rendered dangerous through similar practices and scriptures. The "yellow peril"—a threat associated at times with
Japanese militarism but more often with the movement into Australia of
Chinese workers—has depended historically on military metaphors of invasion; on aquatic metaphors of "flooding" and "swamping" (along with

"swarming," as of locusts); and on disease metaphors of cancer (the modern social curse) and plague (the biblical one).

Just as the White in Australia has changed, so too has the meaning of Asia in relation to it. Australia was constituted in 1901 as a British-Australian nation. Construction of a shared racial kinship and common desire to exclude "yellow" people allowed the separate colonies to suppress their differences and form a nation-state. Australia was founded in the racial relationship of Briton (white) to Asiatic (yellow).

Taken together, the growing economic importance of the Asia-Pacific region (especially of such countries as Indonesia), the abandonment of racial quotas in immigration policy, and the effects of the Vietnam War have worked to transform legal Asian immigrants from a racial category into an ethnic group. In the process, national identity vis-à-vis Asia has been unsettled. Australians were described as "white Asians" in the 1960s. They have been constituted more recently as celebrators of diversity, a uniquely multicultural nation that welcomes everyone to its family and protects their rights via the 1975 Race Relations Act. Simultaneously rebuffed have been "boat people" specifically or immigrants from Asia more generally.

The unsettling of Australian identity through shifting relations with Asia has been compounded by renewed debate about Australia's British head of state. First aired in the 1820s, the suggestion that Australia recognize its national sovereignty by becoming an independent republic (as South Africa did in 1961) has sparked ongoing discussion since the founding of the Australian Republican Movement (ARM) in 1991. Aided by the Labour government's goal of republican status by the year 2001 (the centenary of federation), the debate has pitted the defenders of all of the symbols of a historically British Australia—its history, royal family, national holidays, anthem, flag, and constitution—against so-called multiculturalists and promoters of an Asian Australia. The ambivalence of Australian identity vis-à-vis Britain has been starkly reexposed.

The rest of this chapter proceeds as follows. Within a context of global power relations, part one highlights efforts to contain and manage movement. Aboriginal Australians have been exterminated, forced onto reserved land in the course of bloody battles for territorial control, and generally expected to both assimilate and become extinct. Justified at times in Darwinian terms, the exclusion of Aborigines from the nation (from the ranks even of human beings) was largely taken for granted until a 1967 referendum placed Aboriginal administration with the federal government. A Labour Party commitment to multiculturalism since 1973 has worked in tandem with antidiscrimination laws and land rights to inscribe Aboriginal people as the original inhabitants of Australia and a historically wronged race.

Yet the national status of Aborigines, even among the best intentioned, remains ambiguous. Acknowledgment of land rights claims means either acceptance of Aborigines as the first Australians—the nation's "founding fathers"—or acceptance of a distinct nation on a separate path to development. Public holidays, such as Australia Day (January 26), that equate national origins with the arrival of the first Britons suggest the latter.

Defined in opposition to a yellow peril, White Australia has been defended through exclusionary immigration policies and other practices of statecraft. In recent years the "philosophies of migrant settlement"[12] that accompany such practices have shifted from assimilation to multiculturalism. Any prospective settler may apply for entry to the Department of Immigration and Ethnic Affairs. Those who wait their turn and meet certain criteria will be accepted regardless of race. But "everyone" is not welcome in Australia, multiculturalism notwithstanding. Also not welcome, at least to current Prime Minister Paul Keating, is something called a global culture.

The second part of the chapter looks at how race and culture have intersected historically. According to White, it was only in the 1940s that the celebration of an Australian "type" gave way to an emphasis on "way of life." Shifts in the location of Australian culture from the body of rural man to the life of urban society have been fairly recent.[13] But regardless of their site, egalitarianism, mateship, leisure, democracy, and the idea of a "fair go" have been celebrated as uniquely Australian attributes.

Definitely *not* celebrated by its conservative opponents are the rewriting of history and openness to difference that multiculturalism might entail. Neo-Darwinist arguments about social programming and national survival illustrate the salience of sociobiology in Australia.

Part three examines the role played in Australian nationalism of legends, myths, and historical memories, particularly those associated with colonial relationships and warfare. It shows also how Aboriginal people have been constructed as "backward" and outside of national development, an inscription both challenged and reinforced by a 1992 legal judgment known as Mabo.

NEW BRITANNIA IN *TERRA NULLIUS*

Britain's Children: Transportation and Colonization

They [Aborigines] seem to have no fix'd habitation but move about from place to place like wild beasts in search of food.
—*Captain James Cook, date unknown*[14]

Australasia float, with flag unfurl'd
A new Britannia in another world!
—*William Charles Wentworth, date unknown*[15]

If the 1988 bicentennial Australia Day celebrations are any indication, 1788 is the official birthday of the Australian nation. The establishment by Captain Arthur Phillip of a British penal colony and naval base on land named New South Wales was apparently undertaken with two purposes in mind: to rid the country of its overflowing prison population and to "contribute to the advancement of British trade and influence in the Far East."[16]

As in South Africa, Britons did not discover the new territory. First came representatives of the Dutch East India Company in the 1600s. All of them recorded sightings, in William Jansz's words, of "savage, cruel, black barbarians," so they knew that the land was inhabited. Jan Carstenz's men killed an Aborigine who was trying to prevent the hanging of another.[17]

Enshrined until 1992 in the legal concept of *terra nullius,* the inscription of Australia as an empty land to be settled stemmed from the same distinction as in South Africa—between occupiers of the land and possessors of it—and not from an absence of population. A combination of Lockean philosophy and Christian thought informed the legal principle of *terra nullius.* In the words of A. T. Yarwood and M. J. Knowling:

> Locke was frequently quoted in justifying the seizure of Aboriginal land. . . . The colonists' reactions to Aboriginal land use . . . offended the English tradition by omitting the vital act of cultivation. It also enabled the inhabitants to lead what appeared to be idle lives, untouched by the punishment imposed by God on the descendants of Adam, who were required to live by the sweat of their brow. We shall see, throughout the experience of Australian colonization, the specific resort to biblical and philosophical texts of this kind, as a justification for the removal of the Aborigines.[18]

The Dutch were followed by British explorers James Cook (who claimed the continent for the Crown in 1770), William Dampier, and Joseph Banks. Dampier's writings influenced the perceptions of the others. As Banks wrote in 1770:

> In the morn we stood in with the land near enough to discern five people who appeared through our glasses to be enormously black; so far did the prejudices which we had built on Dampier's account influence us that we fancied we could see their Colour when we could scarce distinguish whether or not they were men.[19]

Banks's portrayal of Aborigines as "but one degree removed from Brutes"[20] may have been derivative of Dampier. The latter described "the inhabitants of this Country" in 1688 as "the miserablest People in the world" who "differ but little from Brutes."[21] If Dampier was influential, though, it was precisely because he did not say anything original. Perceptions of animality, savagery, barbarism, and general nastiness were conditioned by a tradition of travel writing to which Dampier in turn contributed.

Presumptions that Aborigines were both treacherous and idle also justified land seizure, rape, and extermination.

Extermination raids broke Aboriginal resistance to colonization, but they were effective only in combination with "disease, prostitution, infanticide [of "mixed-race" children], and the loss of a will to live."[22] Armed confrontation and violence remained common practice even after missionaries began attempting to "civilize" Aboriginal children.

Britons in New South Wales did not long remain (if they ever were) a homogeneous group. An increasing number of convicts, mostly male, have been scripted in some nationalist histories as the founding fathers of the nation and the bearers of its class-based, democratic values (the so-called mateship tradition).[23] McQueen has disagreed with the notion that convicts were merely victims of poverty or political prisoners from Ireland. He describes them as "déclassé small proprietors, dispossessed laborers and professional criminals."[24] Following transportation, "divisions which split the outside world—nationality, religion, and social class—also divided the convicts"[25] and were overlaid by a later distinction between felon and ex-felon. The latter were a motley crew of small landholders (the recipients of a 1789 land grants scheme), rum traders, storekeepers, policemen, soldiers, and bushrangers (who occasionally joined with Aborigines to rob and murder farmers).[26]

Whatever solidarity existed among convicts, it was fueled by resentment of colonial authorities who used Aboriginal guards and trackers (after 1804) to prevent the escape of prisoners.[27] But its consequence was neither mateship (according to McQueen) nor national identity. Convicts and ex-felons were no more possessed of national consciousness than the Trekkers from the Cape, and they were much less of a nation than the Afrikaners who stayed behind.

There was also the growing ranks of those who departed the British Isles free of leg irons and chains. Emigrants to Australia were driven by opportunities for economic gain; by assisted migration schemes (after 1832); by an image of the colony as a haven for the poor (less charitably, as a sinkhole of the unsuccessful); and by humanitarian concerns for Aborigines. But emigration was impelled as much by social change in Britain as by visions of Australia. It occurred (in McQueen's words) "in the context of a relentlessly expanding industrial capitalism which destroyed the old ways of independence and agriculture."[28] The will to found a new society was less a driving force, according to White, than the wish to reclaim an older one: "Supporters of emigration saw Australia becoming the sort of society they imagined England to have been in the past."[29]

Romantic visions of rural Britain were not tempered by the reality of life overseas. Obstacles to a new Britannia were acknowledged by its adherents, but these were described in the language of racial degeneration and not in terms of economic constraint. Convicts and ex-felons were often thought of as a "criminal type," a racialization facilitated perhaps by the Irish origins of many transportees. Agitation against the transportation that conditioned colonial expansion in Australia until its cessation in 1868 was expressed as fear of the convict "type." Bad blood would supposedly contaminate the Pacific region if left unstaunched.

White has argued that those who benefited from convict labor rejected notions of inherited depravity. The native-born children of convicts were referred to as "currency" Australians and described (by one Peter Cunningham in the 1820s) as "a fine interesting race."[30] Still, the racial differences tempered in Britain by recurring warfare and fears of invasion from France enjoyed free rein in colonial New South Wales.

Political grievances over such matters as self-government (granted to New South Wales in 1856), transportation (which ceased there in 1840), freedom of the press, and control of Crown lands were often framed as conflicts between the government in London and colonial opinion. The formation of the Australian Patriotic Society in 1835 might suggest an emergent national consciousness founded in opposition to British rule. But even then the term *Australian* referred to liberal policies and not to all settled inhabitants of a bounded territory.[31]

By the middle of the nineteenth century, colonial grievances and physical distance from the mother country were not sufficient to transform Britons into Australians. Emigrants to both Australia and America thought of themselves as Britain's transplanted children (its "juvenile delinquents"), not as founders of independent nations. Since "words such as brash, young, egalitarian, materialistic, provincial, braggart, were applied to all of them,"[32] the "children" identified as much with each other as they did with their motherland. This explains the relative ease with which Australia later shifted allegiance from Britain to the United States. But its immediate effect was to suppress a common identity.

Australia for the White Man: Movement and the Yellow Peril

> By noble bonds of race,
> By closer ties of blood,
> That nought can e'er efface,
> We Britishers have stood
> Together in the past;
> And in the future will
> Our Greater Britain last,
> Till Time himself stood still.
> —*British-Australian Cantata, 1884*[33]

Imperial Federation was a monstrous plot to institute aristocra-
cy and privilege in democratic Australia, to destroy the decen-
cy and livelihood of the working man by opening the country
to 'leprous Mongols' and every unwashed tribe of the British
dominions.   —*The Bulletin, 1887*[34]

The paradox of Australian nationalism in the late nineteenth century is
summed up by McQueen, who has dubbed it "British race patriotism."[35] By
then New South Wales coexisted with the five other British colonies
(Victoria, South Australia, Queensland, Western Australia, and the island of
Tasmania) that federated as an Australian state in 1901. Until the 1880s,
according to White, separate identities and colonial rivalries were the order
of the day: "The general trend was toward a widening of the gap between the
six colonies, at least politically."[36]

The trend was reversed by a shared demand for restrictive immigration
from other parts of the empire, one expressed as the necessity to maintain a
British character in Australia via racial control—hence the paradox of an
Australian nation founded in opposition to British imperial policy suppress-
ing colonial differences in the name of a unified British race.

As early as 1779, the same Joseph Banks who had spied "enormously
black" Aborigines advocated the importation of Chinese workers to Britain's
proposed new territory. Apparently the use of Aboriginal labor was not seri-
ously entertained. But Banks's advocacy fell on deaf ears in London. Labor
requirements were to be met by convicts, not "coolies."

With labor shortages in New South Wales in the 1820s came renewed
debates about importing labor from Asia. The Colonial Office remained
opposed to its use, although for different reasons than previously. Instead of
being unnecessary, Asian workers were cast as a deterrent to the emigration
of unemployed Britons. Private recruitment by Australian pastoralists was
not forbidden, but demands for labor contracts with India and China were
ignored in favor of assisted migration from the British Isles.

Also opposed to indenture were those who derived privilege from labor
scarcity. Struggle was against transportation and emigration from the motherland—the very processes that brought Britons to Australia in the first
place—as well as from Asia, so the interests of white workers did not coin-
cide exactly with those of the Colonial Office. But there was some commonality of purpose on the issue.

On the other side were "squatters" who sought labor that was "cheap"
and "unencumbered."[37] Without prohibitions on private recruitment there
was nothing to prevent the arrival in the late 1830s of Indians and Afghanis,
otherwise known as Hindoos.[38] But pastoralists did not rush en masse to use
Hindoo labor, because "paganism" and "color" offset for many the advan-
tages of cheapness and independence.[39] If cheap labor could be acquired
from Britain, so much the better.

Within this context, the 1841 Immigration Committee in New South Wales ruled against the importation of indentured labor. Although the ending of convict transportation the previous year meant probable labor shortages, the committee argued that the arrival of servile aliens would spell deterioration for the colony. Prominent individuals such as W. C. Wentworth argued for the "preservation of the British character of the community" via continued immigration from Britain.[40]

Thanks to the Indian government's 1839 ban on recruitment, Indian workers were unavailable no matter what the committee decided. But the fact that a principle of restriction was established at a time when immigrants were few and their ranks unlikely to swell is not immaterial—for a couple of reasons. First, it illustrates that racial fears do not depend solely on numerical superiority. Like convicts, Indians were constructed as a contaminant and so invested with destructive potential. Second, restrictive immigration predated the gold rush era of the 1850s by several years and so was not a simple response to it. Like Jewish artisans in Britain, Chinese men on the goldfields were rendered a threat by virtue of their economic prowess. They were also slotted into an established racial discourse.

Among those attracted to the goldfields of Victoria, South Australia, and New South Wales were men from the Flowery Land (as China was sometimes called) and from British Hong Kong. As the numbers of Chinese rose in Victoria—from 2,000 in 1853 to 10,000 in 1855—Governor Sir Charles Hotham spoke of a "weekly invasion" and the necessity for "self-defence" of the colony.[41] Sir Charles Fitzroy wrote of the need for immigration of "persons of British origin" instead of "the importation of male adults of the colored race."[42]

Despite the maintenance of opposition to Asian immigration, the Colonial Office could not exclude the Hong Kong Chinese, as British subjects, from Australian territory. So marked the onset of anti-British feeling in the six colonies, a resentment impelled more by Britain's contradictory global interests than by its principled support for laissez-faire immigration.

In a 1920s defense of White Australia, Myra Willard described the colonies' response to Chinese immigration with the following aquatic metaphors:

> Victoria received the yellow tide first. Measures she took to prevent it from flooding the country, after a few years turned its strength toward New South Wales. The latter was forced to take energetic measures which in a short time brought about a subsidence. . . . Chinese immigrants remained as separate and distinct from the rest of the people on the goldfields as oil from water. Their customs, mode of living, dress, and even physical appearance set them apart even from the very heterogeneous mass of humanity to be found there. . . . The total dissimilarity of these immigrants who came in bodies, quickly attracted general attention to their presence.[43]

"General attention" took the form in Victoria of anti-Chinese riots. These led to the appointment in 1855 of a Royal Commission of Inquiry, followed by a Restriction Act and the appointment of a protector for the Chinese. Neither measure was particularly effective. By the middle of 1857 there were up to 40,000 Chinese in Victoria alone. Riots broke out on one of the goldfields that year, and the Miners' Anti-Chinese League was formed.[44]

Passenger limitations on ships, entrance taxes, and denial of naturalization rights soon followed in South Australia (1857) and New South Wales (1861). Having just signed a treaty with China allowing British colonies to obtain Chinese workers, the British government opposed the 1861 Chinese Immigration Restriction Act.[45] Some colonists opposed the act as well, in terms reminiscent of more recent debates about the need for skilled immigrants to aid the development of a multicultural society. Racial prejudice was cast as "unworthy of a civilized people." Britons should allow immigration from a similarly "industrious and civilized race" (the Chinese), no matter how different they might be. If British claims to territory depended on improving its value through cultivation, then Britons could not legitimately exclude those who displayed the same abilities.[46]

Such arguments were pilloried by those who railed against "a swarm of human locusts"[47] and spoke of the necessity to "drive the moon-faced barbarians away."[48] Again reminiscent of more recent debates, colonists in favor of exclusion cast all Chinese as a threat even when forced to acknowledge some evidence of industriousness and efficiency. Chinese immigrants were said to lack the free and independent spirit supposedly characteristic of European adventurers. Mining abilities were of no use if gold were sent back to China, and "coolies" were undeserving of respect in any case. An "inferior" element from a "filthy" race, the Chinese were described as a "sore" that would develop into a "plague-spot" impossible to eradicate. Their presence meant the cheapening of labor and the discouragement of immigration from Britain.[49]

The British government was blamed for failing to take "adequate measures for reducing the inflow from the East."[50] But even as official friendship with China prompted resentment toward the motherland, questions about the British identity of the colonies drove debates over immigration. Did the admittance into a British body politic of an alien male population foster development and progress, or deterioration? Did the presence of the Chinese mark the British as "civilized," or did it (as one colonist asked in 1861) drag them down to the level of Hottentots?[51]

Underlying the entire debate was a nagging conviction that the British character of the colonies was already compromised by convict and working class origins as well as by climate. According to Mandle, the presence of "short Australians" on Melbourne streets prompted one Victoria newspaper to remark that "the Anglo-Australians in this colony promise to be as stunted in their growth as the former possessors of the soil."[52] Advocacy of Asian labor for tropical Queensland was driven by "a general belief among employers . . . that whites should not labor in the hot, steamy north."[53] It reflected fear that the Anglo-Saxon race would degenerate in such an environment.

Added to this was concern that the colonies' admiration for U.S.-style democracy was a recipe for anarchy. Comparisons to the United States became ever more prevalent after the California gold rushes of the 1850s.[54] As White has argued, Australian colonies in the mid–nineteenth century tended to site themselves on a spectrum between Great Britain at one end and the United States at the other.[55] But there was no universal agreement as to which society constituted the preferred model, no consensus as to where exactly the colonies stood in relation to each pole, and no shared sense of a common identity binding the colonies together.

Shared frustration with British imperial policy provided the necessary glue, but only after each colony acted against Chinese immigration. Restrictions briefly rescinded in the 1860s were back in place in three of the colonies by 1881. The Queensland legislature—having once sought Chinese labor for the gold and sugar industries—argued in 1876 that a "foreign race" must not be allowed to occupy a territory still one-third unsettled. A Goldfields Act Amendment Act imposing on "Asiatic and African aliens" heavier licensing fees to mine was sent to the governor for approval but disallowed. This sparked outrage over British interference in the colony's affairs and a demand for self-government, followed by passage of the Chinese Immigration Restriction Act of 1877.[56]

Again showing the power of U.S. example, the Queensland move was justified by reference to events in California. Restrictive measures had been adopted there after an official commission described Chinese immigration as "ruinous to our laboring classes, promotive of caste, and dangerous to free institutions."[57] Suggesting that the "flood" of Chinese diverted from the Pacific state of California might wash up in Queensland, C. S. Mein swayed the legislature with the following argument:

> I have read the report as testimony of the result to a civilized community of the same race as ourselves, possessing similar institutions to our own, from the coming among them of a large Chinese population, and from the unrestricted invasion of the country by an inferior race. That is what this country will arrive at unless we take steps to protect ourselves against this invasion.[58]

Restriction was also a response to labor unrest over the use of Chinese strikebreakers. McQueen cites a Queensland maritime dispute of 1878 as a key moment, not because the numbers involved in either the strike or subsequent riots were large, but because fears of economic competition gar-

nered widespread sympathy once they were expressed in racist/nationalist
language. For example, an argument against letting "aliens of inferior mental and physical capacity or endurance . . . supersede . . . the indomitable
valor of British seamen" prompted the following response from *The
Illustrated Sydney News:*

> It may be a foolish prejudice that neither reason nor religious principle can
> justify, but we cannot get over our repugnance to the race, whose tawny,
> parchment colored skins, black hair, lank and course, no beards, oblique
> eyes and high cheek bones distinguish them so widely from ourselves, and
> place them so far beneath our recognized standards of manliness and beau-
> ty.[59]

Claiming to uphold "the power and prestige and glory of the British
nation," the seamen described Chinese men as unclean and immoral.[60]
Colonial towns in general were unsanitary and prostitution common, yet an
epidemic of smallpox was quickly blamed on recent arrivals from China.
Reports of leprosy in San Francisco and the apparent arrival in Queensland
in 1880 of eleven Chinese lepers reinforced the idea of a "filthy" race.[61]

If there was yet an impediment to concerted action against Chinese
immigration, it was the frailty of an Australian identity linking all six
colonies together. In the absence of war, the foundation for national identity was laid with sports, specifically the England/Australia cricket match of
1877. A victorious Australian team seemed evidence of what was possible
when all pulled together and reassurance that Anglo-Australians were not
that short. According to an editorial in *The Australasian* that year: "The
event marks the great improvement which has taken place in Australian
cricket; and shows, also, that in bone and muscle, activity, athletic vigor, and
success in field sports, the Englishmen born in Australia do not fall short of
the Englishmen born in Surrey or Yorkshire."[62]

Pulling against a common identity were four somewhat related factors.
First, references to Anglo-Australians and to "Englishmen born in Australia"
reflected the weakness of British (let alone Australian) nationalism in the
colonies, that is, a tendency for English emigrants to identify with each other
only. Second, the association of hot climates with racial degeneracy meant
that those who went north were sometimes compared to the "lower Latin
type" of southern Europeans, especially when a few Italians arrived to work
in agriculture.[63] Although his pamphlet was entitled *The Future Australian
Race* (singular), climatic considerations may have informed Marcus
Clarke's 1877 prediction of the rise of *two* Australian nations. One was a
northern, tropical state along the lines of Egypt and Mexico; the other was a
southern republic.[64]

Possibly related to the second point was the reliance of first Queensland
and then Western Australia on "coolie" labor in agriculture. The latter

agreed to restrictions only in 1886, when gold discoveries at Kimberley threatened to turn a "tidal wave" of Chinese northward. The final obstacle to British race patriotism was colonial demarkations themselves, divisions that worked as in South Africa to contain nationalist sentiment behind territorial lines. One effect of separate governments, for example, was the maintenance of individual armies. This enabled New South Wales to send a contingent of troops to the Sudan in 1885 to help restore British authority there. But in the absence of shared battle, the Australian man was a New South Welshman first. In the words of William Bede Dalley, premier of Australia's oldest and longest self-governing territory:

> We do not stop to question; we only know that British blood—that Australian blood—has been shed in the defence of England's rights, and we respond accordingly. . . . We have leapt from infancy to national manhood at a bound. . . . [Our action] has given us a place in the world's opinion, which years of wise legislation and unheard of prosperity could never have procured for us.[65]

Perhaps to offset separate nationalisms, the premier of Victoria, James Service, described Sudan as an event that had "precipitated Australia, in one short week, from a geographic expression to a nation."[66] This description rooted the nation in Australian soil and appeared inclusive. But the boundaries of Australia clearly stopped short of Asian workers and "aboriginal natives," who could neither vote nor mine in any of the colonies.

Founded in 1871 to campaign against Asian immigration, the Australian Natives Association was a promoter of British race patriotism. Britons rather than Aborigines (who were thought on the road to extinction or assimilation) were constructed as the original, native race of Australia. The association invoked the presence of dangerous "Asiatics" in order to produce a unified British race, and relied on *terra nullius* assumptions to justify land claims and entitlements.

If the shared demand for restrictive immigration marked the birth of a transcolonial Australia, the nation was only 100 years old when it celebrated its bicentennial in 1988. Asian immigration was apparently in decline at the time of the 1888 Intercolonial Conference, but the recent arrival from China of a commission of inquiry gave rise to rumors of assisted migration schemes. The colonies asked Britain to negotiate a treaty on their behalf, as well as to pressure China to restrict emigration from its shores. Also requested was "the right of the Australian authorities to frame such laws as they may consider necessary to ensure on this continent the preponderance of the British race."[67]

Nothing came of the treaty negotiations. Britain signed a commercial treaty with Japan in 1894, whereupon the colonies asked at the Intercolonial

Conference of 1896 for restrictions on "all colored races" and "Asiatic immigrants."[68] In sympathy with the Australians, Britain was placed again in a position where it could not agree to racially explicit legislation without risk of offending an important trading partner.

The British colonial secretary, Joseph Chamberlain, suggested in 1897 that "it may be possible for us to arrange a form of words which will avoid hurting the feelings of any of Her Majesty's subjects, while at the same time it will amply protect the Australian Colonies against any invasion of the class to which you would justly object." Chamberlain advocated a policy devoid of reference to race or class, one that made immigration contingent only on the ability to write a European language—preferably English. Japan voiced no objection to a policy used successfully by colonial Natal to exclude Indians, and the "Natal method" was immediately adopted by New South Wales, Western Australia, and Tasmania.[69]

The British-Australian Constitution

> No motive power operated more universally on this continent, or in the beautiful island of Tasmania, and certainly no motive power operated more powerfully in dissolving the technical and arbitrary political divisions which previously separated us than the desire that we should be one people, and remain one people, without the admixture of other races.
>
> —*Alfred Deakin, date unknown*[70]

> The question is whether we would desire that our sisters or our brothers should be married into any of these races to which we object.   —*Prime Minister J. C. Watson, 1901*[71]

The endorsement of the Natal method by three colonies did not meet with universal approval, not only because it shattered unanimity but also because of its hypocrisy. Yet adoption of the method may have strengthened the case (first made in the Victorian Parliament in the 1850s) for a federal union to "prevent the surreptitious entrance of Chinese into any of the Colonies."[72] The 1901 Immigration Restriction Act of the new Australian Common-wealth was built in large measure upon the Natal method.

Described by Willard as "a distinct concession to Empire" and a way to ensure British support for Australian subimperialism in the Pacific, the 1901 legislation was passed into law over the objections of those who preferred a less "back-door method" of exclusion. The act prohibited immigration of anyone who "when asked to do so, fails to write out at dictation, and sign in the presence of an officer, a passage of 50 words in length in a European lan-guage." Like the 1905 Aliens Act that worked to exclude European Jews from Britain, Australia's Immigration Act precluded entry of "criminals, persons diseased in body or mind, those likely to be a charge on the public purse, and those who might be prepared to come under contract to work for [low] wages."[73]

A piece of legislation that made no explicit reference to race was racist in a threefold sense. First, and most obviously, the "motive power" of the act was a common desire for racial exclusion. Second, the act was racist in application as well as motivation. The key words were "when asked to do so," because it was made apparent during parliamentary debate on the bill that no European would ever be asked to take the dictation test.[74] Finally, race was evident in the cultural codes of criminality, disease, and poverty. As Chamberlain said in 1897, it was through such language that "exclusion can be managed with regard to those whom you really desire to exclude."[75]

Japan protested the act, first to the Australian Commonwealth and then to Britain. But it did so only after Parliament decided against conducting the dictation test in English only. English was apparently acceptable because it put Japan on the same symbolic footing as Europe. A "European" examination, on the other hand, would place Japan with "Kanakas, Negroes, Pacific Islanders, Indians, and other Eastern peoples" and was "hardly warranted."[76]

Newly independent Australia made no attempt to appease Japan until 1905, when destruction of the Russian fleet by Britain's Pacific ally induced panicked fears of a military threat.[77] The text of the original act was amended to read "50 words in any prescribed language," and a clause was inserted (with India as well as Japan in mind) that allowed for temporary residence of "students, merchants, and other visitors."[78]

The twin pillars of the White Australia policy were the 1901 Immigration Act and the Naturalization Act of 1903, which limited the right of naturalization to Europeans only. These two measures constituted in principle an Australian nation that was European and not simply British. Nonetheless, the argument made earlier that *White* was a synonym for *British* until after World War II is shown in two ways. First, it was assumed that the prohibitive cost of unassisted migration from Europe and the "preference for the closer American lands . . . puts such an emigration to Australia beyond the bounds of probability." A country of 98 percent British origin (the largest non-British populations were of German and Chinese descent) was to be protected by the Immigration Act. "Very dissimilar" Europeans were simply not an issue.[79]

Second, discussion in Parliament linked restriction to the survival of "a nation of the British type." Economic competition from "cheap alien workers" was to be avoided because "it would arouse a primary instinct to fight for the right of existence" of such a nation,[80] one intending to remain a loyal member of the British Empire. As one senator expressed it, "Nothing could tend to solidify and strengthen the Empire so much as that we should build up in these Southern lands a British race."[81]

"Instinct" as a justification for racial exclusion was couched in the language of natural evolution as well as national survival. *The Bulletin,* for example, defended the White Australia policy in 1902 in the following terms:

> The instinct against race-mixture which Nature has implanted to promote her work of evolution . . . may not be good ethics. But it is Nature . . . the Caucasian race, as a race, has taken up the white man's burden of struggling on towards "the upward path," of striving at a higher stage of evolution. . . . If he were to stop to dally with races which would enervate him, or infect him with servile submissiveness, the scheme of human evolution would be frustrated.[82]

Confident of U.S. support, nationalists remained loyal to Britain to secure the country's independence. Australian troops supported Britain in the Boer War despite some identification with the Afrikaner republics, and a contingent of soldiers was sent to China during the Boxer Rebellion. But even as "a British race" was defended, its Britishness was in some doubt.

At least since the famed cricket match of 1877, there had been talk of a "coming man" with a rather adolescent set of personality traits: "independence, manliness, a fondness for sport, egalitarianism, a dislike of mental effort, self-confidence, a certain disrespect for authority."[83] According to White, women who were clever with horses or who were "tomboys" earned a sort of second-rate manliness. But "more often, women were portrayed as a negation of the type, at best as one who passively pined and waited, at worst as one who would drag a man down."[84]

It was in warfare for Britain that the "coming man" arrived. The physical prowess of colonial troops was noted with favor during the Boer War and attributed to a now hospitable climate and racial purity. But if one war is associated more than any other with a "typical Australian," it is World War I, because of the emotive power of a single battle—Gallipoli.

As Mandle has portrayed it, the defeat suffered at Gallipoli in 1916 lent itself to tales of national heroism and sacrifice: "This image is recalled each Anzac Day in moving rituals of remembrance and in just celebration of the deeds of great if humble men." Mandle has claimed that Gallipoli "rightly provided Australia with a self-image of itself in war" because "it sees its soldiers as tough and inventive, loyal to their mates beyond the call of duty, a bit undisciplined . . . chivalrous, gallant, sardonic." The "conspicuous, almost foolhardy bravery at Pozières" the same year has been forgotten, and only the "developing Australian virtue of mateship, that strange blend of individualism and interdependence that on Gallipoli had shown itself as powerful in war as in the bush," has been remembered.[85]

Described in 1995 as one of the twelve great myths of Australian history,[86] Gallipoli was significant at the time because it provided a national character and evidence of racial prowess. Defeat could be blamed on British officers. What mattered was that tall, healthy Australians compared favorably to despised races and to British soldiers. Now, apparently, "It was clear a new and finer race, at least in physical terms, was developing in the Antipodes."[87]

White has shown that Australia was identified at the turn of the century with "purity, innocence, wholesomeness, sanity." Symbolized by the wattle (a flower incorporated into the Australian coat of arms in 1912 and now given to naturalized Australians at their citizenship ceremony), the wholesome image reflected a larger nationalist preoccupation (found elsewhere as well) with purity and efficiency. Australian troops were urged to return clean from the war to father a pure-blooded Australian race, while women were expected to stay home and bear as many children as possible.[88]

The soldiers who returned from Gallipoli and Pozières found a country in turmoil. Its constitution as the home of one race did not prevent Australia from being rift by social tensions. According to Mandle, there were five principal fault lines of division: the economic impact of the war; Britain's handling of the 1916 Easter Uprising in Dublin (which threatened to tear apart Australia's fragile "Anglo-Celtic alliance"); the conduct of the war and Australian losses; Labour opposition to conscription (which went to a divisive referendum in 1916); and the departure from the Labour Party of a Billy Hughes–led coalition.[89]

These divisions were attributed to anything but national differences. All that was threatening, White has argued, "was seen as being foreign" and the work of either "Russian Bolshevism or Irish Sinn Feinism." After an epidemic of "Spanish flu" broke out in 1919, "disease became a popular metaphor for those seeking to depict communism as an evil foreign influence attacking the healthy but vulnerable Australian body politic."[90]

Metaphors of war and disease were soon transferred from working-class organizations to racialized minorities. Threats in the 1920s were not typically attributed to the "brown race" of Indian residents given the franchise in 1925. They were not read into the behavior of the "yellow race" of Chinese who formed less than 1 percent of the population. And they bypassed completely the "black race" of Aborigines who were not even counted in the census. The problem was supposedly the "white race" of Italians—either the descendants of earlier migrants or wartime recruits to industry. Sometimes beaten during labor disputes (such as the Melbourne Waterfront Strike of 1928),[91] Italians were described in the same terms once reserved for "Asiatics." *Smith's Weekly,* for example, wrote of "that greasy flood of Mediterranean scum that seeks to defile and debase Australia" and of "dirty Dago Pests."[92] Tellingly, Italians were nicknamed "the Chinese of Europe."[93]

Attention was diverted from Italians by the Great Depression, a time of economic crisis that revived fears of the "money power" of Jewish financiers. Australian bank crashes in the 1890s had been blamed on a Jewish-Japanese conspiracy.[94] In 1930, they were blamed on a British-Jewish imperialism personified in Sir Otto Niemeyer, director of the Bank of England, who came to prescribe doses of unpalatable economic medicine.[95] When Niemeyer was followed in 1933 by a visiting English cricket team, one that supposedly won by resorting to unscrupulous "bodylining" tactics, insecurities over British trustworthiness were revived.[96]

These insecurities did not prevent Australia from responding to Britain's call for help in fighting World War II. But when the Pacific side of the struggle seemed subordinated to the European one, the time to untie the apron strings had apparently arrived.

Asian Australia Under America's Umbrella

Australia asks for a concerted plan evoking the greatest strength at the Democracies' disposal, determined upon hurling Japan back. . . . Australia looks to America, free of any pangs as to our traditional links or kinship with the United Kingdom.   —*Prime Minister John Curtin, 1941*[97]

The immigration program has been one of the historical forces which has broadened Australia's cultural and economic focus from one narrowly focused on the United Kingdom to one that embraces the world.
    —*Department of Foreign Affairs and Trade, 1994*[98]

If British Australia was founded in opposition to Chinese workers, European Australia was fashioned in opposition to the economic and military might of Japan. The immediate effect of the onset of war in the Pacific in 1941 was restrictions on entry from Japan and China, as well as fears that "tribal people . . . might go over to the enemy."[99] By 1942, Australian troops were in combat against a Japanese army that inspired no respect or admiration.[100] The town of Darwin had been bombed by Japanese aircraft in February of that year; Australia was primed for invasion; and the Curtin government "looked to America" for aid "until the tide of battle swings against the enemy."[101]

Australia's wartime relationship with the United States was not without its tensions. U.S. servicemen were called home-wreckers, and they were reminded of the suspicious deaths in the United States of two great

Australian heroes—the boxer Les Darcy and the horse Phar Lap.[102] But in the strategic arena, the alliance with a country described by Hughes in 1918 as "our great ally"[103] worked well enough. The New Guinea campaign of late 1942 was "in every way a joint Australian-American exercise."[104]

The more lasting effects of military conflict with Japan were set in train once the war ended. Differentiated in wartime from authoritarian Nazis and barbaric "Japs," Australians were exhorted to populate or perish. While they were doing so, the Labour government guaranteed their safety via a two-pronged approach: the new Department of Immigration would solicit people willing to live "the Australian way of life," and the Department of Defence would cement a military alliance with the United States.

Had circumstances permitted, the character if not the pace of prewar immigration would not have changed. Official policy had long consisted of active assistance to potential British migrants; of a laissez-faire attitude toward northwestern Europeans; of limits on immigration from southern and eastern Europe; and of sharp restrictions on Asians. By these means, 87.8 percent of the Australian population was of British descent in 1947.[105]

Unlike immigrants from Europe, Britons could become Australian citizens without relinquishing their existing citizenship.[106] Until 1973 they could become citizens after only one year in Australia, in contrast to English-speaking Europeans who had to wait three years and non-English-speaking Europeans who had to wait five.[107] But an immigration growth rate of 1 percent per year (one designed to foster industrialization as well as to populate areas of low density) could not be achieved without promotion of non-British settlement. Manpower shortages in the United Kingdom acted as a brake on emigration. The Australian government's Nationality and Citizenship Act of 1948 may also have checked immigration from Britain. Designed to deter those who became Britons via the British Nationality Act of 1948, the act required registration certificates from all British applicants for Australian citizenship.[108]

Australia's population was to be swelled with continental Europeans, even with those described in living memory as "scum" and "pests." Throughout the 1950s and early 1960s, displaced persons from Eastern Europe were encouraged to settle in Australia along with migrants from further south, especially from Italy and Greece.

Planned assimilation has been less than complete if largely nonviolent. "Ethnics" (particularly women) continue to occupy mainly marginal economic positions, and even their Australian-born children have been labeled "migrants." Nonetheless, racial statecraft after 1945 was to reconstitute White Australia as European instead of British. It is a project revealed not only in modifications to immigration policies but also in changes in classification of immigrant groups. Percentages of reported migrant sources in 1947 were: United Kingdom and Republic of Ireland (72.7); Other Europe

(14.9); Oceania (6.6); Asia (3.2); and Other (2.6). By 1990, the first two categories had been collapsed into one. By far the largest percentage of immigrants that year came from Asia (50.1); followed by Europe (26.6); then Other (14.3); and finally Oceania (9.0).[109]

In the immediate postwar period, arguments for looser policies vis-à-vis Asia fell on deaf ears. The rationale (as in the past) was economic development, and the response (as before) was an invocation of barbarism. The 1951 Anzus Treaty formalized Australia's alliance with the United States and excluded, at the former's insistence, the membership of Japan and the Philippines. Australia objected to the peace treaty signed a year later between Japan and the United States but acquiesced because of perceived security guarantees in Anzus. During parliamentary debate on the treaty, representative Eddie Ward argued as follows:

> The Japanese have not changed. . . . Japan will also have the right, under the treaty, to use the atomic bomb. I have no doubt that the Australian people will be horrified to think that a barbarous nation, which is controlled by the militarists, is to be put in possession of that devastating instrument of warfare.[110]

Restrictions on Asian entry to Australia were modified somewhat in 1956 and again a decade later. The first amendment allowed for the extended stay of qualified workers, as well as for the permanent residence of Japanese war brides and other foreign spouses of Australian citizens. The second gave preference to those who could integrate and show "positive skills." But numerical quotas remained in place for the continent, and individual migrants from outside Europe received no official assistance.[111]

Change reflected pressure from churches and immigration reform groups, both of which argued for a more humane policy and harmony with Asian neighbors.[112] More fundamentally, the "motive power" of change was the shifting economic and strategic role Australia played in the Asia-Pacific region. Although arguably a junior partner to the United States in Anzus, Australia was somewhat in the position once occupied by Great Britain. The necessity (as Chamberlain had put it) to "avoid hurting the feelings" of regional allies complicated restrictions on immigration.

Prime Minister Harold Holt paid an official visit in 1967 to Cambodia, Laos, Taiwan, and South Korea. In a seemingly remarkable reversal, a magazine that had once taken as its slogan "Australia for the white man" and defended the White Australia policy in Darwinian terms reacted by asking if Australians were "white Asians." Alan Reid's article in *The Bulletin* suggested that the "average Australian" no longer considered himself a "transplanted European" but "an Asian of European extraction." An "average" man himself, Holt was said to act not as "a European leader intruding into

Asian affairs" but as "an Asian leader dealing with neighbors—fellow Asian leaders."[113]

The metamorphosis of Australians from European to Eurasian was tied to an assessment that economic development required a friendly Asia, not to anything the "average Australian" had said.[114] The article rendered "Asian" a matter of geography only and compared the "European extraction and culture" of the nation to the alien traits of its neighbors. The historic reluctance of Australians to work in the tropics was forgotten, and their willingness to perform manual labor there was cited as evidence of "our egalitarianism." The "long-established and prosperous parliamentary democracy" of Australia was contrasted to the difficult political road ahead "for them." And Holt's rendition of an Australian national character that was fair and honest was cited with approval.

Meanwhile, commitment to U.S.-initiated wars—an echo of earlier willingness to fight for Britain—was to have lasting consequences. Involvement in the Vietnam War began in 1962 with the dispatch of Australian military instructors. Conscription was reintroduced in 1964 and the decision to send troops to Vietnam announced a year later. The first of those conscripted under a so-called lottery of death departed in 1966, just as immigration policies were undergoing modification. The national debate surrounding conscription may have diverted attention away from immigration reform, because according to Mandle, 1966 was a "year of division in Australian society."[115]

Another diversion the following year was a referendum on the constitutional status of Aborigines, one that promised to "remove any ground for the belief that, as at present worded, the Constitution discriminates in some ways against people of the Aboriginal race."[116] The stakes involved in constitutional change were summed up in *The Bulletin* as follows:

> If, by some dreadful accident, emotionalism and muddle should produce a "No" vote . . . on the question of whether we should, in our census, count the Aborigines as human beings and whether the Commonwealth should be allowed to legislate for them, Australia is going to be in a frightful mess. We would stand up in the councils of the world looking like racialist lunatics (which we are not) committed to a Nazi-like *untermenschen* doctrine. It is the duty of every Australian to see that this does not happen. If it happened through stupidity rather than design we might well consider ourselves to be a nation of clowns.[117]

Despite a higher percentage of "no" votes in the three states with the largest percentage of Aborigines (Western Australia, South Australia, and Queensland), an overwhelming 90.77 percent of voters seemed not to be "lunatics" or "clowns." Perhaps they agreed with the government that "our personal sense of justice, our commonsense, and our international reputation

. . . require that we get rid of this out-moded provision."[118] Then again, the "yes sayers" may simply have "decided in unprecedented numbers to make these changes to the Constitution because it was not seen as any type of threat to the status quo."[119]

International reputation apparently prompted the formal abandonment of the White Australia policy. According to Prime Minister Gough Whitlam in 1972, "The number one objective of my Government is to strengthen relations with Indonesia," the country from whence most Asian immigration had come since 1966. But despite all the fanfare about the removal of quotas from the Asian continent and of discrimination from the assisted passage scheme, the change did not signify a new openness to Asia as a whole. On the contrary, immigration was to be scaled down and preference given to the relatives of existing settlers—who were still mainly British. As *The Times* noted, "colored" applicants would still be judged "on their qualifications and likelihood of 'blending' into Australian society," and the government even "soothingly hinted that colored immigration will fall proportionally with white."[120]

Given this background, it is not surprising that "the true turning point: the non-symbolic end of White Australia" is said to have begun later than 1973, and only as a consequence of the end of the Vietnam War.[121] Reminiscent of Britain's response to Jews fleeing Hitler, the Australian government evacuated only seventy-eight Vietnamese refugees in 1975. The small Indo-China Refugee Association formed to argue that national honor demanded a concerted resettlement scheme. Echoing earlier claims about how a "civilized people" should behave, the president of the Victoria branch, Robert Manne, suggested in 1984 that anything less than a major role in refugee resettlement was "barbarous" and unworthy of a country known for "ethnic pluralism and religious toleration."[122]

Having scripted Australia as normally civilized, Manne described the media's response to the 1977 arrival of 400 Vietnamese "boat refugees" as "extraordinary." But in historical context that reaction was not atypical, invoking as it did traditional fears of invasion, disease, flooding, and destruction:

> It was suggested that this "invasion" portended an "armada" of at least sixty boats with two thousand refugees on board. They were rumoured to be, on the one hand, extremely wealthy . . . or, on the other, to be potential disease carriers. Stories surfaced about their bringing here an exotic strain of syphilis. . . . The Melbourne *Sun* warned that the arrival of these refugees raised the question of our willingness to struggle for the survival of a white civilization in the Antipodes. "Suppose" [it] wrote "that today's trickle of Vietnamese is a foretaste of the mass human flotsam that will drift south when political and economic convulsions engulf Indonesia, the Philippines and tribal New Guinea."[123]

After its victory in the 1977 federal election, the Fraser government agreed to take more Vietnamese refugees if Indonesia and Malaysia would stop aiding the boats. An annual program to settle 9,000 Indo-Chinese (the old limit for Asian migrants was only 10,000) was announced in May of 1978. "The first large and visible Asian immigration programme in [Australian] history"[124] was an attempt to manage and control movement— of Vietnamese people initially and then of Cambodians and Chinese as well.

Nationwide discussion of the "non-symbolic end of White Australia" was evident in 1984, with the onset in March that year of the so-called Blainey debate. The Enoch Powell of Australian politics, historian Geoffrey Blainey was quickly lambasted for getting his facts wrong about immigration.[125] "Far from being an Australian nationalist," a man with known connections to mining capital was dismissed by McQueen as "an apologist for the uneasy alliance of British and US domination of this country."[126] Perhaps McQueen was right. But Blainey nonetheless gained a prominence enjoyed by few academics.

In an article entitled "The Asianization of Australia,"[127] Blainey claimed only that "the pace of Asian immigration should be slower" and not that it should be halted. But he began by rejecting a view taken to be "widely held in the Federal Cabinet, that some kind of slow Asian takeover of Australia is inevitable." The White Australia policy was faulted because it supposedly "saw the yellow peril as inevitable." A new policy driven by "a strong strand of guilt" over Vietnam was no improvement because it "sees us as powerless unless we adopt extreme policies." What exactly a better policy would be, Blainey did not say.

Lest anyone think there was ample space for immigrants, Blainey shrank "the real Australia" to "two coastal strips" with no room for "a disproportionate number of refugees." The capacity of the cities to "absorb migrants and give them a contented way of life" was said to be limited by unemployment, which generated unease about "the increasing rate of Asian immigration." Workers were supposedly unhappy to see their taxes "paying the dole to Asians flocking into [their] neighborhood." An immigration program that shunned "a vital section of public opinion" in the name of a multicultural society could not hope to succeed as far as Blainey was concerned.

Australian society had apparently "come to terms with the Aborigine" by realizing "that they too *had* a civilization" (my emphasis) and thus "that they have rights in this land." But neither a past civilization (let alone a present one) nor rights in Australia were accorded to Asians. Ultimately "Australia, to be a nation worth living in, must be monocultural as well as multicultural . . . we should not undermine our gains."

In professing to speak for "the poorer people in the cities," Blainey revived justifications for the old White Australia policy even as he described it as "extremist and unbalanced." Asians with jobs would exacerbate unemployment, while refugees were a charge on the public purse. Accompanying the article was a graphic illustration of a blindfolded white woman bearing the scales of justice across her shoulders and a "coolie" hat on her head. Here was the Australian equivalent of Powell's aged Britannia: an indiscriminate legal system unable to see the cultural effects of its self-inflicted blindness.

If articles published up to ten years later are any indication,[128] Blainey stimulated a level of debate about immigration that even he may not have predicted. His detractors have tried to "assuage the fears he aroused by setting the record straight" and by asking, "What are the facts?" The former quote is from an academic named J. A. C. Mackie.[129] He pointed out in 1987 that "the 'Asian' proportion of our population" was only 2 percent and argued that in any case the term *Asian* would lose its meaning over the next generation because "nearly all of them think like Australians . . . and are in many respects 'assimilated' (an appallingly question-begging word) as effectively into the Australian way of life as their counterparts from Greece, Italy, Poland, Ireland or London."[130] Unlike Blainey, Mackie did not hearken back to an Australia that existed circa 1901. But he revived a pre-1973 faith in assimilation to reassure people that "the Australian way of life" remained unthreatened by Asians and multiculturalists.

The second quote is from Prime Minister Bob Hawke in 1988.[131] Instead of offering reassurance that nothing need change, Hawke reinvoked an earlier idea of certain immigrants as "industrious and civilized." Professional and qualified Asians were tied to economic development, national maturity, and regional respect. "The story I hope the historians will write," he said, was of a country that went from "the sheep's back to a robust industrial economy" and from "an insular economic and cultural outpost of Britain" to "an accepted, respected partner of the most dynamic region in the world." Australian development since World War II had been "shaped by successive waves of immigrants and their cultures." The country could not afford to "fossilize" now by retreating "into its own memory, frightened of its own success and overcome by nostalgia for a mythical past."

To "see the way ahead," Hawke wanted Australians to recognize the skills that Asian immigrants brought. They were to treat multiculturalism as "entirely separate" from immigration, and they were to understand that "the one thing needful to be a true Australian is a commitment to Australia." Ultimately, Australians must understand that "economic livelihood is now enmeshed with that of Asia. It is a relationship we endanger at our own peril."

Renewed celebration of "industrious Asiatics" as a means to national development mystifies the extent to which Australian immigration policy remains indebted to criteria established in 1901. The section of the application form that deals with "character" makes clear that entry is still precluded for criminals, drug addicts, and debtors, while the "health requirements" weed out anyone with "serious communicable disease." Even more fundamentally, the current emphasis on "English-language competence" in the "skilled migration" category instantiates a once-planned Natal test in English only.

Certainly more Asians are able to qualify for entry now than before, and the small number who enter under the refugee and humanitarian program (4,800 people in 1992) need not speak English at all.[132] But when a few illegal boats carrying Sino-Vietnamese people from southern China docked in Australia at the end of 1994, reactions were predictable. *The Sydney Morning Herald* reported that "the Government is to toughen its refugee laws immediately in the face of a feared flood of boat people from China,"[133] even as others described the numbers involved as "minuscule"[134] and begged the ruling Labour Party not to turn people away without investigating the causes of movement.[135]

Another echo of the past in discussion of Asia concerns that other historic enemy, Japan. The third largest investors in Australia after Britain and the United States are Japanese mining companies, trading houses, banks, real estate brokers, and tourist developers. A 1990 *Bulletin* article described Australia as the "target" of an investment "flood," "wave," and "flow," and said that Australians feel there is too much Japanese investment in the country.[136] Even celebrants of Japan as a peacetime ally have described the country as "dearest enemy"[137] and its culture as "hierarchical."[138]

Ambivalence about Asia has been seized upon by Australians Against Further Immigration. This small group has described the "cultural swamping" it associates with "mass immigration and its Trojan horse, multiculturalism" as "grounds for revolution."[139] But it has not prevented Australia from being scripted as a country "striving to be Asian"[140] and its people as a "white tribe of Asia."[141]

Prime Minister Paul Keating espouses the view that Australia is naturally a part of Asia. He also supports those who think that an Australian head of state would make that position clearer.

Republicans and Monarchists

Are we part of Asia, or are we (spiritually at least) moored in the mid-Atlantic between New York and London? . . . A real nation is perceived as such by other nations. When Indonesians, or Malaysians or Japanese look at our coins, they see the woman they know to be the Queen of England. And if they are confused, who can blame them?
—*Malcolm Turnbull, 1992*[142]

> The establishment of an Australian republic is essentially a
> symbolic change, with the main arguments, both for and
> against, turning on questions of national identity rather than
> questions of substantive change to our political system.
> —*Republic Advisory Committee, 1993*[143]

Australia remains a monarchical polity despite a 1942 declaration of constitutional independence. The decision to wrest greater sovereignty from Britain did not—as Attorney-General H. V. Evatt put it at the time—"weaken the Imperial tie."[144] With continued use of English as the country's official language (even as Australian schoolchildren are encouraged to become "Asia-literate" by learning other tongues),[145] the retention of the British queen as Australian head of state has worked against the strengthening of an Asian identity.

The idea of an Australian republican body without a British head is not a new one. But according to ARM's Malcolm Turnbull, republicans before 1991 "were generally regarded as being 'ratbags' or, more generously, eccentric." The establishment of ARM has turned a "non-issue" into "a national discussion,"[146] particularly since Paul Keating established the Republic Advisory Committee in April 1993.

While constitutional scholars argue over the impact of change on the Australian political system, the popular debate favored by ARM centers on such symbols of identity as flags, anthems,[147] national holidays, and the figure of the queen. A popular T-shirt displays an Australian flag absent the Union Jack and the words "Jack Off!" When a sculpture of a naked Queen Elizabeth and Prince Philip was placed on a park bench in Canberra in 1995, "vandals" soon lopped off the queen's head. This symbolically charged act prompted monarchist Carey McQuillan to "protect the dignity of the sovereign" by covering the statue with a T-shirt.[148] After subsequent decapitation of the prince and widespread discussion (as well as protestations of republican innocence from an ARM representative),[149] the remains of "Down by the Lake with Liz and Phil" were removed by the sculptor to prevent further damage.

As happened when Britons debated the EC, republicanism has entailed rethinking the meaning and significance of the national past as well as symbolic acts of political vandalism. While describing opposition as "cave-man conservatism,"[150] republicans have sought to strengthen the appeal of a republic with a new flag and its own anthem by casting Britain as a historically neglectful parent. In the words of Turnbull:

> To use a commercial metaphor, the Imperial relationship was rather like
> that of a family company with grown up children. . . . Far from Australia
> seeking independence, quite the reverse is true. Australia increasingly

undertook the responsibilities of nationhood because it had been turned out
by its Mother Country. Our nationhood was forced on us. We did not fight
for it.[151]

The theme of imperial desertion in warfare has not been absent from the
speeches of Paul Keating, a prime minister who sparked a monarchist furor
in 1992 when he laid a hand on the back of the visiting queen. That same
year Keating accused Britain of leaving Australia to the mercy of Japan fifty
years earlier and turned his Anzac Day speech into a tribute to the 1942 New
Guinea campaign.

If letters to the press are any indication, such calculated attempts "to
wrest the symbolism of Australia's military heritage from an imperialist to a
nationalist cause"[152] have borne some fruit. As one reader of *The Australian*
argued in 1993, the defeat at Gallipoli should not be eulogized every year
because "our presence there underlines our lack of real independence at that
time. . . . How can we be a true nation without an unambiguous national
day?"[153]

Since then Keating has dropped the theme of imperial neglect, to suggest only that a mature national body requires a head "who is truly one of
us." Insisting in a 1995 speech that "we are not as we once were, in a par-
ent-child relationship" with Britain, Keating went on to say that because
Australia "occupies a unique place in the world and makes a unique contribution to it," the country's head of state "should embody and represent
Australia's values and traditions, Australia's experience and aspirations. We
need not apologize for the nationalism in these sentiments."[154]

Ranged against the republicans are organized groups such as
Australians for Constitutional Monarchy (ACM), self-styled prophets of
"constitutional disaster" who insist that no good reason for change has yet
been offered.[155] Among monarchist sympathizers stands Geoffey Blainey.
After stating in 1992 that Keating's "childhood idol, Ireland, did nothing to
save the democratic world" from Hitler and Japan, Blainey bemoaned the
"state of flux" of Australian loyalties. He treated social division—of which
"anti-Englandism" is but one component—as a serious detriment to economic competitiveness globally.[156]

Whether Lloyd Waddy's ACM enjoys much popular support is difficult
to discern. Like reggae music in Britain, harmless pleasures have been cast
as un-Australian by republicans. According to Terry Durack for *The Sydney
Morning Herald,* for example, "The traditional Christmas dinner flies in the
face of all we have learned about easy summer entertaining, about living in
this sunny, happy-go-lucky country, about enjoying our few days off work,
and about embracing our own identity as Australians." A "mature, unapolo-
getic Australia" is one that eats local fruits and seasonal vegetables.[157]

The republican issue may be settled by the centenary of federation in

2001, as the Keating government would like. But the context and conduct of the republican debate raises a larger question about national identity than the nature of Christmas dinners. If Australia is spiritually a part of Asia, and the head of the queen on Australian currency stands for nothing more malevolent than a neglectful parent, what is to hold Australia together? In other words, is there no longer an alien force against which the Australian nation is defined?

Global Invasions

> Boat People. The do-gooders say they should stay; the realists disagree. Who will win as the next invasion looms?
> —*Cover of The Bulletin, 1994*[158]

> The revolution in information technology and the wave of global mass culture potentially threatens that which is distinctly our own. That is why we must address the information revolution and the new media, not with fear and loathing, but with imagination and wit.
> —*Prime Minister Paul Keating, 1994*[159]

Peter Fray noted in 1994 that "even left-wing politicians now see no problem in sitting often trenchant criticism of the boat people beside their broad libertarian approach to most other social issues."[160] The most prominent candidate for alien threat is simply an updated yellow peril, one aided not by British imperial interests but by the international conventions on the rights of refugees to which Australia is a signatory.

It is not the sheer numbers of boat people from the Asian continent—people detained for months, even years, while their applications for refugee status are processed—that recall earlier eras. Nor is it just that distinctions are rarely made between Cambodians, Vietnamese, and Chinese, who are all functionally "Asiatic." Continuity inheres above all in inscriptions of illegality.

People who take to the high seas without recourse to legal channels have been scripted as a criminal charge on the public purse. Immigration Minister Nick Bolkus has condemned "do-gooders . . . who work on the principle if you come here on a boat, you are a refugee."[161] Balkus defended plans for tougher refugee laws in 1995 by citing the need "to prevent any people without claims on Australia from abusing our processes and tying up considerable public resources."[162]

Whether or not they abuse the law and cost public money, recent arrivals on Asian boats have been victims of guilt by association. According to Fray, "There is now reasonable concern within the government and the bureaucracy that Australia may become a target of the global, organized crime trade in human flesh." One in three boat people is apparently a "genuine refugee." But in a climate of social intolerance of queue jumping, "the public is unlikely to want to listen anyway."[163]

A different candidate for global threat is more amorphous and less easily embodied in a particular group of people. Dubbed his "creative nation" speech, Prime Minister Keating's announcement of new funding for the arts spoke less of money than of Australia's cultural past. True to his republican credentials, Keating erased British colonialism from the picture and equated national constitution with the founding of the federal state. William Charles Wentworth's desire for a "new Britannia" was contrasted to "the distinctly Australian voice that emerged with the birth of the nation 100 years ago." What followed were the "cringe" and the "strut," cultural attitudes toward the rest of the world that Keating considered "over for good." They have apparently been superseded in "contemporary, multicultural, urban Australia" by a "more complex web of traditions . . . than Henry Lawson could ever have imagined." Like the multicultural family itself, the nation's cultural riches have supposedly come from international and local sources, and from "the magnificent heritage of the oldest civilization on earth—the civilization of Aboriginal and Torres Strait Islander people."[164]

Keating's "creative nation" has room for Aborigines and Torres Strait Islanders, but not for cultural imperialists. Also excluded is something called a "global mass culture." Whatever that is, it is not so dangerous that it cannot be treated with "imagination and wit" as opposed to "fear and loathing." Apparently "global mass culture" can be fended off with the development of a high-technology information industry, one funded to the tune of $84 million over a four-year period.[165] A "creative nation" is one that protects its culture with the capture of global markets, not the detention of illegal aliens. Despite tarnished images in recent years, the heroes of such a nation are more likely to be "globe-trotting" capitalists like Alan Bond and Rupert Murdoch than an Aboriginal or Torres Strait Islander person.[166]

FAIR DINKUM AUSSIES

Anzac Parade should continue as the nation's Spiritual Place— a celebration of the heroic and acknowledgement of the sacrifice, but not exclusively in a military sense. Areas of achievement such as the arts, culture, democracy and justice could also be celebrated here.

—*National Capital Planning Authority, 1994*[167]

Original Australians

> All white men who come to these shores—with a clean
> record—and who leave behind them the memory of the class-
> distinctions and the religious differences of the old world . . .
> are Australian. . . . No nigger, no Chinaman, no lascar, no
> kanaka, no purveyor of cheap colored labor is an Australian.
> —*The Bulletin, 1887*[168]

> The negro race cannot very well be compared with Asiatic
> peoples possessed of civilizations in many respects of a won-
> derful and admirable character, civilizations that had been
> evolved long before the first rudiments of Western civilization
> appeared.   —*Myra Willard, 1923*[169]

White has argued that Aborigines were the first "type" discovered in
Australia by those willing to grant a modicum of humanity to "black barbarians." But compliments were few. Racial scientists deduced the moral
character of Aborigines from their physiognomy. In an 1844 lecture, popular phrenologist George Combe said of Aborigines that their "characteristic
vice and failing is indolence . . . phrenologically speaking, their tempera-
ment partakes largely of the lymphatic quality." A colleague of his concluded from skull measurements that Aborigines were "rather deceitful, suspicious, slippery, time servers or dissemblers."[170]

Aborigines were given the same attributes as black people everywhere:
idleness, criminality, and treachery—hence the use of the term *Hottentot* in
the Australian context. Aborigines and "Asiatics" have been referred to collectively as "colored." But they have also been given different characters
and abilities. Whereas the "negro race" was expected in the nineteenth century to become extinct, "Asiatic peoples" were thought capable of destruction of the body politic.

This does not mean that Asians were never deemed inferior or as analogous to Aborigines. They were supposedly effeminate and nonconformist,
dirty and diseased. But like European Jews in Britain, Asian immigrants
were rarely considered idle. On the contrary, they were invested with such
"positive" qualities as a capacity for tireless labor. That same logic of separation informs the federal placement of ethnic affairs in the Department of
Immigration, and Aboriginal affairs in its own bureau. Legal Asian immigrants are now "ethnics," like Italians or Greeks. Only Aborigines remain a
separate race.

Australia has experienced nothing akin to the "race riots" that gripped
Britain in the 1980s: "By international and historical standards, Australia is

a very quiet place."[171] Yet the idea that Aboriginal and Asian people are on the whole less honest and law-abiding than whites has not died. The criminality of Aborigines is associated with high rates of incarceration for minor offenses such as public drunkenness. A Royal Commission of Inquiry into Aboriginal deaths in custody reported in 1991 that the criminalization of Aboriginal peoples (who do *not* have higher rates of alcoholism than the general population) has been a function of marginality and despair induced by a history of colonization and oppression. Media coverage of the findings acknowledged "our entrenched racism"[172] while the government promised to act on the commission's findings.[173] But as *Time* noted in 1992, the attitude that police surveillance of urbanized Aborigines (such as those in Redfern in Sydney) is warranted by lawlessness "looms large in the white Australian psyche."[174]

Reflecting traditional stereotypes, Asian criminals have been portrayed as much smarter and therefore more threatening than drunken Aborigines. A 1991 article in *The Bulletin,* for example, described the work of federal antidrug police as "Australia's war against the burgeoning infiltration by Asian crime groups." The "battle against the South-East Asian drug cartels" was necessitated by "the new ethnic makeup of Australia" that had "brought with it a proportionately rapid increase in major criminal activity." Singled out for attention were "ethnic Chinese drug dealers" with practiced "ingenuity"; Vietnamese teenagers described by police as "particularly ruthless and cruel"; and "Japanese crime bosses" from the Yakuza money-laundering group. While "allowing that only a small percentage of Asian migrants is involved in serious crime," the article cited with approval a "concerted battle plan" against "the cleverest and most daring criminals to target Australia."[175]

"Colored" peoples have all been excluded from the Australian nation. As the quote from *The Bulletin* makes clear, Aborigines ceased to be Australian once that term was appropriated for "white men." Despite the arbitrariness of division, Australian nationalism has had relatively little difficulty drawing cultural boundaries between white and colored. The more significant problem has been how to differentiate the national child from other members of the imperial family.

The Australian Type and His Way of Life

As Australia has changed, the conventional definitions of national identity have struggled to keep up. They are still haunted by a 19th Century image of Australia: colonial, pioneering, masculine, distinctive for its landscape more than its society.   —*Graeme Turner, 1994*[176]

Australians in the nineteenth century were like Britons or Americans. Anthony Trollope saw them as more English than the English and described the country as "rather a repetition of England than an imitation of America."[177] Others assumed that Anglo-Saxons transplanted to Australia shared more in common with transplants elsewhere than with family members back home. The United States was the political model of a radical democracy. But the image of a U.S. society of small farmers and pioneers "in the midst of a benighted and savage region of the world" also captured the imagination of nationalists. According to White, "words such as 'squatter,' 'homestead,' and even 'the bush' were borrowed from America."[178]

The "real" Australia at the end of the nineteenth century was not Blainey's "two coastal strips" but the bush, a place apparently invented by urban intellectuals in attempts to found a national culture in something other than cricket. Expressed in art and literature from the 1880s onward, a revolt against British culture took the form of an idealization of the "common man." Often a bushman, the Australian was always white and sometimes a member of a "chosen race" in the poems of Bernard O'Dowd, A. H. Adams, and Henry Lawson.[179] In the pages of *The Bulletin,* the environment ceased to be hostile and became associated with "sunlight, wattle, the bush, the future, freedom, mateship, and egalitarianism." The irony was that such "symbols and principles" not only were "essentially artificial," but "were themselves imported from Britain as part of the international urban culture."[180]

Given the "man in the bush" motif, Australia was often drawn in cartoons and other illustrations as a kangaroo (in contrast to the British lion) or as an ordinary working man. But these images coexisted with others that captured the sense of the nation as a growing adolescent. "He" was sometimes a "she," either a Little Bo Peep herder of the country's sheep or a younger version of Britannia.

The male equivalent of England's John Bull was a little boy from Manly.[181] Modeled on an actual child who sent pocket money to the Sudan campaign, the national youngster was portrayed as independent, generous, and impetuous—the same traits then ascribed to his "brothers" at Gallipoli.

The celebration of Anzac Day in all states since 1927 has kept alive a male-gendered nation. When it was suggested in 1934 that the Sydney War Memorial feature a female, "the ensuing outcry led to its replacement by a naked male warrior."[182] In the center of that memorial is a Christlike statue of a male upon a sword. He is borne aloft by a trinity of women who "represent the sacrifice Australian women must bear in the death of their men." With its domed roof and templelike appearance, the Australian War Memorial in the "spiritual" city of Canberra is for Bruce Kapferer "the central symbol of the Australian nation."[183]

While an idealized manhood continued to inform the notion of an Australian "type" in the 1930s, his image as a demobilized bushman was questioned in two different ways. In a context of economic hardship and the rise of fascist movements in Europe, artists and poets sought for the first time to root a distinctive national culture in the soil of Aboriginal Australia. Founded by Rex Ingamell in 1938, the Jindyworobak movement (an Aboriginal term meaning "to join") "searched both for spiritual values and a true bond between human beings and the natural world."[184] They were savaged at the time by the Angry Penguins of Max Harris, a group that sought a return to European avant-garde.

Although the legacy of the Jindyworobaks may live on in the popular music of bands such as Midnight Oil,[185] they tend to be remembered with ill-concealed contempt by later nationalists. Mandle, for example, has described them as "prophets retreating into the deserts . . . to seek parochial refuge in Aboriginal vocabulary and odes to the gum tree."[186] The preferred alternative is not the "metropolitan, English tradition" of the Angry Penguins but the "Sydney classicist" school that succeeded it. According to Mandle:

> All critics would agree that since World War II Australian literature has achieved *maturity* [my emphasis]. Patrick White is the supreme example of an Australian author. . . . Nationalistic Australian verse soon realised that it could draw upon stockriders and drovers, swagmen and bullockies, the "Man from Snowy River" and Middleton's "Rouseabout" to mark lines of demarcation between Australian and English society.

The "gone native" nationalism of the Jindyworobaks seemed to fly in the face of the federal government's assimilation policy for "lighter caste" Aboriginal people. Adopted at a national conference in 1936, the plan was to remove part-Aboriginal children to institutions where they could be taught "useful skills." Their "full blood" relatives were to be left to the discretion of individual states.[187] All Aboriginal people were brought under the administrative control of the federal government after the 1967 referendum. But before then it seemed fruitless to learn from a culture destined for extinction.

The second challenge to the bushman image came from the opposite direction—not from poets "retreating into the deserts" but from semiurban man in more leisurely surroundings. In representations of Australia overseas, the country was symbolized in the 1930s by Bondi Beach and its nation by a bronzed lifesaver. Bondi was a powerful symbol because it could be bent to fit established images. Phalanxes of lifesavers parading in martial formation on the beach recalled the nation's "diggers" (its World War I soldiers). Those who prevented the mass drowning of hundreds of people caught in freak waves in 1938 became national heroes who risked their lives for their compatriots. And a place supposedly devoid of "class distinction" was said to unite people "in the democracy of sun and sea worship."[188]

Depending on the angle of vision of the photographer, Bondi can stand for either urban development or the timelessness of an untamed environment. But as in Max Dupain's famed 1937 photograph of a lone beached male, "The Sunbaker," this is a sunlit Australia where the Anglo-Saxon "type" has been able to thrive.

The shift from a language of racialized types to an emphasis on national *way of life* came after World War II. White has argued that the term often "lacked definition" and was wielded against any number of nonconformists. Communist nationals as well as aliens were rendered a threat to an unspecified Australianness. But the cultural image became more closely tied to that of an urban, industrial, consumer society as Australia aligned more fully with the United States:

> Whereas the Australian "type" had been seen as an extension of the British "type," and Britain had set the standard against which the developing Australian character was measured, it was the United States which provided the standard against which Australia, and other Western nations, measured their "way of life."[189]

The shift in focus from a rural to an urban lifestyle was reflected in Blainey's placement of the "real" Australia in the cities (where the majority of the country's residents live). It was shown as well in Keating's "creative nation," one he described as "multicultural" and "urban." But along with reconstructions of the national culture have come continuities. Politically but also economically and socially, Australia has continued to be associated with egalitarianism, democracy, opportunity (giving people a "fair go"), and honesty. These traits inhere above in a supposedly distinctive attitude toward work.

What is cast as "properly Australian," according to Tim Rowse, is "a pragmatic rather than moral attitude toward work" and a "celebration of leisure." The idea is to work hard—unlike the "dole bludgers" in the Aboriginal population—but not as hard as immigrants from "authoritarian societies."[190] A "fair dinkum Aussie" knows when to retreat to the beach (the "sunbaker"), or to the pub for a beer that is neither warm ("English") nor low alcohol ("effeminate").[191]

Australia is no longer symbolized by the bronzed lifesaver on Bondi Beach. He was followed by the Snowy Mountains (electricity generation) Scheme in the 1950s and 1960s, by the Sydney Opera House in the following decade, and more recently by either *Crocodile Dundee* or the new

Parliament House in Canberra (itself a city of symbols). These icons display continuity as well as change, for they recall man in relation to nature in ways that the Voortrekker monument in Pretoria or the Houses of Parliament in London do not. Designed to resemble yachts on Sydney harbor, the Opera House invokes an affluent Australia at play in its most American of cities. The new Parliament, "dug into a hill, with the rather sad look about it of a disused quarry," hearkens back according to White to an Australia of mining and the outback while mystifying the displacement of the bushman by U.S. and Japanese multinationals.[192]

It is important to remember the Aboriginal designs on the floor of the entranceway to the new Parliament, a visual sign of federal control over Aboriginal affairs since 1967. But Parliament has not been captured by latter-day Jindyworobaks, and Aboriginality does not symbolize Australia's "way of life" in the 1990s. Multiculturalism, in Graeme Turner's words, means learning "how to think of Australian identities as hybrids, constituted through complex patterns of difference."[193]

In industry commercials on television, the country's sheep have been manufactured into "lamb, the multicultural meal." The product of the government-funded Australian Film Institute, the mythical Crocodile Dundee is also a hybrid character. A bushman often in the company of a totemic kangaroo,[194] Mick Dundee was apparently adopted by Aborigines. His best friend describes him in *Crocodile Dundee II* as "more like an Aborigine than a white man."

Even more multicultural visions of Australia are found in two popular films of 1994, namely *Muriel's Wedding* and *Priscilla Queen of the Desert.* Both portray urban Sydney as a safe space for marginalized nationals— overweight women and transsexual men, respectively—while the bush is the welcoming province of friendly Aborigines. The "wider world" spoken of by Keating is represented in both films through Asian motifs. In *Muriel* the heroine's father solicits for Asian investment; *Priscilla* ends with a life-sized, naked rubber doll landing on a Buddhist monk.

If government publications on immigration are any indication, the preferred symbol of the nation is not a person, a place, or a particular film. According to the Department of Foreign Affairs and Trade, one of the "most visible symbols" of "the concept of multiculturalism" is "the Special Broadcasting Service [SBS], a nationwide radio and television network funded by the Australian government to provide programs in a variety of foreign languages as well as English."[195]

To understand the significance of these different symbols, it is necessary to look more closely at the different meanings of the term *multiculturalism,* because, like the visions of the nation it inspires, there is not one definition but many.

The Multicultural Family

> I have spoken on other occasions of "the family of the nation."
> . . . It is not a cliché, but a fundamental objective. Unless we
> achieve unity of purpose, unless we are joined—all thirteen
> million of us—in common purpose, how can we succeed as a
> nation?   —Al Grassby, 1973[196]

> "Multicultural" is more than a descriptive term to designate a
> society made up of different ethnic groups. It is also an
> approach to policy formulation and resource allocation which
> seeks to provide for equality of access and opportunity. It des-
> ignates a society which supports a common group of institu-
> tions, legal rights and obligations, while leaving individuals
> free to maintain their religion, language and cultural customs.
>   —Bob Hawke, 1984[197]

Jan Pettman has pointed out that "ethnicity, like multiculturalism, came to Australia in the 1970s"[198] with the formal end of the White Australia policy. Reflected in the above speeches, multiculturalism has been associated with an ethos of racial tolerance and equality of opportunity. Or as the Department of Foreign Affairs and Trade now tells prospective immigrants, multiculturalism "serves as a backdrop to the tolerance towards migrants that prevails in most of Australia." It expresses the rights of new settlers "to equality of treatment and opportunity regardless of race, religion, language and birthplace."[199]

Exemplified in the 1975 Race Discrimination Act passed by the Liberal (conservative) Party of Malcolm Fraser, multiculturalism might mean no more than nonracial liberalism, an attempt to create a legally race-blind nation for the sake of global reputation and honor. If Australia is multicul-tural in those terms, so too is Britain for its antidiscrimination laws. But Australian multiculturalism cannot be dismissed so easily as a misnomer. It soon developed a "Jekyll and Hyde" quality by taking off in directions described as "conservative and radical" by an opponent of both:

> The multiculturalism of the Fraser government was concerned with explic-
> it support for ethnic pluralism, as a means of maintaining social cohesion.
> It was associated with two different enterprises: the improvement of post-
> arrival services for migrants and the fostering of the cultures and languages
> of the ethnic groups. Not only interpreter services but also Latvian folk-
> dancing now had the blessing and financial support of the State. . . . Under
> the patronage of Mr. Grassby, multiculturalism became the basis of a radi-
> cal ideology which sought to transform Australia from an "Anglo-domi-
> nated racist colony" into a new paradise.[200]

Grassby's Liberal predecessor, Bill Sneddon, stated that "if migration implies multicultural activities within Australian society, then it was not the type Australia wanted." Sneddon associated a national culture "with everyone living in the same way, understanding each other and sharing the same aspirations," and insisted that "we do not want pluralism."[201] Opponents have lambasted "conservative" multiculturalism for wasting state funds on SBS, interpreter services, and "Latvian folk-dancing."

Far from considering it a waste of money, academic analysts such as Bill Cope and Mary Kalantzis have described multiculturalism as an "extremely cost-effective element in the neo-conservative pruning and reconstruction of the welfare state," one "based on real cutbacks in government funding."[202] Such divergent interpretations reflect quite different assessments of the changing nature of the Australian state—a book project in itself and thus beyond the scope of this chapter. Addressed briefly in what follows are attacks on multiculturalism that go beyond questions of money to issues of national identity.

According to the Australian Association for Cultural Freedom, a backlash against "the distinctly anti-British edge of multiculturalism and its association with the quest for new flags and anthems" was inevitable. A "radical ideology" that considered "Australian history before 1972 as a simple saga of racism" was "extremely insensitive to the culture and values of old Australians, treating Australia before the coming of the post-war migrants as a racist hell and cultural desert."[203] Here the enemy is not simply foreign immigrants but republicans, not just an Asianized Australia but a European one as well.

Given the associations between multiculturalism and immigration, it is not surprising that what may begin as defense of "a common British culture" frequently ends with demands for the "survival" of the nation from "a vast flow of immigrants from very many different countries." In the age-old terms of yellow peril nationalism picked up by some of Blainey's disciples, Asians with skills are again rendered a threat and a problem because "their virtues . . . make them sharp competition for a lot of people . . . who are least able to compete."[204]

The more sophisticated opponents of multiculturalism do not mention immigrants at all and confine themselves to critical analyses of the term's meaning. A decade after the debate he sparked, Blainey replaced fears of "slow Asian takeover" with more focused predictions of trouble. He warned instead of possible separatism among Aborigines (who "form the only race and culture that diverge widely from the dominant culture in Australia"); of social rifts between Islam and "secular, laid-back" Australian values ("What may happen if Islam eventually constitutes 10% of Australia's population and 30% of the people living in one city?"); and of conflict created by the presence of the traditionally industrious Chinese ("If by 2050 the Chinese, with their drive and family loyalties, dominate much of Australian commerce and such key professions as law and medicine, there will be resentment").[205]

The older Blainey challenged the notion that multiculturalism denotes "racial tolerance and cultural equality." What it denoted for Blainey in 1994 was the public confrontation of powerful cultures—those that share power in dominant institutions and practices such as law, Parliament, language, and sports. If Australia has remained peaceful, according to Blainey, it is because different groups have only "folk-danced at each other's restaurant" and not undermined the "long-established, Anglo-Celtic culture and institutions." That there might be something undemocratic about such cultural monopoly was not acknowledged by Blainey. On the contrary, he thought it "fair to say that multiculturalism, like many other manifestations of political correctness, is not fully at ease with democracy and the idea of majority rule."[206]

Blainey has not been alone in suggesting that Australia is not actually a multicultural society. Education lecturer Brian Bullivant has also equated multiculturalism with the plural control and management of public institutions:

> The fully culturally pluralist or multicultural society would be one in which several "cultural" groups set up their own systems of education, law, defence, social welfare, government, bureaucracy, and economics, right up to the national . . . level, and run them according to their own cultural standards and values. It does not take much perception to see that conflict and competition between cultural groups would be inevitable.[207]

Bullivant's major concern was to show why educators should avoid leaping aboard the multicultural bandwagon. He endorsed instead a model of "integrated polyethnicity" wherein the public domain remains the cultural province of the "Anglo-Celtic majority." What is noteworthy about Bullivant's argument is the assumptions of sociobiology that inform it. Culture is defined as "a form of socio-biological survival program evolved by a society to cope with the types of environment in which it is situated." Ethnic minorities may not like Australian culture but they must nonetheless "accept the situation" as necessary "to ensure survival of Australia as a nation-state."[208]

In summary, multiculturalism at its most superficial refers to nothing more than the willingness of the federal government to fund folk festivals and English-language programs for ethnicized minorities. But to supporters and detractors alike, multiculturalism also conjures up Asian immigration, state spending, antidiscrimination policies, republicanism, foreign languages, educational reform, and a rewriting of national history.

MEMORIES OF CHILDHOOD

Pioneers, Saints, and Soldiers

Now it's Australia Day 1995 and I am plagued with doubts
about our national day of jubilation. . . . Aboriginal people
have reminded us that we are celebrating an invasion, not just
a new beginning for the British empire. . . . It throws an evil
shadow on the spirit of discovery.   —*Mimi Ivey, 1995*[209]

In making a nation those early Australians worked long hours;
they were more conscious than we are of the need to save
money; they were willing to experiment with new ways of
doing daily tasks, whether bringing in the harvest or cutting
forest. . . . Democracy, like prosperity, is another early achievement to be celebrated each Australia Day.
                                    —*Geoffrey Blainey, 1995*[210]

National days are occasions to rethink the national past, to identify with
those whom Blainey called "our pioneers," or to celebrate traditional elements of national culture. Australia Day 1995 was no different than any
other in that regard. But nationalism does not wait for official birthdays,
notions of its "rebirth" in Australia and elsewhere not withstanding.[211]
Events occurring a few weeks prior to January 26, 1995, fostered as much
nationalist activity as that day itself.

Glorifications of the ordinary man and the common soldier—summed
up in celebrations of mateship, democracy, and the "little Aussie battler" trying to make a living in difficult times—have robbed Australia of a founding
parent or single, heroic national figure. There has been no Elizabeth I or
Nelson Mandela to rally the country; the Captain Phillip who founded New
South Wales in 1788 was a British officer. By the same token, there is no
obvious tradition of Christian-nationalism, no correspondence between an
official religion and the nation in Australia as there is in South Africa and
Britain.

The least likely symbol of Australia's cultural past or present is surely a
Catholic nun. Yet her beatification by Pope John Paul II made Blessed Mary
of the Cross (as Mother Mary MacKillop is henceforth known) into a national if not an actual saint. The front-page headline "A Nation Consecrated" in
The Australian was actually inspired by a papal speech. Pope John Paul II
was quoted as saying:

The beatification of Mother Mary MacKillop is a kind of consecration of
the people of God in Australia. Through her witness the truth of God's love

and the value of his kingdom have been made visible in this land, values
which are at the very basis of Australian society. May your whole nation
remain true to its Christian heritage.[212]

The real Mary MacKillop was excommunicated from the Catholic
Church then reinstated. She has been read as something of a feminist, "an
unconscious member of the Australian sisterhood," as Edmund Campion
called her.[213] As an Australian sister as well as Catholic Mother, Mary the
symbol stands for the Australian woman once excluded from the nation but
now given her due place among the blessed.

The symbolic Mary stands for more than a feminized nation. Resisting
the feminist inscription as historically anachronistic and calling her instead
a "battling nun," James Murray asked: "What can the beatification of
Mother Mary MacKillop possibly mean to the average Catholic, let alone
the average Australian?" According to Murray, her beatification "established
Mother Mary MacKillop as a role model for contemporary Australians,
migrants and Aborigines among them." Mary's sex, religion, and race were
to be of no consequence to the "average Australian." Instead, "she tri-
umphantly shows that a determined individual, single-minded about some
great issue, can still achieve it in the technological age."[214]

If the nation needs an updated version of the soldiering "digger" who
fought in World War I, it may thus be found in the "battling" figure of a consecrated nun. But a novel vision of the Australian landscape, one that
enforces reconsideration of the place of Aboriginal people in Australian
time, may require something more.

The Development of *Terra Non-Nullius*

Australia's treatment of her Aboriginal people will be the thing
upon which the rest of the world will judge Australia and
Australians—not just now, but in the greater perspective of history.   —*Gough Whitlam, 1973*[215]

Terra Nullius was the very foundation of our society. Mabo has
given Australians a unique chance to make amends. It also
offers us a reason to look squarely at ourselves. We can only
pray that justice may help the Aborigines to forgive and forget.
                                               —*Frances Letters, 1993*[216]

With the symbolic end of the White Australia policy in 1973 came the offer
of a new deal for the 150,000 Aborigines who had survived extermination
and assimilation. The Whitlam government promised freehold title to
Aboriginal reserves and other settlements. It established the Department of

Aboriginal Affairs in Canberra and promised to act on the results of the 1967 referendum by passing antidiscrimination laws on behalf of Aborigines. The politics of land rights since 1973 has involved the federal government in a complex web of relationships with individual states, Aboriginal organizations, citizen groups (such as the short-lived Rights for Whites movement), and defenders of economic development (mining and agricultural lobbies, primarily). Detailed analysis of that politics is available elsewhere.[217] Of relevance here is David Mercer's insight that political struggles over land have been underpinned by two competing visions of Aborigines. There is a minority view that celebrates their spirituality and contributions to the nation's cultural development; there is also a more dominant interpretation that treats them as a social problem and the unworthy recipients (along with Asian immigrants) of social welfare.[218]

The celebratory perspective is bound up with established understandings of national culture and originality. In addition to being spiritual, Aborigines have been constructed "as the beings who have most successfully adapted to the material requirements of their extreme environment" and thus as the most authentically Australian of the people on the land.[219] This construction reflects the opening up of a national space for Aborigines since 1967. It also reflects continued ambivalence about the capacity or willingness of transplanted Europeans to adapt to a foreign environment, to a land they are sometimes seen as having destroyed in "an act of irrational violence."[220]

On the other side, "Aboriginal demands for land rights are often portrayed by their opponents as standing in the way of mining and other important projects that potentially could be earning Australia millions of dollars in much-needed foreign exchange."[221] Here Aborigines are recreated as "backward," as incapable of cultivation or of contributions to national development.

The transference of Ayres Rock—a symbol of Australia and earner of tourist dollars—to "traditional owners" in 1988 was bound to be contested by the opponents of land rights claims. It occurred in the year that Australia celebrated its official bicentennial, a national birthday that distilled in unprecedented fashion a debate about the place of Aborigines in Australian society and history. Historian Manning Clark suggested that "now, in an age of doubt about everything, the descendants of the British have at last become soul-searchers."[222]

Soul-searching was reflected in a decision by the minister for Aboriginal affairs, Gerry Hand, to boycott the celebrations in solidarity with those Aboriginal groups that proclaimed 1988 a year of national mourning. Responding to criticisms of official irresponsibility, Hand argued that the anniversary of British settlement had had a positive impact on relations between Aboriginal people and the rest of the population:

> One of the greatest problems we have had in this country has been a con-
> siderable lack of knowledge in the broader community of Aboriginal his-
> tory and culture. It is not a subject that has been taught in schools, nor is it
> an area that has been treated very seriously in the media. In 1988 Australia
> finally started to look seriously at the Aboriginal history of the past two
> hundred years.[223]

The bicentennial may not have focused as much attention on school curriculum as Hand seemed to hope. Proposed changes to the high school geography syllabus by the minister for education in 1992 prompted resistance
from private school principals in Sydney. They were quoted as complaining
that students would be forced to "think like an Aboriginal" and that the syllabus committee intended to "change our Judaeo-Christian mind-set and
way of looking at the world."[224] Some readers of *The Sydney Morning
Herald* associated that same "Judaeo-Christian mind-set" with the "near
extinction of the Australian Aborigines" and with "anglo-centric prejudice."[225]

Australia's 200th official birthday did less for reconsideration of the
colonial past—as opposed to Aboriginal history and treatment—than did the
conclusion four years later to one momentous court case. Mounted on behalf
of Murray Islanders in the state of Queensland by the late Eddie Mabo, the
so-called Mabo case took land rights claims from the political arena into the
country's highest court. In the words of Nonie Sharp, the High Court's
acceptance in 1992 of oral history as a valid basis for land entitlements
"sweeps away forever the force of past judgements which upheld the legal
invention that Australia was unoccupied land at the time of white settlement."[226] Mabo shredded one of the founding myths of White Australia, that
colonists were "settlers rather than conquerors."[227]

While callers to radio talk shows worried that Aboriginal people might
lay claim to their property, Judge Hal Wootten cautioned that Mabo meant
"simple justice" and was "no cause for hysteria."[228] Alongside public panic
stood contrasting assessments of the implications of Mabo for further development. One issue has been whether the recognition and provision of land
rights for Aboriginal people will facilitate *their* development. Many people
who identify as Aboriginal have a continuing, spiritual relationship to the
land and may well benefit from so-called native title. But just as many (the
residents of Redfern, for instance) do not. To suggest that all people who
identify as Aboriginal are closer to nature (wherever they might be) than
other Australians is to revive the old category of "native." This freezes contemporary Aboriginal people in the past time of the nation and recreates
them as an unchanging, unchanged race.

Another equally contentious issue concerns the meaning of Mabo for
Australian development and nationhood. Centered most vocally in mining

companies and the state government of Western Australia, opponents have predicted separate development under separate laws—the sort of multiculturalism that Blainey and others consider a recipe for conflict. Western Mining Corporation's Hugh Morgan has gone further, calling Mabo a "crisis which contains the seeds of the territorial dismemberment of the Australian continent and the end of the Australian nation as we have known it."[229]

Not all critics predict an Australia headed into South Africa's apartheid past. In the wake of the High Court ruling, the Keating government worked to produce "historic legislation" on land ownership. After months of wrangling involving Aboriginal groups, state leaders, farmers, and the mining lobby, a Native Title Act acceptable to all was passed into law in December 1993.[230]

Geoffrey Blainey's assessment of that act sounds rather like Enoch Powell's views on Britain's antidiscrimination legislation. Although deserving of "a fairer deal," Aborigines and other minorities apparently should not be "singled out for undue protection." To do so would threaten majority rights, for Blainey, in a country in "economic decline." Instead of a matter of simple justice, Blainey has described native title law as "a new form of racial discrimination." Fighting discrimination is one thing; "imposing it on the land tenure of vast areas of Australia might prove to be a short-sighted policy as well as muddled thinking."[231]

South Africa's apartheid past, Britain's postcolonial present, or a uniquely multicultural future—these are the three visions of national development that *terra non-nullius* apparently inspires.

NOTES

1. See the advertisement "Australian Citizenship: Welcome to Our Family," *The Canberra Times,* November 11, 1994.
2. White as a racial category will be written with a capital *W* when it refers to the country's official policy of exclusion.
3. White, *Inventing Australia: Images and Identity, 1688–1980,* ix.
4. McQueen, *A New Britannia: An Argument Concerning the Social Origins of Australian Radicalism and Nationalism,* 10–11.
5. de Lepervanche, *Indians in a White Australia: An Account of Race, Class and Indian Immigration to Eastern Australia,* 32.
6. Whether colonists were conquerors or settlers remains open to some dispute; neither term is neutral.
7. McQueen, *A New Britannia,* 9.
8. White, *Inventing Australia,* 112.
9. Mandle, *Going It Alone: Australia's National Identity in the Twentieth Century,* 121.
10. Willard, *History of the White Australia Policy to 1920,* 207.

11. de Lepervanche, *Indians in a White Australia*, 32.

12. The phrase is that of the Australian Association for Cultural Freedom (AACF). See AACF, "The Perils of Multiculturalism."

13. White, *Inventing Australia*, 161–162.

14. From the journals of Captain Cook, written prior to penal settlement in 1788. Quoted in Yarwood and Knowling, *Race Relations in Australia: A History*, 31.

15. Wentworth's poem describes the vision of Australia supposedly held by British colonists. Quoted in Meaney, *Australia and the World: A Documentary History from the 1870s to the 1970s*, 8.

16. Meaney, *Australia and the World*, 8.

17. Yarwood and Knowling, *Race Relations in Australia*, 25.

18. Yarwood and Knowling, *Race Relations in Australia*, 17.

19. Quoted in Yarwood and Knowling, *Race Relations in Australia*, 29.

20. Quoted in White, *Inventing Australia*, 8.

21. Quoted in White, *Inventing Australia*, 27.

22. Yarwood and Knowling, *Race Relations in Australia*, 45.

23. The major exponent of this view is Russel Ward, in Ward, *The Australian Legend*.

24. McQueen, *A New Britannia*, 130.

25. McQueen, *A New Britannia*, 135.

26. Yarwood and Knowling, *Race Relations in Australia*, 56.

27. Yarwood and Knowling, *Race Relations in Australia*, 62–63.

28. McQueen, *A New Britannia*, 121.

29. White, *Inventing Australia*, 34.

30. White, *Inventing Australia*, 26.

31. White, *Inventing Australia*, 52.

32. White, *Inventing Australia*, 48.

33. Cited in McQueen, *A New Britannia*, 11.

34. Quoted in McQueen, *A New Britannia*, 23. The title of this section, "Australia for the White Man," was the founding motto of *The Bulletin*, from which the quote was taken.

35. McQueen, *A New Britannia*, 12.

36. White, *Inventing Australia*, 63.

37. Willard, *History of the White Australia Policy*, 4.

38. de Lepervanche, *Indians in a White Australia*, 12.

39. According to Willard, the "paganism" and "color" of the immigrants caused "a good deal of hesitation." See Willard, *History of the White Australia Policy*, 4.

40. Willard, *History of the White Australia Policy*, 3–6.

41. Quoted in Willard, *History of the White Australia Policy*, 22.

42. Quoted in Willard, *History of the White Australia Policy*, 12.

43. Willard, *History of the White Australia Policy*, 18–19.

44. Willard, *History of the White Australia Policy*, 23–25.

45. Willard, *History of the White Australia Policy*, 33–34.

46. Willard, *History of the White Australia Policy*, 30.

47. *The Empire* newspaper, February 1861. Quoted in Willard, *History of the White Australia Policy*, 19.

48. *The Miner and General Advertiser,* March 1861. Quoted in McQueen, *A New Britannia*, 32.

49. Willard, *History of the White Australia Policy*, 18, 27, 29.

50. Willard, *History of the White Australia Policy*, 36.

51. Letter to *The Empire,* February 1861. Quoted in Willard, *History of the White Australia Policy,* 31.

52. Mandle, *Going It Alone,* 28.

53. de Lepervanche, *Indians in a White Australia,* 50.

54. White, *Inventing Australia,* 55.

55. White, *Inventing Australia,* 49.

56. Willard, *History of the White Australia Policy,* 41–51.

57. Quoted in Willard, *History of the White Australia Policy,* 41.

58. Quoted in Willard, *History of the White Australia Policy,* 42.

59. Quoted in McQueen, *A New Britannia,* 32–33.

60. Willard, *History of the White Australia Policy,* 52–54.

61. Willard, *History of the White Australia Policy,* 61–62.

62. Quoted in Mandle, *Going It Alone,* 28.

63. de Lepervanche mentioned the hostility of British settlers toward Italian rural workers. See *Indians in a White Australia,* 52. White suggested a distinction existed between "real" white men and those from the "lower Latin type" who were "only technically white." See *Inventing Australia,* 82.

64. Mandle, *Going It Alone,* 29.

65. Speech delivered to the New South Wales parliament, March 1885. Quoted in Meaney, *Australia and the World,* 73–74.

66. Quoted in White, *Inventing Australia,* 73.

67. Quoted in Willard, *History of the White Australia Policy,* 80.

68. Willard, *History of the White Australia Policy,* 109–110.

69. Willard, *History of the White Australia Policy,* 112–113.

70. Deakin was attorney general of the first federal government of Australia. Quoted in Willard, *History of the White Australia Policy,* 119.

71. Quoted in McQueen, *A New Britannia,* 34.

72. Quoted in Willard, *History of the White Australia Policy,* 119 (footnote 1).

73. Willard, *History of the White Australia Policy,* 120–121.

74. Willard, *History of the White Australia Policy,* 120–121.

75. Quoted in Willard, *History of the White Australia Policy,* 113.

76. Japanese consul E. Eitaki, quoted in Willard, *History of the White Australia Policy,* 122.

77. McQueen, *A New Britannia,* 60.

78. Willard, *History of the White Australia Policy,* 125–27.

79. Willard, *History of the White Australia Policy,* 207.

80. Willard, *History of the White Australia Policy,* 200–201.

81. Senator Staniford, Commonwealth Parliamentary Debates, 1901–1902. Quoted in Willard, *History of the White Australia Policy,* 206 (footnote 64).

82. Quoted in White, *Inventing Australia,* 81.

83. White, *Inventing Australia,* 76.

84. White, *Inventing Australia,* 83.

85. Mandle, *Going It Alone,* 4–8.

86. "The Twelve Great Myths of Australian History," *The Sydney Morning Herald,* June 10, 1995.

87. Mandle, *Going It Alone,* 12.

88. White, *Inventing Australia,* 115–118, 127.

89. Mandle, *Going It Alone,* 16.

90. White, *Inventing Australia,* 115, 140–141.

91. See Mandle, *Going It Alone,* chapter 3.

92. Quoted in White, *Inventing Australia,* 141.

93. de Lepervanche, *Indians in a White Australia,* 70.

94. See McQueen, *A New Britannia,* 104, 204.

95. See Mandle, *Going It Alone,* chapter 4.

96. The issue was whether a new practice of trying to hit the batsman constituted bad sportsmanship. See Mandle, *Going It Alone,* 32–34.

97. "Asian Australia Under America's Umbrella" is the title of an article by Lord Chalfont that appeared in *The Times,* September 21, 1993. Curtin quoted in Meaney, *Australia and the World,* 473.

98. Australian Department of Foreign Affairs and Trade (Overseas Information Branch), "Immigration," 1.

99. Jack McPhee in Morgan, *Wanamurraganya: The Story of Jack McPhee,* 146.

100. The Australian army after the Battle of Gona was "completely puzzled," according to I. Morrison, by the Japanese refusal to surrender honorably as the "Germans and Italians" might. See Mandle, *Going It Alone,* 127.

101. Prime Minister John Curtin, quoted in Meaney, *Australia and the World,* 473.

102. On the nationalist myths surrounding the deaths of these two icons see Mandle, *Going It Alone,* chapter 2.

103. Quoted in McQueen, *A New Britannia,* 57.

104. Mandle, *Going It Alone,* 127.

105. Carens, "Nationalism and the Exclusion of Immigrants: Lessons from Australian Immigration Policy," 44.

106. See Stewart Harris, "Britons Can Keep Their Citizenship in Australia," *The Times,* December 28, 1972.

107. After 1973, all new settlers, including ones from Britain, had to wait three years for citizenship. See Stewart Harris, "Australia to Cut Britons' Privileges as Settlers," *The Times,* April 12, 1973.

108. de Lepervanche, *Indians in a White Australia,* 71.

109. Australian Department of Foreign Affairs and Trade, "Immigration," 2–3.

110. Quoted in Mandle, *Going It Alone,* 134.

111. See Peter Evans, "Race Board Accuses Australia of Color Discrimination in Assisted Passage Scheme," *The Times,* December 22, 1971, 2.

112. de Lepervanche, *Indians in a White Australia,* 72.

113. Alan Reid, "Are We White Asians?" *The Bulletin,* May 20, 1967, 32–33.

114. As Reid put it, "Australia not only wants a stable and prosperous Asia, but indeed must have one if it is to survive and to continue the development that has brought it the highest living standard in the area."

115. On Vietnam see Mandle, *Going It Alone,* 39–44.

116. The Commonwealth of Australia, "Referendums: The Arguments for and Against," Canberra, April 6, 1967.

117. See "'Yes' Voters, Please Turn Over," *The Bulletin,* May 27, 1967; and "When Aborigines Become People," *The Bulletin,* May 20, 1967.

118. "When Aborigines Become People."

119. Scott Bennett, "The 1967 Referendum," 30.

120. See "Australia to Drop Racial Immigration Policy," *The Times,* December 27, 1972; and "Australia's New Rules for Immigrants," *The Times,* December 28, 1972.

121. AACF, "The Perils of Multiculturalism," 9.

122. Robert Manne, "The Blainey View—the Politics of Asian Immigration to Australia, 1975–1984," 13.

123. Manne, "The Blainey View," 15.

124. Manne, "The Blainey View," 16.

125. See, for example, Collins, "Why Blainey Got It Wrong," 11–13.

126. McQueen, "Blainey and Multiculturalism," 40–43.

127. Geoffrey Blainey, "The Asianization of Australia," *The Age,* March 20, 1984, 11.

128. See the eight-page special "The Blainey Debate—10 Years On," *The Australian,* March 15, 1994; and "Did Blainey Get It Right? Immigration a Decade On," *The Bulletin,* August 30, 1994, 22–27.

129. Mackie, "Asian Immigration to Australia: Past Trends and Future Prospects," 104–109.

130. Mackie, "Asian Immigration to Australia," 107.

131. Hawke, "An Open Letter by the Prime Minister," 34–36.

132. There is also a "family migration" scheme that offers to unite Australian citizens and permanent residents with extended family members. However, Asians (and others) without "positive skills" do not qualify for this because "the selection criteria is a 'points test' which is essentially a labor market test. . . . Some applicants in this category have to demonstrate that they speak English at a level necessary to find employment in their profession in Australia." See Australian Department of Foreign Affairs and Trade, "Immigration," 2.

133. Margo Kingston, "Tougher Law to Keep Out Boat People," *The Sydney Morning Herald,* December 31, 1994.

134. James Jupp, "Don't Panic: Our Influx Is Not Huge by World Standards," *The Canberra Times,* December 31, 1994.

135. Kerry Murphy, "Government Overreacts on New Arrivals," *The Sydney Morning Herald,* January 3, 1995.

136. Glenda Korporaal, "Japan's Super-Rich Target Australia," *The Bulletin,* May 1, 1990, 38–42.

137. James Dunn, "Dearest Enemy," *The Bulletin,* August 18, 1992, 24.

138. According to John Stackhouse, "It is a facet of Japanese culture that they see the world in hierarchical terms." See "Why Tokyo Takes Top Priority," *The Bulletin,* January 14, 1992, 42–43.

139. See William Branigin, "Australia Questions 'Open Door' Policy to Asiatic Migrants," *The Guardian Weekly,* April 11, 1993, 18.

140. David Sanger, "Australia Is Striving to Be Asian, But How Asian?" *The New York Times,* August 16, 1992, 3.

141. Patrice de Beer, "Australia—'White Tribe of Asia's' Dilemma," *The Guardian Weekly,* March 7, 1993.

142. Turnbull, "Why We Need the Republic," 105.

143. Republic Advisory Committee, *An Australian Republic: The Options—an Overview,* 22.

144. Quoted in Meaney, *Australia and the World,* 477.

145. See Greg Roberts, "Speaking in Other Tongues," *The Bulletin,* April 19, 1994, 20–21.

146. Turnbull, "Forward," xi.

147. Australia has its own anthem—"Advance Australia Fair." An Australian flag retaining a small Union Jack in one corner was authorized by the Flags Act of 1953. When the Labour Party advocated a new design for the flag in 1992, "overnight, the benches of Her Majesty's Loyal Opposition sprouted little Australian flags, like a thin blue line of royalist defence, and battle commenced." Love, "Old Lang's Sign," 6.

148. Carey McQuillan, "I Acted to Protect Her Dignity," *The Sydney Morning Herald*, April 17, 1995.

149. See Bryan Lobascher, Letters to the Editor, "Nothing to Do with Republicans," *The Canberra Times*, April 18, 1995.

150. Turnbull, "Why We Need the Republic," 104.

151. Turnbull, "Why We Need the Republic," 104.

152. Love, "Old Lang's Sign," 6.

153. Eric Proust, "Tobruk or Kokoda," *The Australian*, October 6, 1993, 14.

154. "An Australian Republic: The Way Forward." Speech by the prime minister, the Honorable P. J. Keating, June 7, 1995, 3 (Australian Publishing Service, Canberra).

155. See Janet Fife-Yeomans, "Prophecy of Disaster, Say Monarchists," *The Australian*, October 6, 1993, 16.

156. Blainey, "Divided Nation."

157. Terry Durack, "A Republican Christmas," *The Sydney Morning Herald*, December 20, 1994.

158. See *The Bulletin*, September 6, 1994.

159. Paul Keating, "Culture Part of Our Common Heritage," *The Sydney Morning Herald*, October 19, 1994, 11.

160. Peter Fray, "Missed the Boat," *The Bulletin*, September 6, 1994, 28.

161. Quoted in Fray, "Missed the Boat," 27.

162. Quoted in Murphy, "Government Overreacts on New Arrivals."

163. Fray, "Missed the Boat," 28.

164. Keating, "Culture Part of Our Common Heritage," 11.

165. See Tony Wright, "Murdoch Studio Plan a Surprise," *The Sydney Morning Herald*, October 19, 1994.

166. See the discussion of "would-be kings battling each other at home and abroad for a growing market share." In D'Arcy Jenish, "Globe-Trotting Aussies," *Maclean's*, May 2, 1988, 50–51.

167. See "Looking to the Future: Australia's National Capital." Canberra, September 1994, 13.

168. Quoted in White, *Inventing Australia*, 81.

169. Willard, *History of the White Australia Policy*, 208.

170. Quoted in White, *Inventing Australia*, 65.

171. Cope and Kalantzis, "Speaking of Cultural Difference: The Rise and Uncertain Future of the Language of Multiculturalism," 14.

172. See "The Black Deaths Report," *The Sydney Morning Herald*, May 10, 1991, 4.

173. See Overview of the Response by Governments to the Royal Commission, *Aboriginal Deaths in Custody*.

174. Damien Murphy and Bill Mellor, "Black Pain, White Blindness," *Time*, March 23, 1992, 27.

175. Tony Barnao and Norm Lipson, "The Asian Connection," *The Bulletin*, April 2, 1991, 86–88.

176. Graeme Turner, "Rebirth of Nationalism," *The Sydney Morning Herald*, December 19, 1994.

177. Quoted in White, *Inventing Australia*, 50.

178. White, *Inventing Australia*, 51.

179. McQueen, *A New Britannia*, 97–112.

180. McQueen, *A New Britannia*, 97–99.

181. White, *Inventing Australia*, 120–123.

182. White, *Inventing Australia*, 136.

183. Kapferer, *Legends of People, Myths of State*, 122, 131.

184. Newton, "Becoming 'Authentic' Australians Through Music," 95.

185. Newton, "Becoming 'Authentic' Australians," 97–100.

186. Mandle, *Going It Alone*, 54, 60.

187. Beckett, "Aboriginalty, Citizenship and the Nation State," 9.

188. The quote is from a 1930s travel book. See in general Game, "Nation and Identity: Bondi."

189. White, *Inventing Australia*, 161–162.

190. Rowse, "Surrendering Australia."

191. Hamilton, "Beer and Being: The Australian Tourist in Bali," 17–29.

192. White, *Inventing Australia*, 171.

193. Turner, "Rebirth of Nationalism."

194. Morton, "Rednecks, 'Roos and Racism: Kangaroo Shooting and the Australian Way."

195. Department of Foreign Affairs and Trade, "Immigration," 4.

196. Labor Minister for Immigration Al Grassby, quoted in Cope and Kalantzis, "Speaking of Cultural Difference," 15–16.

197. Hawke, "Australia: A Multicultural Society," 317–318.

198. Pettman, *Living in the Margins*, 119.

199. Department of Foreign Affairs and Trade, "Immigration," 4.

200. AACF, "The Perils of Multiculturalism," 10.

201. Bill Sneddon while minister for immigration in 1969. Quoted in Cope and Kalantzis, "Speaking of Cultural Difference," 14.

202. Cope and Kalantzis, "Speaking of Cultural Difference," 16.

203. AACF, "The Perils of Multiculturalism," 10.

204. Dunn, "All Cultures Are Good, Except Our Own."

205. Geoffrey Blainey, "Melting Pot on the Boil," *The Bulletin*, August 30, 1994, 22–25.

206. Blainey, "Melting Pot on the Boil," 25.

207. Bullivant, "Pluralism in Australia—Clarifying the Issues," 11.

208. Bullivant, "Pluralism in Australia," 10–17.

209. Mimi Ivey, "The Wrong Symbols," *The Australian*, January 26, 1995, 11.

210. Geoffrey Blainey, "Silent Thank-You to Our Pioneers," *The Australian*, January 26, 1995.

211. See Turner, "Rebirth of Nationalism."

212. Quoted in Errol Simpert and D. D. McNicoll, "A Nation Consecrated," *The Australian*, January 20, 1995, 1.

213. Edmund Campion, "A Nun's Feminist Tale," *The Bulletin*, January 17, 1995, 23–25.

214. James Murray, "Battling Nun Practiced What She Preached," *The Australian*, January 20, 1995, 6.

215. Quoted in Stewart Harris, "White Man Speaks Without Forked Tongue," *The Times*, April 30, 1973.

216. Frances Letters, "Justice at Last for an Invisible People," *The Guardian Weekly*, August 29, 1993, 24.

217. See, for example, Libby, *Hawke's Law: The Politics of Mining and Aboriginal Land Rights in Australia*.

218. Mercer, "*Terra Nullius*, Aboriginal Sovereignty and Land Rights in Australia."

219. Lattas, "Aborigines and Contemporary Australian Nationalism: Primordiality and the Cultural Politics of Otherness," 53.

220. Lattas, "Aborigines and Contemporary Australian Nationalism," 52.

221. Mercer, "*Terra Nullius*," 305.

222. Quoted in Andrew Bilski, "A Nation's Troubled Bicentennial," *Maclean's,* February 8, 1988, 24.

223. Hand, "The Bicentenary: A View," 23.

224. Paola Totaro, "Reconsider Changes to Syllabus: Chadwick," *The Sydney Morning Herald,* July 11, 1992.

225. "A Worrying 'Judaeo-Christian Mind-Set,'" Letters to the Editor, *The Sydney Morning Herald,* July 11, 1992.

226. Sharp, "Scales from the Eyes of Justice," 56.

227. "The Twelve Great Myths of Australian History."

228. Hal Wootten, "Mabo Means Simple Justice, and No Cause for Hysteria," *The Sydney Morning Herald,* July 29, 1993.

229. Quoted in Glen Haigh, "Prophet of Doom," *The Weekend Australian,* July 31, 1993.

230. See "A Land for All Australians," *The Australian,* December 24, 1993, 13.

231. Blainey, "Silent Thank-You to Our Pioneers."

6

National Families
in Global Space

The connections between national identity and race examined in previous chapters, the insistence that nationalism cannot be neatly divided into two ideal types (be they good/bad, civic/ethnic, political/cultural, or some other), and the fact that nationalism is not simply a movement for statehood that comes and goes (like a reincarnated human spirit) suggest that it is fruitful to return to the question of how national identities and boundaries are conditioned by global forces. This chapter begins with a brief summary of the book's major arguments. It then highlights contemporary practices and movements that challenge the traditional boundaries of international relations and comparative politics, as well as nationalist distinctions between national kin and alien kind.

The issues chosen pertain to real families and households. They reinforce earlier claims that nationalism is not merely a function of social modernization or state collapse. Nationalist practices are sustained and affected by wider processes of both change and continuity in international relations and global political economy.

Novel patterns of marriage and adoption, transplantation, and settlement have aroused nationalist fears of boundary transgression and redoubled efforts to prevent or regulate movement. They have also generated ethical debates and concerns about human rights violations and the exploitation of human bodies and resources (particularly those of women and children). To what extent colonial power relations have been transcended with formal independence from European rule is but one of the questions raised for future research.

THE PRACTICE AND PROMISE OF NATIONALISM

The arguments of earlier chapters may be summarized as two key points. The first is that nationalism's relationship to global politics is inevitably paradoxical. The twin concepts of national and alien cannot exist independently of each other; both are simultaneously brought into being by nationalist scriptures that operate as political religions. Difference is found in forces that transgress and contest boundaries—in movement, transmission, and flows. The racialized alien can always be found within sovereign boundaries, but the alien within is usually linked, imaginatively, to aliens without. The demise of national identity does not necessarily follow from the globalization of cultural modes of life such as capitalism, as earlier prophets now realize. Demise is not inevitable, because without global politics the manufacture of alien difference would be much more difficult.

The paradox inheres in how nationalism operates as a narrative performance. As previous chapters demonstrate, one of the principal (multifaceted) practices of nationalism is the creation of boundaries between national and alien. Another complex practice involves the policing and maintenance of those borders. Management, containment, and capture of global forces are essential components of nationalism everywhere, *not* modern states or demands for statehood (which have certainly been evident as well).

Albert Memmi noted in his study of colonialism that the wished-for "disappearance of the usurped" is a death wish for the usurper of power. This is because colonial relationships have "chained the colonizer and the colonized into an implacable dependence, molded their respective characters and dictated their conduct."[1] By the same token, the disappearance of the alien would mean the elimination of the national. Nationalism may assimilate or exterminate certain proscribed groups of aliens, but the *idea* of the alien must be ever revived. That is why moments of incorporation of once racialized groups entail the search for new differences.

The second point relates to nationalism as promise as well as practice. In academic scholarship the dichotomous separation of foreign policy from domestic policy is effected routinely. In disciplines such as international relations, the foreign is taken to be that which is "outside" the nation-state (the realm of anarchy or another sovereign power), while the domestic is the sphere of the "inside" (the space where political differences within a sovereign community are negotiated and resolved). Such imaginary divisions have been challenged—for example, in critical analyses of the politics of identity in the United States.[2] But of relevance here is how nationalism on a global scale depends on re-creation of that same foreign/domestic dichotomy.

In nationalist scripture, the sign of the domestic functions as a rallying cry to unity and a promise of security. Its key indicators are home and family—the metaphor of the household and the concept of kinship, respectively. These are recurred to continually, even though the family home may be a site of danger and violence—thus of extreme *in*security—and there can be no absolute certainty (unless one is a Siamese twin) of consanguineous kinship. Domesticity endures in nationalist scripture for three reasons: First, it reinvents the fiction that like families, nations (in whatever guise is the social norm for both) are naturally given and divorced from politics. Second, domestic metaphors reflect the incorporation of biblical myths of human origin and community into nationalism, or more generally the continued authority of racial and religious traditions. And third, the sign of the domestic implies the more modern, contingent idea of the domestic realm as a private space—an autonomous realm guaranteed by the state and protected from external incursions.

Here it is worth recalling Max Weber's insight that the separation of commercial activity from the family house is a novel capitalist phenomenon. For although the subcontracting of employment to home-based workers (known euphemistically as "outworkers") is globalizing so-called cottage industry,[3] the realm of the domestic still connotes autonomy from the workings of the market. As the constitutive principle of international relations, state sovereignty is supposed to enable the autonomous national family to manage its private domestic economy and to develop within its own cultural and territorial space.

THE GLOBALIZATION OF KINSHIP

> The fundamental distinction between "real" kinship and "pseudo"-kinship—or between literal and figural structure—is the topic of a still-unresolved debate about whether kinship is essentially a matter of biology or sociology. . . . The traditional distinction between literal and figural family, or between real and nominal kinship, erodes as family is conflated with nation—or with species.   —*Marc Shell, 1993*[4]

Nationalism displays little tolerance for those who threaten defenses and bureaucratic routines by crossing boundaries in "waves." Aquatic metaphors have been applied with regularity to two groups of transgressors. One is the people who seek safe refuge from conditions of terror, such as Jewish refugees from Nazi Germany. The other is those who seek settlement, either legally or illegally, in a different country.

Within the category of settler, inscriptions of danger (expressed often in military metaphors) have been applied to male workers deemed "unencumbered" competitors for jobs and women. The national women who form relationships with such men have attracted more nationalist opprobrium than the national men (often military servicemen) with foreign partners. This has been the case whether the women's motives are for love or for money (the so-called green card marriage in the United States is an example of the latter). In either case the fertile woman is the key to the reproduction or subversion of the boundaries of the nation, while the children born of national/alien pairings are considered embodiments of national decline and contamination.

Warning signs of doom have been hung as well over the dependents (usually wives and children) of "encumbered" men, those who threaten to swell numbers and take control of population growth away from the managers of immigration policy.

While established patterns of refuge and settlement continue, they have been joined by two other processes of a rather different sort. Instead of alien men sending for wives and/or children from abroad, national men in a number of countries have availed themselves of commercial services known disparagingly (in Australia at least) as the mail-order bride business. And rather than children crossing boundaries in the company of their natal mothers, a growing number adopted through transnational agencies are arriving without literal kinship ties to any member of the nation in residence.

Intermarried, International

> The term "mail-order bride" is not appropriate to those Filipinas who marry Australians. Australia has a strict requirement that anyone who wishes to migrate to Australia as a spouse or fiancée of an Australian resident must be personally acquainted with their future partner.
>
> —*Australian Ambassador John Holloway, 1987*[5]

A 1994 study of love and sex in the United States refuted research linking sexuality to "the whims of our hormonal surges and even genetic predispositions." Robert T. Michael and coinvestigators argued instead that "whether or not marriage is the object, people usually have sex with people who are remarkably like themselves—in age, race or ethnicity, and education. More than 90 percent of couples—married or dating—are from the same race or ethnic group." Although the study did not speak directly to such issues as the growth of a commercial trade in Russian wives for American men, it suggested that "most couples in the study met in conventional ways. They were introduced by family members or friends. They met at work. They met at a party. They met at church."[6]

Ruth Frankenberg has used the term *border infractions* to describe marriages or partnerships that cross the boundaries of racial/national division.[7] Although marriage is a contract, such relationships are only sometimes commercial. For example, many of the Filipinas in Australia (who have attracted attention simply by outnumbering Filipinos)[8] are professional or clerical women. One study found that only 30 percent of Filipinas planning to marry

Australian men were technically mail-order brides.[9] But commercial or not, transgressional associations are not hermetically sealed from societal norms and family pressures. In reference to what he called his own "mixed marriage," for example, Memmi "discovered that the couple is not an isolated entity, a forgotten oasis of light in the middle of the world; on the contrary, the whole world is within the couple."[10]

Border infractions can be an effect of traditional inscriptions of difference and not a beacon of transcendence. The Philippine embassy in Austria reported in 1987 that local advertisements described Filipinas as "docile, exotic, and available as bed partners and domestic help at the same time." Equally reflective of constructed images, women from the Philippines married to Australian men were found in one study to expect either release from poverty or a husband "more attuned than Filipino men to notions of sexual equality."[11] Racial thought conditions sexuality and desire, which is why Frantz Fanon argued that "if one wants to understand the racial situation psycho-analytically, not from a universal viewpoint but as it is experienced by individual consciousnesses, considerable importance must be given to sexual phenomena."[12]

Germane to this chapter is how such complex personal choices and decisions have become the object of nationalist attention. On the Philippine side of the mail-order bride equation, efforts began in 1987 to criminalize arranged marriages between foreign men and Filipinas. Senator Ernesto Maceda, cosponsor of one of two government bills, argued that "for many years our women have been treated like commodities to be bought and sold at leisure by shameless, perverted exploiters whose only motive is greed and whose main goal is money."[13] The women seemed to symbolize to Maceda and others (such as the curiously named Cardinal Sin) either a gross abuse of the rights of women to fair treatment, or a neocolonial world economy run on the continued exploitation of developing countries' bodies and resources.

On the Australian side, the passage of Philippine legislation in 1990 that banned mail-order bride businesses was welcomed by officials of the Department of Immigration and Ethnic Affairs.[14] Two factors would seem pertinent to that welcome. One is that the Philippines in 1987 was already the third-largest source of immigrants to Australia after Britain and New Zealand.[15] Further entry from a country once excluded from the Anzus Treaty at Australia's insistence may not have been wanted.

The other, related factor is that over half of all visas issued for settlement in Australia in 1992–1993 (the last year for which figures are available) were allocated from the "family migration" category. Those adjudged "extended family members" must meet certain established requirements; that is, they must pass "a labor market test" and "demonstrate that they speak English at a level necessary to find employment in their profession in Australia." By contrast "close family members"—such as spouses, fiancés, parents, and natural or adopted children—are subject to no such test when they apply "to be reunited with Australian citizens and permanent residents."[16]

Once transformed into citizens or permanent residents themselves, "close family" may seek reunion with other relatives. This means that unregulated personal relationships have the potential to swell the overall numbers of Filipinos and Filipinas who migrate to Australia without desired qualifications or English-language skills.

The small numbers of "boat people" who aroused so much concern at the end of 1994 will be repatriated to China if they cannot summon Australian family, economic skills, or refugee status. The still limited numbers of Asian people (mainly wives and children) who apply for reunion must demonstrate that they were united at least once before. But what counts as "personally acquainted" with an Australian may not always be that clearcut. The greater the room for interpretation, the less airtight the bureaucratic controls on entry.

Transgressional Children

> Inter-racial adoption, which most inter-country adoption is, usually takes the child out of their own community or cultural group and places them in a European family which is not part of the ethnic or cultural group from which the child comes, and is not likely to be living in the areas where those immigrant ethnic and cultural groups reside.
>
> —Brian English, 1990[17]

English's essay showed that the extent and pace of interracial, intercountry adoption varies from one state to the next. In Australia, the number of children adopted from overseas has risen steadily since the end of the Vietnam War in 1975, at the same time as "policy and practice now prohibit the interracial adoption of an Aboriginal child." Sweden, Norway, and Holland have been destination points since the 1960s for children adopted from such countries as Korea, India, Pakistan, and Colombia. Among countries with sizable racialized minorities, "Britain has large numbers of inter-racial adoptees, but few inter-country adoptees. The United States of America has large numbers of both inter-country and inter-racial adoptees."[18]

Adoption by white families of children from other racialized groups is an object of established debate, at least in the United States and Australia. When Senator Howard Metzenbaum introduced a bill into the U.S. Senate in 1993 designed to limit the ability of federally funded agencies to block transracial adoption, supporters and detractors regrouped their forces. Pitted against the requirements of children in foster care for "a loving family" were arguments about those same children's needs for a cultural heritage and sense of identity.

The most vocal critics of adoption across boundaries of race were affiliated with the New York branch of the Association of Black Social Workers. But there were precedents for its position outside the New York black community in particular and the United States more generally. The state of Minnesota's Heritage Preservation Act mandates that adoption agencies "search for relatives or families of the same racial or ethnic heritage before considering transracial placements."[19] In Australia, Western Australia's Adoption Legislative Review Committee recommended in 1990 that "every child placed for adoption shall be placed with adoptive parents of the same broad ethnic and cultural background as the child, thus ensuring the child's cultural and ethnic identity is not lost as a consequence of the adoption."[20]

Frankenberg has argued that concerns for children as "victims" of border infractions committed by their parents proceed from "notions of belonging or identity as fundamentally based on biology, of racial difference as absolute, on the presumption that cultural communities exist entirely separately from one another, and on an exactly symmetrical distaste of all cultural communities for one another."[21] When infractions are clearly transnational as well, as in intercountry adoptions, those same assumptions may be operative even as other issues come into play.

English concluded from his review of intercountry adoption research that a good deal more attention has been focused "on the adjustment and identity of the adoptee" than on "the impact of the adoption on the whole family." Defenders of the children, according to English, enframe their arguments within somewhat different "paradigms." One is the "welfare and/or aid paradigm" that considers adoption in terms of universal rights to family assistance. The other is "the paradigm of the market," where debates are about whether "some participants are inevitably exploited by those with greater access to resources and those able to exercise greater muscle in the market place."[22] Like attempts in Manila to ban mail-order brides, the contrast is between human rights and the workings of the world economy.

Aside from children's adjustment and the age-old question of whether identity is socially produced or innate, the increased resort of "'older' would-be parents"[23] to cross-border adoption raises a larger question about the management of global forces. This is especially so because the rights of citizens to determine family composition often clash with the objectives of the nation's guardians.

According to English, "Many people now believe, with whatever justification, that everyone has a right to parenthood and to expect assistance from the State to achieve it by one means or another."[24] Since existing bureaucracies have been largely ill-equipped to cope with demand, Beth Wilson has reported that "in some cases potential adopting parents simply went overseas, got the child and brought it home." The larger question for Wilson is "who should run the intercountry adoption program and according to what principles." Apparently this was a question not even posed until after a legal struggle for the custody of one Indian child came to the attention of the Australian media.[25]

Known as the Baby Kajal case, the battle was between the initial adoptive parents, the Wagners, and a couple named Morgan given the baby for potential adoption by Community Services Victoria after Mrs. Wagner became pregnant. While the media berated an inefficient bureaucracy and took sides between the two sets of would-be parents, the focus of administrative investigation shifted from the particular case to intercountry adoption more generally. A 1989 review conducted by the Family and Children's Services Council wrote of the need for "clear and well understood arrangements for the operation of the program with the overseas countries involved, and with the Commonwealth Government."[26] The review was properly driven, Wilson felt, by "the broader issues of who is controlling intercountry adoptions in Australia."[27]

GLOBAL BODIES POLITIC

Settlement and Transplantation

> The worldwide growth in commerce in human organs and its surprising diversity . . . are attracting the close attention of national governments and international agencies such as the World Health Organization. . . . No nation can afford to ignore the human organ trade.   —The Bulletin, 1991[28]

Nationalism has paid attention historically to two modes of settlement: One is the transplantation of nationals abroad; the other is the transplantion of aliens at home. Indicative of racial thought, the former has excited fears of the deterioration of the national race when moved outside its natural environment and climate. Reflective of the power of body metaphors, the latter has aroused images of a healthy body politic injected with alien viruses or contaminated with cancerous cells. Ill health and decline are imagined to originate from outside the national space and to be founded in the transplanted elements rather than in the receiving body. In both sorts of settlement, it is fully intact human beings who constitute the actual transplants.

Again, these established practices and inscriptions of danger have not disappeared. But they have been accompanied by concerns over transplantations from one literal human body to another. The stuff of debates within medical ethics, the global trade in human organs has expanded the supply of available transplants and also broadened the source. As well as dead accident victims or living relatives (the normal point of origin), transplants are coming from living donors with no known relationship to the recipient of the spare part.

With demand for kidneys, eyes, even skin far outstripping supply, organ brokers operate openly in many countries. A village in India is known as "the kidney colony" because so many poor families have sold their organs.[29] At the other end of the process, the Association for Organ Donations and Mutual Human Substitution in Germany "will pay as much as $45,000 each for human kidneys suitable for transplants."[30]

Nothing is beyond commodification in a capitalist world economy, including the innermost parts of the human body. Revulsion at the trade proceeds in some cases from the premise that the market should not be allowed to capture one of the few remaining sites of personal autonomy and free exchange. In the words of a spokesperson for the United Kingdom Transplant Service, for instance, "It is abhorrent, appalling and simply unethical to sell parts of the human body for money."[31] The fact that the sellers "are mostly destitute and from the Third World," while the traffickers and buyers are not,[32] reflects the unequal and uneven development of capitalism on a global scale as well as its expansion into all avenues of human life.

After a long history of allowing commerce in blood and other tissues, the United States enacted a ban on organ sales via the 1984 National Organ Transplant Act.[33] A 1989 scandal involving the activities of a Turkish "kidney gang" apparently conning poor people out of their organs prompted Britain to follow suit. Legislation enacted that year was designed to prohibit trade in organs as well as anonymous transplants between living people. However, there was no ban on transplantation from one living person to another if the two were "genetically related."[34]

In 1989, the World Health Organization (WHO) set out to prepare a code of global guidelines informed by "clear ethical principles." Since the principle of personal autonomy was not accepted by all delegates, the WHO advisory body focused on two others:

> The first was that of distributive justice and equity, which requires that donated organs be made available to sick patients on the basis of medical need and not on the basis of financial or any other consideration. The other rule proceeds from the belief, based on evidence before the WHO, that commerce in human tissues inevitably leads to exploitation of the weakest members of society. . . . It was held that the human body and its parts cannot ethically be the subject of commercial transactions.[35]

The WHO resolution was only a recommendation to member states that they take into account the two accepted principles in formulating their own

policies. Even if legislation similar to the British and U.S. laws were enacted in other countries, effective policing of anonymous transplantations
between living people is complicated by two constraints. One is that the latest medical technology can determine genetic relatedness only to a point:
"Tissue matching and blood testing can confirm a close family relationship
but are much less reliable when the parties describe themselves as cousins
or more distant relatives."[36] Disparities in dress or physical appearance
might well inform the assessments of relatedness made by individual doc-
tors. But in that case, judgment emerges from the realm of social condition-
ing, not from the province of scientifically objective machinery.

The other constraint is posed by the effects of transplantion on the bodies of both donor and recipient. Healthy bodies need one of everything, not
two. The second organ, or eye, or limb, is only a natural insurance policy
against failure. Success rates for transplantation are increasing, which
means that "no doctor wishes to see a patient die when restoration to good
health is available from a willing donor."[37]

Perhaps there is a lesson for nationalism in the simple fact that global
transplantation means life, not death.

NOTES

1. Memmi, *The Colonizer and the Colonized,* 53–54, ix.
2. See in general Campbell, *Writing Security.*
3. Maria Mies has tied the use of the labor of Third World women in their own homes to the globalization of the category "housewife." She argued that "their work, whether in use value or commodity production, is obscured . . . and can hence be bought at a much cheaper price than male labor." See Mies, *Patriarchy and Accumulation on a World Scale,* 116. It should be noted, though, that "outworkers" are not all female or poorly paid. J. Wajcman and B. Probert have distinguished on the high-technology end of the labor process between highly skilled computer pro-grammers (mainly men) and relatively unskilled word processors (typically women). "Outworking" may thus reflect established gender inequalities and labor relations even as it reinforces them. See Wajcman and Probert, "A New Breed of Outworker."
4. Shell, *Children of the Earth,* 3–4.
5. Quoted in Philip Chubb, "Mail-Order Brides from Manila," *Time,* November 30, 1987, 17.
6. Robert T. Michael et al., "Sex in America," *Glamour,* November 1994, 177.
7. Frankenberg, *White Women, Race Matters: The Social Construction of Whiteness,* 103.
8. A 1988 study noted that "the fact that of the 33,727 Filipinos resident in Australia, 23,347 or two thirds are females draws public debate and the attention of policymakers." See Cauchi, "Filipino Families in Australia: A Comment," 10.
9. Cooke, "Australian-Filipino Marriages in the 1980s: The Myth and the Reality."
10. Memmi, *The Colonizer and the Colonized,* vii.
11. Both quotes are from Chubb, "Mail-Order Brides."

12. Fanon, *Black Skin, White Masks,* 160.

13. Chubb, "Mail-Order Brides."

14. Payne, "Ban On Mail-Order Bride Businesses Welcomed."

15. Chubb, "Mail-Order Brides."

16. Australian Department of Foreign Affairs and Trade (Overseas Information Branch), "Immigration," 2.

17. English, "Inter-Country Adoption: The Context of Recent Developments and the Need for Research," 19.

18. English, "Inter-Country Adoption," 18–19.

19. Charisse Jones, "Debate on Race and Adoptions Is Being Reborn," *The New York Times,* October 24, 1993.

20. Quoted in Dickey, "Mixed-Race Adoptions," 590.

21. Frankenberg, *White Women, Race Matters,* 126.

22. English, "Inter-Country Adoption," 18–19.

23. According to English, "The vast majority of Australians marry relatively young and have their children early in marriage. Adoptive parents rarely reflect this norm." See English, "Inter-Country Adoption," 16.

24. English, "Inter-Country Adoption," 18.

25. Wilson, "Treating People Like Babies," 188.

26. Quoted in Wilson, "Treating People Like Babies," 189.

27. Wilson, "Treating People Like Babies," 189.

28. Russell Scott, "Australia and the Human Organ Trade," *The Bulletin,* October 1, 1991, 34–35.

29. Scott, "Australia and the Human Organ Trade," 34.

30. "Kidneys for Sale," *The Bulletin,* November 29, 1988, 109.

31. Quoted in Lisa Beyer, "Chilling Tales of the Flesh Trade," *Time,* February 20, 1989.

32. Beyer, "Chilling Tales of the Flesh Trade."

33. Scott, "Australia and the Human Organ Trade," 35.

34. Scott, "Australia and the Human Organ Trade," 34.

35. Scott, "Australia and the Human Organ Trade," 35.

36. Scott, "Australia and the Human Organ Trade," 34.

37. Scott, "Australia and the Human Organ Trade," 34.

Bibliography

BOOKS AND ARTICLES

AACF (Australian Association for Cultural Freedom). "The Perils of Multiculturalism." *Quadrant* 34 (June 1989): 9–10.

Adam, Heribert, and Hermann Giliomee. *Ethnic Power Mobilized: Can South Africa Change?* New Haven and London: Yale University Press, 1979.

Almog, Shmuel. *Nationalism and Antisemitism in Modern Europe 1815–1945.* New York: Pergamon Press, 1990.

Almond, Gabriel, and G. Bingham Powell. *Comparative Politics: A Developmental Approach.* Boston: Little, Brown, 1965.

Alter, Peter. *Nationalism.* London and New York: Edward Arnold, 1989.

Anderson, Benedict. *Imagined Communities: Reflections on the Origin and Spread of Nationalism.* 2d ed. New York: Verso, 1991.

Appiah, Kwame Anthony. *In My Father's House: Africa in the Philosophy of Culture.* New York: Oxford University Press, 1992.

Ardrey, Robert. *The Territorial Imperative.* London: Collins, 1967.

Ashcraft, Richard. *Revolutionary Politics and Locke's Two Treatises of Government.* Princeton: Princeton University Press, 1986.

Ashforth, Adam. *The Politics of Official Discourse in Twentieth Century South Africa.* Oxford: Clarendon Press, 1990.

Ashley, Richard K. "Untying the Sovereign State: A Double Reading of the Anarchy Problematique." *Millenium* 17 (1988): 227–262.

Balibar, Etienne. "Paradoxes of Universality." In *Anatomy of Racism,* edited by David Theo Goldberg. Minneapolis: University of Minnesota Press, 1990.

Balibar, Etienne, and Immanuel Wallerstein. *Race, Nation, Class: Ambiguous Identities.* London: Verso, 1991.

Banton, Michael. *White and Colored: The Behavior of British People Towards Colored Immigrants.* London, Jonathan Cape, 1959.

———. *Racial Theories.* Cambridge and New York: Cambridge University Press, 1987.

Barker, Anthony J. *The African Link: British Attitudes to the Negro in the Era of the Atlantic Slave Trade, 1550–1807.* London: Frank Cass, 1978.

Barker, Martin. "Biology and the New Racism." In *Anatomy of Racism,* edited by David Theo Goldberg. Minneapolis: University of Minnesota Press, 1990.

Barnett, Anthony. "Iron Britannia." *New Left Review* (special issue) 34 (July– August 1982): 16–89.

Beckett, Jeremy. "Aboriginality, Citizenship and the Nation State." *Social Analysis* 24 (1988): 9.

Bennett, Scott. "The 1967 Referendum." *Australian Aboriginal Studies* 2 (1985): 26–31.

Bennington, Geoffrey. "Postal Politics and the Institution of the Nation." In *Nation and Narration,* edited by Homi K. Bhabha. London and New York: Routledge, 1990.

Benyon, John. "Going Through the Motions: The Political Agenda, the 1981 Riots and the Scarman Inquiry." *Parliamentary Affairs* 38 (Autumn 1985): 409–422.

Bevan, Vaughan. *The Development of British Immigration Law.* London and Sydney: Croom Helm, 1986.

Bhabha, Homi K. "DissemiNation: Time, Narrative, and the Margins of the Modern Nation." In *Nation and Narration,* edited by Homi K. Bhabha. London and New York: Routledge, 1990.

Biko, Steve. *I Write What I Like.* London: Heinemann, 1978.

Blainey, Geoffrey. "Divided Nation." *Australian Business Monthly* (April 1992): 106–107.

Bloomberg, Charles. *Christian-Nationalism and the Rise of the Afrikaner Broederbond in South Africa, 1918–1948,* edited by Saul Dubow. Bloomington: Indiana University Press, 1989.

Boesak, Allan. "Liberation Theology in South Africa." In *Third World Liberation Theologies: A Reader,* edited by Deane William Ferm. Maryknoll, N.Y.: Orbis Books, 1986.

Botha, Jan. *Verwoerd Is Dead.* Cape Town: Books of Africa, 1967.

Breuilly, John. *Nationalism and the State.* 2d ed. Manchester: Manchester University Press, 1993.

Brink, Elsabe. "'Maar 'n Klomp "Factory" Meide': Afrikaner Family and Community on the Witwatersrand During the 1920s." In *Class, Community and Conflict: South African Perspectives,* edited by Belinda Bozzoli. Johannesburg: Ravan Press, 1987.

Bullivant, Brian M. "Pluralism in Australia—Clarifying the Issues." *Polycom* 30 (March 1982): 10–17.

Burleigh, Michael, and Wolfgang Wipperman. *The Racial State: Germany 1933–1945.* Cambridge: Cambridge University Press, 1991.

Campbell, David. *Writing Security: United States Foreign Policy and the Politics of Identity.* Minneapolis: University of Minnesota Press, 1992.

Carens, Joseph H. "Nationalism and the Exclusion of Immigrants: Lessons from Australian Immigration Policy." In *Open Borders? Closed Societies? The Ethical and Political Issues,* edited by Mark Gibney. New York: Greenwood, 1988.

Cauchi, J. "Filipino Families in Australia: A Comment." *Family Research Bulletin* 15 (June 1988): 9–10.

Center for Contemporary Cultural Studies. *The Empire Strikes Back: Race and Racism in 1970s Britain.* London: Hutchinson, 1982.

Ceserani, David, and Tony Kushner. *The Internment of Aliens in Twentieth Century Britain.* London: Frank Cass, 1993.

Chatterjee, Partha. *Nationalist Thought and the Colonial World: A Derivative Discourse?* London: Zed Books, 1986.

Coetzee, J. M. *White Writing: On the Culture of Letters in South Africa.* New Haven and London: Yale University Press, 1988.

Colley, Linda. *Britons: Forging the Nation, 1707–1837.* New Haven and London: Yale University Press, 1992.

Collins, Jock. "Why Blainey Got It Wrong." *Australian Society* 3 (September 1984): 11–13.

Conversi, Daniele. "Reassessing Current Theories of Nationalism: Nationalism as Boundary Maintenance and Creation." *Nationalism and Ethnic Politics* 1 (Spring 1995): 73–85.

Cooke, F. M. "Australian-Filipino Marriages in the 1980's: The Myth and the Reality." Australian-Asia Papers No. 37. Queensland: School of Modern Asian Studies, Griffith University, 1986.

Cope, Bill, and Mary Kalantzis. "Speaking of Cultural Difference: The Rise and Uncertain Future of the Language of Multiculturalism." *Migration Action* 9 (1987): 14–16.

Crick, Bernard, ed. *National Identities: The Constitution of the United Kingdom.* Cambridge, Mass.: Blackwell, 1991.

Davis, Stephen. *Apartheid's Rebels: Inside South Africa's Hidden War.* New Haven and London: Yale University Press, 1987.

de Klerk, Willem. *The Puritans in Africa: A Story of Afrikanerdom.* London: Rex Collings, 1975.

Delacampagne, Christian. "Racism and the West: From Praxis to Logos." In *Anatomy of Racism,* edited by David Theo Goldberg. Minneapolis: University of Minnesota Press, 1990.

de Lepervanche, Marie M. *Indians in a White Australia: An Account of Race, Class and Indian Immigration to Eastern Australia.* Sydney: Allen and Unwin, 1984.

Der Derian, James. *Antidiplomacy: Spies, Terror, Speed, and War.* Cambridge, Mass., and Oxford: Blackwell, 1992.

Deutsch, Karl. *Nationalism and Social Communication: An Inquiry into the Foundations of Nationality.* New York: John Wiley and Sons, 1953.

———. "Nation and World." In *Contemporary Political Science: Toward Empirical Theory,* edited by Ithiel de Sola Pool. New York: John Wiley and Sons, 1967.

De Villiers, Marq. *White Tribe Dreaming: Apartheid's Bitter Roots as Witnessed by Eight Generations of an Afrikaner Family.* New York: Penguin, 1987.

De Villiers, Rene. "Afrikaner Nationalism." In *The Oxford History of South Africa,* vol. 2, edited by Monica Wilson and Leonard Thompson. New York: Oxford University Press, 1971.

Dickey, A. "Mixed-race Adoptions." *Australian Law Journal* 64 (September 1990): 590.

Doty, Roxanne. *Imperial Encounters: The Politics of Representation in North/South Relations.* Minneapolis: University of Minnesota Press, 1996.

Dubow, Saul. "Afrikaner Nationalism, Apartheid, and the Conceptualization of 'Race.'" Paper presented at the Thirty-third Annual Meeting of the African Studies Association, Baltimore, November 1990.

Dunn, Frank. "All Cultures Are Good, Except Our Own." *Quadrant* 34 (June 1989): 40–43.

Du Toit, André, and Hermann Giliomee. *Afrikaner Political Thought, Volume I: 1780–1850.* Berkeley and Los Angeles: University of California Press, 1983.

Elstain, Jean Bethke. "Sovereignty, Identity, Sacrifice." In *Gendered States: Feminist (Re)Visions of International Relations Theory,* edited by V. Spike Peterson. Boulder and London: Lynne Rienner Publishers, 1992.

Emerson, Rupert. *From Empire to Nation: The Rise to Self-Assertion of Asian and African Peoples.* Cambridge: Harvard University Press, 1960.

———. "Nationalism and Political Development." *Journal of Politics* 22 (February 1960): 3–28.

English, Brian A. "Inter-Country Adoption: The Context of Recent Developments and the Need for Research." *Children Australia* 15 (March 1990): 16–20.

Fabian, Johannes. *Time and the Other: How Anthropology Makes Its Object.* New York: Columbia University Press, 1983.

Fanon, Frantz. *Black Skin, White Masks.* New York: Grove Press, 1967.

Fitzpatrick, Peter. "Racism and the Innocence of Law." In *Anatomy of Racism,* edited by David Theo Goldberg. Minneapolis: University of Minnesota Press, 1990.

Foot, Paul. *Immigration and Race in British Politics.* Baltimore: Penguin, 1965.

Foucault, Michel. *Discipline and Punish: The Birth of the Prison.* New York: Vintage Books, 1979.

Frankenberg, Ruth. *White Women, Race Matters: The Social Construction of Whiteness.* Minneapolis: University of Minnesota Press, 1993.

Game, Ann. "Nation and Identity: Bondi." *New Formations* 11 (Summer 1990): 105–121.

Gellner, Ernest. *Nations and Nationalism.* Ithaca: Cornell University Press, 1983.

———. *Encounters with Nationalism.* Oxford and Cambridge, Mass.: Blackwell, 1994.

Geyser, O., ed. *B. J. Vorster: Select Speeches.* Cape Town: Printpak, 1977.

Giliomee, Hermann. "The Development of the Afrikaner's Self-Concept." In *Looking at the Afrikaner Today,* edited by Hendrik H. Van Der Merwe. Cape Town: Tafelberg, 1975.

Gilman, Sander. "'I'm Down on Whores': Race and Gender in Victorian London." In *Anatomy of Racism,* edited by David Theo Goldberg. Minneapolis: University of Minnesota Press, 1990.

Gilroy, Paul. *There Ain't No Black in the Union Jack: The Cultural Politics of Race and Nation.* Chicago: University of Chicago Press, 1991.

———. *Small Acts: Thoughts on the Politics of Black Cultures.* London: Serpent's Tail, 1993.

Glazer, Nathan. "The Scarman Report: An American View." *Political Quarterly* 53 (April-June 1982): 111–127.

Goldberg, David Theo. "The Social Formation of Racist Discourse." In *Anatomy of Racism,* edited by David Theo Goldberg. Minneapolis: University of Minnesota Press, 1990.

———. "Modernity, Race, and Morality." *Cultural Critique* (Spring 1993): 193–227.

———. *Racist Culture: Philosophy and the Politics of Meaning.* Cambridge, Mass.: Oxford University Press, 1993.

Goldstein, Joshua S. "The Emperor's New Genes: Sociobiology and War." *International Studies Quarterly* 31 (March 1987): 33–43.

Greenfeld, Liah. *Nationalism: Five Roads to Modernity.* Cambridge, Mass., and London: Harvard University Press, 1992.

Grimm, The Brothers. *Grimms' Tales for Young and Old.* New York: Doubleday, 1977.

Hall, Stuart. *Policing the Crisis: Mugging, the State, and Law and Order.* London: Macmillan, 1978.

Hamilton, Annette. "Beer and Being: The Australian Tourist in Bali." *Social Analysis* 27 (April 1990): 17–29.

Hand, Gerry. "The Bicentenary: A View." *Social Alternatives* 8 (1989): 23–25.

Harris, Nigel. *National Liberation.* London: Penguin, 1990.

Harrison, David. *The White Tribe of Africa.* Berkeley and Los Angeles: University of California Press, 1981.

Hawke, Bob. "Australia: A Multicultural Society." *Australian Foreign Affairs Record* 55 (April 1984): 317–318.

———. "An Open Letter by the Prime Minister." *Migration Action* 10 (1988): 34–36.

Hepple, Alexander. *Verwoerd.* Baltimore: Penguin, 1967.

Hobbes, Thomas. *Leviathan: Of the Matter, Forme and Power of a Commonwealth, Ecclesiasticall and Civil.* London: Collier Books, 1962.

Hobsbawm, E. J. *Nations and Nationalism Since 1780: Programme, Myth, Reality.* Cambridge: Cambridge University Press, 1990.

Holiday, Anthony. "White Nationalism in South Africa as Movement and System." In *The National Question in South Africa,* edited by Maria Van Diepen. London: Zed Books, 1988.

Holmes, Colin. *A Tolerant Country? Immigrants, Refugees, and Minorities in Britain.* London and Boston: Faber and Faber, 1991.

Horowitz, Donald L. *Ethnic Groups in Conflict.* Berkeley and Los Angeles: University of California Press, 1985.

Ignatieff, Michael. *Blood and Belonging: Journeys into the New Nationalism.* New York: Farrar, Strauss and Giroux, 1993.

Inkeles, Alex, and David H. Smith. "Becoming Modern." In *Development and Underdevelopment: The Political Economy of Inequality,* edited by Mitchell A. Seligson and John T Passé-Smith. Boulder and London: Lynne Rienner Publishers, 1993.

Irving, Helen. "Who Are the Founding Mothers? The Role of Women in Australian Federation." Lecture given at Parliament House, Canberra, Australia, November 18, 1994.

Jobson, Richard. *The Golden Trade.* London, 1623.

Kapferer, Bruce. *Legends of People, Myths of State: Violence, Intolerance, and Political Culture in Sri Lanka and Australia.* Washington and London: Smithsonian Institution Press, 1988.

Kearney, Hugh. "Four Nations or One?" In *National Identities: the Constitution of the United Kingdom,* edited by Bernard Crick. Cambridge, Mass.: Blackwell, 1991.

Kellas, James. *The Politics of Nationalism and Ethnicity.* London: Macmillan, 1991.

Koerner, Lisbet. "Linnaeus' Floral Transplants." *Representations* 47 (Summer 1994): 144–169.

Kohn, Hans. *The Idea of Nationalism.* New York: Macmillan, 1944.

Kristeva, Julia. *Nations Without Nationalism.* Translated by Leon S. Roudiez. New York: Columbia University Press, 1993.

Lattas, Andrew. "Aborigines and Contemporary Australian Nationalism: Primordiality and the Cultural Politics of Otherness." *Social Analysis* 27 (April 1990): 52–53.

Lawrence, Errol. "Just Plain Common Sense: The 'Roots' of Racism." In *The Empire Strikes Back: Race and Racism in 1970s Britain,* edited by the Center for Contemporary Cultural Studies. London: Hutchinson and Company, 1982.

Layton-Henry, Zig, and Paul B. Rich, eds. *Race, Government and Politics in Britain.* London: Macmillan, 1986.

Leatt, James, Theo Kneifel, and Klaus Nurnberger, eds. *Contending Ideologies in South Africa.* Grand Rapids: Eerdmans, 1986.

Lenin, V. I. "Critical Remarks on the National Question." In V. I. Lenin, *Collected Works,* vol. 20. Moscow: Progress Publishers, 1977.

Lerner, Adam J. "The Nineteenth-Century Monument and the Embodiment of National Time." In *Reimagining the Nation,* edited by Marjorie Ringrose and Adam J. Lerner. Buckingham, Pa.: Open University Press, 1992.

Lerner, Daniel. *The Passing of Traditional Society.* 2d ed. New York: Free Press, 1964.

Lewis, Gavin. *Between the Wire and the Wall: A History of South African "Coloured" Politics.* New York: St. Martin's Press, 1987.

Lewsen, Phyllis, ed. *Voices of Protest: From Segregation to Apartheid, 1938–1948.* Craighall, South Africa: A. D. Donker, 1988.

Libby, Ronald T. *Hawke's Law: The Politics of Mining and Aboriginal Land Rights in Australia.* University Park: Pennsylvania University Press, 1992.

Lijphart, Arend. *Democracy in Plural Societies: A Comparative Exploration.* New Haven: Yale University Press, 1977.

Lijphart, Arend, and Bernard Grofman, eds. *Choosing an Electoral System: Issues and Alternatives.* New York: Praeger, 1984.

Lipset, Seymour Martin. "Values, Education, and Entrepreneurship." In *Promise of Development: Theories of Change in Latin America,* edited by Peter F. Klaren and Thomas J. Bossert. Boulder and London: Westview Press, 1986.

Locke, John. *Two Treatises of Government.* Cambridge: Cambridge University Press, 1960.

Loubser, J. A. *The Apartheid Bible: A Critical Review of Racial Theology in South Africa.* Cape Town: Longman, 1987.

Love, Peter. "Old Lang's Sign." *Australian Left Review* 140 (June 1992): 6–7.

Mackie, J. A. C. "Asian Immigration to Australia: Past Trends and Future Prospects." *Australian Outlook* 41 (August 1987): 104–109.

Macmillan, John, and Andrew Linklater, eds. *Boundaries in Question: New Directions in International Relations.* London and New York: Pinter, 1995.

Mandle, W. F. *Going It Alone: Australia's National Identity in the Twentieth Century.* London: Allen Lane, 1977.

Manne, Robert. "The Blainey View—the Politics of Asian Immigration to Australia, 1975–1984." *Dyason House Papers* 11 (September 1984): 13–16.

Manzo, Kathryn A. (Kate). "Modernist Discourse and the Crisis of Development Theory." *Studies in Comparative International Development* 26 (Summer 1991): 3–36.

———. "The Limits of Liberalism." *Transition* (53): 115–124.

———. *Domination, Resistance, and Social Change in South Africa: The Local Effects of Global Power.* New York: Praeger, 1992.

Manzo, Kate A., and Pat McGowan. "Afrikaner Fears and the Politics of Despair: Understanding Change in South Africa." *International Studies Quarterly* 36 (1992): 1–24.

Marx, Karl. "The German Ideology: Part I"; "On the Jewish Question"; and "On Imperialism in India." In *The Marx-Engels Reader,* edited by Robert C. Tucker. 2d ed. New York: W. W. Norton, 1978.

Mboya, Tom. *The Challenge of Nationhood.* London: Heinemann, 1970.

McClelland, David. *The Achieving Society.* Princeton: Van Nostrand, 1962.

———. "The Achievement Motive in Economic Growth." In *Development and Underdevelopment: the Political Economy of Inequality,* edited by Mitchell A. Seligson and John T Passé-Smith. Boulder and London: Lynne Rienner Publishers, 1993.

McClintock, Anne. "'No Longer in a Future Heaven': Women and Nationalism in South Africa." *Transition* (51): 104–123.

McNeill, William H. *Poly-ethnicity and National Unity in World History.* Toronto: University of Toronto Press, 1986.

McQueen, Humphrey. *A New Britannia: An Argument Concerning the Social Origins of Australian Radicalism and Nationalism.* London: Penguin, 1976.

———. "Blainey and Multiculturalism." *Island Magazine* 21 (Summer 1984): 40–43.

Meaney, Neville. *Australia and the World: A Documentary History from the 1870s to the 1970s*. Melbourne: Longman, 1985.

Meinecke, Friedrich. *Cosmopolitanism and the National State*. Princeton: Princeton University Press, 1970.

Meli, Francis. "South Africa and the Rise of African Nationalism." In *The National Question in South Africa*, edited by Maria Van Diepen. London: Zed Books, 1988.

Memmi, Albert. *The Colonizer and the Colonized*. 2d ed. Boston: Beacon Press, 1991.

Mercer, David. "*Terra Nullius*, Aboriginal Sovereignty and Land Rights in Australia." *Political Geography* 12 (July 1993): 299–318.

Mies, Maria. *Patriarchy and Accumulation on a World Scale*. London: Zed Books, 1986.

Miller, Christopher. *Blank Darkness: Africanist Discourse in French*. Chicago: University of Chicago Press, 1985.

Mitchell, Joshua. *Not by Reason Alone: Religion, History, and Identity in Early Modern Political Thought*. Chicago: University of Chicago Press, 1993.

Moodie, T. Dunbar. *The Rise of Afrikanerdom: Power, Apartheid, and the Afrikaner Civil Religion*. Berkeley and Los Angeles: University of California Press, 1975.

Moore, Robert. *Racism and Black Resistance in Britain*. London: Pluto, 1975.

Morgan, Sally. *Wanamurraganya: The Story of Jack McPhee*. Fremantle: Fremantle Arts Centre Press, 1989.

Morris, Desmond. *Intimate Behavior*. London: Cape, 1971.

Morse, Bradford, and Thomas R. Berger. *Sardar Sarovar: The Report of the Independent Review*. Ottawa: Resource Futures International, 1992.

Morton, John. "Rednecks, 'Roos and Racism: Kangaroo Shooting and the Australian Way." *Social Analysis* 27 (April 1990): 30–49.

Mudimbe, V. Y. *The Invention of Africa: Gnosis, Philosophy, and the Order of Knowledge*. Bloomington and Indianapolis: Indiana University Press, 1988.

Newton, Janice. "Becoming 'Authentic' Australians Through Music." *Social Analysis* 27 (April 1990): 95–100.

Ngugi, wa Thiong'o. *Decolonizing the Mind: The Politics of Language in African Literature*. London: James Currey, 1986.

Nixon, Rob. "Mandela, Messianism, and the Media." *Transition* (51): 42–55.

Nkrumah, Kwame. *Ghana: The Autobiography of Kwame Nkrumah*. New York: International Publishers, 1971.

Nott, Josiah. *Types of Mankind: Or Ethnological Researches Based Upon the Ancient Monuments, Paintings, Sculptures, and Crania of Races and Upon Their Natural Geographical, Philological, and Biblical History*. Philadelphia: 1854.

O'Meara, Dan. *Volkskapitalisme: Class, Capital and Ideology in the Development of Afrikaner Nationalism, 1934–1948*. Cambridge: Cambridge University Press, 1983.

Opitz, May, Katharina Oguntoye, and Dagmer Schultz. *Showing Our Colors: Afro-German Women Speak Out*. Amherst: University of Massachusetts Press, 1991.

Orwell, George. *England Your England*. London: Secker and Warburg, 1953.

Outlaw, Lucius. "Toward a Critical Theory of 'Race.'" In *Anatomy of Racism*, edited by David Theo Goldberg. Minneapolis: University of Minnesota Press, 1990.

Overview of the Response by Governments to the Royal Commission. *Aboriginal Deaths in Custody*. Canberra: Commonwealth of Australia, 1992.

Parsons, Talcott. *The Social System*. New York: Free Press, 1951.

Patterson, Sheila. *The Last Trek: A Study of the Boer People and the Afrikaner Nation.* London: Routledge, 1957.

Payne, J. "Ban on Mail-Order Bride Businesses Welcomed." *Migration* 79 (June–July 1990): 3.

Pettman, Jan Jindy. *Living in the Margins: Racism, Sexism, and Feminism in Australia.* North Sydney: Allen and Unwin, 1992.

Phillips, Mike. "Black Britain Explodes." *Africa* 120 (August 1981): 12–18.

Pilkington, Edward. *Beyond the Mother Country: West Indians and the Notting Hill White Riots.* London: I. B. Tauris and Company, 1988.

Plamenatz, John. "Two Types of Nationalism." In *Nationalism: the Nature and Evolution of an Idea,* edited by Eugene Kamenka. New York: St. Martin's Press, 1976.

Portes, Alejandro. "On the Sociology of National Development: Theories and Issues." In *Development and Underdevelopment: The Political Economy of Inequality,* edited by Mitchell A. Seligson and John T Passé-Smith. Boulder and London: Lynne Rienner Publishers, 1993.

Racioppi, Linda, and Katherine O'Sullivan See. "Nationalism Engendered: A Critique of Approaches to Nationalism." Paper presented at the Thirty-sixth Annual Convention of the International Studies Association, Chicago, February 1995.

Reed, John, and Clive Wake, eds. *Senghor: Prose and Poetry.* London: Heinemann, 1976.

Renan, Ernest. "What Is a Nation?" In *Nation and Narration,* edited by Homi K. Bhabha. London and New York: Routledge, 1990.

Republic Advisory Committee. *An Australian Republic: The Options—an Overview.* Canberra: Commonwealth of Australia, 1993.

Revised Standard Version of the Holy Bible. Cleveland and New York: World Publishing, 1962.

Rex, John. *Race, Colonialism and the City.* London and Boston: Routledge and Kegan Paul, 1973.

———. "The 1981 Urban Riots in Britain." *Urban Praxis* (1981): 99–113.

Ricardo, David. "On Foreign Trade." In *The Theoretical Evolution of International Political Economy: A Reader,* edited by George T. Crane and Abla Amawi. New York and Oxford: Oxford University Press, 1991.

Rich, Paul. *Race and Empire in British Politics.* Cambridge: Cambridge University Press, 1986.

Richard, Pablo, et al. *The Battle of the Gods.* Maryknoll, N.Y.: Orbis Books, 1984.

Rose, Lawrence. *Revolutionary Antisemitism in Germany from Kant to Wagner.* Princeton: Princeton University Press, 1990.

Rowse, Tim. "Surrendering Australia." *Meanjin* 43 (1984): 379–391.

Sahlins, Peter. "Fictions of a Catholic France: The Naturalization of Foreigners, 1685–1787." *Representations* 47 (Summer 1994): 85–110.

Sen, Sudipta. "The Patriarchal Economy of Imperialism: On Domesticity and Dominion in British-India." Presentation given at the symposium "Colonialism, Sexuality, and the State in Modern India," Johns Hopkins University, Baltimore, April 8, 1994.

Senghor, Léopold Sédar. "The Struggle for Negritude" and "We Are All Cultural Half-Castes." In *Senghor: Prose and Poetry,* edited by John Reed and Clive Wake. London: Heinemann, 1976.

Shapiro, Michael J., and Hayward Alker, eds. *Challenging Boundaries.* Minneapolis: University of Minnesota Press, 1995.

Sharp, Nonie. "Scales from the Eyes of Justice." *Arena* 99/100 (1992): 56.

Shaw, R. Paul, and Yuwa Wong. "Ethnic Mobilization and the Seeds of Warfare: An Evolutionary Perspective." *International Studies Quarterly* 31 (March 1987): 5–31.

Shell, Marc. *Children of the Earth: Literature, Politics, and Nationhood.* New York: Oxford University Press, 1993.

Shiva, Vandana. *Staying Alive: Women, Ecology, and Development.* London: Zed Books, 1988.

———. *Monocultures of the Mind: Perspectives on Biodiversity and Biotechnology.* London: Zed Books, 1993.

Slater, John. "History and Controversy in the Classroom." *History Today* (January 1987): 6–7.

Slezkine, Yuri. "Naturalists Versus Nations: Eighteenth-Century Russian Scholars Confront Ethnic Diversity." *Representations* 47 (Summer 1994): 170–195.

Smith, Anthony D. *Theories of Nationalism.* London: Harper and Row, 1971.

———. *National Identity.* London: Penguin, 1991.

Smith, Geoffrey. "Britain in the New Europe." *Foreign Affairs* (Fall 1992): 158–164.

Smith, John. "Of the Naturall Inhabitants of Virginia." In *Narratives of Early Virginia, 1606–1625,* edited by Lynn Gardiner Tyler. New York: Charles Scribner's, 1907.

Smithies, Bill, and Peter Fiddick. *Enoch Powell on Immigration.* London: Sphere Books, 1969.

Snead, James. "European Pedigrees/African Contagions: Nationality, Narrative and Communality in Tutuola, Achebe, and Reed." In *Nation and Narration,* edited by Homi K. Bhabha. London and New York: Routledge, 1990.

Solomon, John. "Problems, But Whose Problems: The Social Construction of Black Youth Unemployment and State Policies." *Social Administration Digest* 56 (February–April 1985): 527–554.

Sparks, Allister. *The Mind of South Africa.* New York: Alfred A. Knopf, 1990.

Stepan, Nancy Leys. "Race and Gender: The Role of Analogy in Science." In *Anatomy of Racism,* edited by David Theo Goldberg. Minneapolis: University of Minnesota Press, 1990.

Taylor, Robert. "A Summer of Discontent." *Europe* (September–October 1981): 34–35.

Thomas, Laurence. "The Evolution of Anti-Semitism." *Transition* (57): 94–108.

Thompson, Leonard. "Great Britain and the Afrikaner Republics, 1870–1899." In *The Oxford History of South Africa,* vol. 2, edited by Monica Wilson and Leonard Thompson. New York: Oxford University Press, 1971.

———. *The Political Mythology of Apartheid.* New Haven and London: Yale University Press, 1985.

Tilly, Charles, ed. *The Formation of National States in Western Europe.* Princeton: Princeton University Press, 1975.

Todorov, Tzvetan. "Xenocide: Antisemitism à la Française." *Transition* (55): 154–159.

Tomaselli, Keyan, and Mewa Ramgobin. "South Africa and the Freedom Charter: Culture and Violence." *Enclitic* (Fall 1988): 86–94.

Torgovnick, Marianna. *Gone Primitive: Savage Intellects, Modern Lives.* Chicago and London: University of Chicago Press, 1990.

Turnbull, Malcolm. "Why We Need the Republic." *The Verbatim Report* 1 (May 1992): 104–105.

———. "Forward." In *The Republicanism Debate,* edited by Wayne Hudson and David Carter. Kensington: New South Wales University Press, 1993.

Van Schaik, J. L. *Groot Woordeboek: Afrikaans/Engels.* Pretoria: Librigebou, 1986.

Vatcher, Henry, Jr. *White Laager: The Rise of Afrikaner Nationalism.* New York: Praeger, 1965.

Vernon, Raymond. *Sovereignty at Bay.* New York: Basic Books, 1971.

Wajcman, J., and B. Probert. "A New Breed of Outworker." *Australian Society* 6 (November 1987): 35–36.

Walker, R. B. J. *Inside/Outside: International Relations as Political Theory.* New York: Cambridge University Press, 1993.

Wallerstein, Immanuel. "The Present State of the Debate on World Inequality." In *Development and Underdevelopment: The Political Economy of Inequality,* edited by Mitchell A. Seligson and John T Passé-Smith. Boulder and London: Lynne Rienner Publishers, 1993.

Walvin, James. *Passage to Britain: Immigration in British History and Politics.* New York and London: Penguin, 1984.

Walzer, Michael. "The Distribution of Membership." In *Boundaries: National Autonomy and Its Limits,* edited by Peter G. Brown and Henry Shue. Totowa, N.J.: Rowman and Littlefeld, 1981.

Ward, Russel. *The Australian Legend.* Melbourne: Melbourne University Press, 1958.

Weber, Cynthia. *Simulating Sovereignty: Intervention, the State and Symbolic Exchange.* New York: Cambridge University Press, 1994.

Weber, Max. *The Protestant Ethic and the Spirit of Capitalism.* New York: Charles Scribner's, 1958.

———. "The Nation." In *From Max Weber: Essays in Sociology,* edited by Hans H. Gerth and C. Wright Mills. New York: Oxford University Press, 1976.

White, Luise. "Alien Nation: The Hidden Obsession of UFO Literature—Race in Space." *Transition* (63): 24–33.

White, Richard. *Inventing Australia: Images and Identity, 1688–1980.* London: Allen and Unwin, 1981.

Willard, Myra. *History of the White Australia Policy to 1920.* 2d ed. London: Frank Cass, 1967.

Williams, Brackette F. "The Impact of the Precepts of Nationalism on the Concept of Culture: Making Grasshoppers of Naked Apes." *Cultural Critique* (Spring 1993): 143–191.

———. "Dick and Jane and 'Just Us.'" Lecture given at Johns Hopkins University, Baltimore, March 15, 1994.

Williamson, Bill. "Memories, Vision and Hope: Themes in an Historical Sociology of Britain Since the Second World War." *Journal of Historical Sociology* 1 (June 1988): 161–183.

Wills, Garry. *Under God: Religion and American Politics.* New York: Simon and Schuster, 1990.

Wilson, Beth. "Treating People Like Babies." *Legal Service Bulletin* 14 (August 1989): 188–190.

Woods, Donald. *Biko.* New York and London: Paddington Press, 1978.

Worsley, Peter. *The Third World.* 2d ed. Chicago: University of Chicago Press, 1967.

Yarwood, A. T., and M. J. Knowling. *Race Relations in Australia: A History.* Melbourne: Methuen, 1982.

NEWSPAPERS AND MAGAZINES

South Africa

Business Day, 1993–1994.
The Daily News, 1993.
Die Burgher, 1993–1994.
The Eastern Province Herald, 1993–1994.
The Natal Mercury, 1993.
The Natal Witness, 1994.
The Pretoria News, 1994.
The South African Press Association, 1993.
The Sowetan, 1994.
The Star, 1993–1994.
The Sunday Times, 1994.
The Weekly Mail, 1993–1994.

Great Britain

The Daily Telegraph, 1994.
The Economist, 1981–1982.
The Guardian Weekly, 1992–1993.
The Independent Magazine, 1993.
The New Leader, 1982.
The New Statesman and Society, 1988–1989.
The Times, 1971–1973, 1976, 1981, 1985.

Australia

The Age, 1984.
The Australian, 1993–1995.
The Bulletin, 1967, 1988, 1990–1995.
The Canberra Times, 1994–1995.
The Sydney Morning Herald, 1991–1995.
Time, 1987, 1989, 1992.
The Weekend Australian, 1993.

France

L'Evénement du Jeudi, 1990.
Le Monde, 1993.
Libération, 1994.

The United States

The Baltimore Sun, 1993.
The Chicago Tribune, 1992.
The Christian Science Monitor, 1987.
Forbes, 1992.
Glamour, 1994.
The Los Angeles Times, 1991.

The New Yorker, 1992.
The New York Times, 1988, 1991–1994.
This Week in South Africa, 1993–1994.
    (published by the South African Consulate, Washington, D.C.)
Vital Speeches of the Day, 1989, 1992.

Other

Maclean's, 1988.
West Africa, 1986.

Index

About the Book

This imaginative and ambitious book takes issue convincingly with common conceptions about the relationship—or lack of relationship—among race, nationalism, and religion.

Manzo sets the modern nation-state in historical, global, and philosophical context to support three key themes. First, she argues that the theoretical literature on nations and nationalism is limited by a too-ready acceptance of modern ideas and modern practices of boundary creation. Second, she shows that the articulation of race with nation continues even in those societies that have long prided themselves on being "nonracial." Finally, she demonstrates that the concept of race, far from being about something as straightforward as black or white, has been created and recreated in various settings as nations have been made and remade, and vice versa; race and nation have been and remain mutually constitutive.

Case studies of South Africa, Britain, and Australia provide strong defense of Manzo's arguments.

Kathryn A. Manzo is lecturer in politics at Keele University (UK). She is author of *Domination, Resistance, and Social Change in South Africa: The Local Effects of Global Power.*